Structures of *Society*

Elise Kimerling Wirtschafter

Structures
of Society

Imperial Russia's

"People of Various Ranks"

NORTHERN

ILLINOIS

UNIVERSITY PRESS

DeKalb

1994

©1994 by Northern Illinois University Press

Published by the Northern Illinois University Press,

DeKalb, Illinois 60115

Manufactured in the United States using

acid-free paper ⊖ ⊕

Design by Julia Fauci

City plan illustrations from *Atlas Moskovskoi gubernii*

(Moscow, 1787) courtesy of Nauchno-tekhnicheskii

arkhiv "Mosoblstroirestavratsiia," Moscow.

Library of Congress Cataloging-in-Publication Data

Wirtschafter, Elise Kimerling.

    Structures of society : Imperial Russia's "people

  of various ranks" / Elise Kimerling Wirtschafter.

      p.   cm.

    Includes bibliographical references and index.

    ISBN 0-87580-190-0 (acid-free paper)

    1. Social classes—Russia—History.

  2. Russia—Social conditions—To 1801.

  3. Russia—Social conditions—1801–1917.

  I. Title.

HN530.Z9S646645   1994

305.5'0947—dc20   94-14632

                   CIP

To my parents,

with the hope that

the grievances and pathologies of 29–30 April 1992

can be rectified,

and with the hope that

the children of Los Angeles and Birmingham

can live in racial peace.

Contents

List of Tables

TRADITIONAL IMAGES OF imperial Russia in the age of serfdom convey a society of rigid, stagnant, and hierarchical relationships. Based upon an exercise in the history of social and political language *(Begriffsgeschichte)*, this study offers an alternative image—one that depicts a society of shifting and indeterminate boundaries, spontaneous development, and multiple structures. The subject here is the category or phenomenon of the *raznochintsy,* literally, "people of various ranks" or "people of diverse origins." The *raznochintsy* comprised a range of interstitial groups defined both within and outside the structure of juridically based social categories *(sosloviia;* sing., *soslovie),* which provided the formal framework for imperial society's development roughly from 1649 until 1861 and to a lesser degree until 1917. Wedged between or overlapping with the primary *sosloviia* of nobility, clergy, urban "citizens," and peasants, the *raznochintsy* tended to be outsiders in the sense of nonmembers of a given category or community. The contours of the category inevitably fluctuated, and in concrete applications the term could encompass virtually any group in society, including nobles, townspeople, and peasants.

Despite its fluidity there was some minimal consistency to the category, which appeared both as an umbrella and a specific group. Social subcategories specifically identified as *raznochintsy* included retired soldiers; lesser state servicemen, specialists, and artisans below the Table of Ranks; children of personal nobles; educated commoners, including a range of proto- and semiprofessionals; non-Orthodox minorities; and single householders. No attempt is made here—nor would it even be possible—to formulate a single, consistently applied definition of the *raznochintsy* for any chronological period. As the chapters that follow will show, no single definition predominated. So rather than ask who the *raznochintsy* were—a question that assumes the existence of an identifiable stratum or subgroup—it is more useful to consider what the category represented (when, where, and to whom) and to determine what the different representations reveal about Russian society and culture, particularly the dynamics of social categorization and the formation of sociocultural identities.

The phenomenon of the *raznochintsy* touches upon a wide range of issues, particularly the very complex problem of defining group identities.

Every student of Russian history is familiar with numerous formal and informal classifications used by government and society to designate individuals, communities, and larger social categories. Leaving aside the fragmented Muscovite ranks—some of which carried over into the eighteenth century—the most common identifiers of formal status from the reign of Peter the Great on included social category or "estate" *(sostoianie, soslovie)*, rank *(chin)*, calling *(zvanie)*, office *(dolzhnost')*, title, academic degree or technical certification, economic privileges, legally prescribed occupation, and tax and service obligations. The informal elements of status included economic (class), occupational, or educational differentiation within formal categories; deliberate or unintentional violations of legal boundaries; and the continuing importance of lineage regardless of rank, office, or wealth. As these overlapping categorizations reveal, it was not always easy to distinguish formal and informal attributes of status. Official policy consistently sought to establish correspondence between the formal components of status, but the ambiguity of definitions and the impact of informal (often illegal) relationships undermined the desired symmetry. Whether one examines statute law or archival documents, it is essential to distinguish legal definitions from social facts.

The phenomenon of the *raznochintsy* reflected with particular clarity the larger problem of fitting people into neat categories. The codification of serfdom in the mid-seventeenth century and the imposition of tax and service obligations in the reign of Peter the Great established the basic framework for structuring social categories—a framework that remained intact until the era of the Great Reforms. Peter required service from all groups in society, but then defined these obligations in terms of a fundamental social divide: the distinction between the unprivileged, who paid the capitation (poll tax), and the privileged, who did not. This seemingly simple designation proved extremely difficult to implement. Only in the late eighteenth century did the government finally determine exactly which groups in society were exempt from the capitation (nobles, clergy, merchants, ranked and unranked officials, and lesser state and military servitors). Still, in order to implement this distinction and its attendant attributes, officials had to register each and every individual, community, or status group in a juridically defined social category.

It was the multiplicity of traditional Muscovite ranks that made it so difficult for officials to assign formal status. From the early eighteenth century until emancipation in 1861, the very existence of the legal designation *raznochintsy* revealed the ultimate failure to achieve full agglomeration into imperial social categories. In its search for educated and semieducated personnel, the government constantly redefined existing social categories and created new ones—a practice that led to a proliferation of formal and informal statuses reminiscent in their particularism of the older Muscovite ranks. For every subcategory that the law effectively delimited, a new group-ing would arise—either formally to meet the technical and economic needs of a growing bureaucracy and army, or informally as a consequence of spontaneous societal development. In addition, there was a significant free-floating population of runaways, laborers, petty traders, and entrepre-neurs—persons who evaded registration altogether, who fled their as-signed place of residence with or without the required passport, and who sometimes managed to change their formal status through lawful or unlaw-ful means.

Even the primary social categories of nobility, clergy, urban "citizens," and peasants contained multiple legal statuses and so were not always easy to identify. Although very specific rights and obligations distinguished for-mal social categories, the definitions themselves and consequently the boundaries separating contiguous groups remained porous and change-able. Formal status was in many instances subjectively and arbitrarily de-fined. Unrecognized claims to nobility and the persistence of illegal enserf-ment revealed that the ambiguity of definition, most readily discernible at the middle levels of society, was a general feature of the Russian social structure. The plasticity of legal definitions, including the absence of any notion of noble derogation, highlighted the importance of informal rela-tionships. Thus the pursuit of profit and the struggle to survive led to fre-quent violations of the law and so undermined society's formal delinea-tions. Legal and illegal economic relationships made it possible for individuals from all categories, including serfs, repeatedly to cross social boundaries. Equally important, the absence of firm definitions, structures, and boundaries produced an underlying insecurity of status that affected all but the most highly placed groups. In this sense, imperial Russia was a society with a decided lack of structure where the vast majority of people could in different contexts be considered *raznochintsy*.

This study began as an examination of terminology, specifically, usages and meanings of the category *raznochintsy* and their relationship to the larger problem of social categorization. After focusing on the develop-mental (legal, administrative, institutional, economic, and cultural) sources of the various definitions of *raznochintsy*, it became a discussion of the underlying dynamics of social categorization and delimitation in impe-rial Russia. Analysis of the relationship of the category *raznochintsy* to other social designations and to broader patterns of historical development re-vealed that social status in both its formal and informal dimensions was fundamentally indeterminate and changeable. Once this ambiguity was recognized, it was necessary to reconsider traditional depictions of imperial social structure. Attention to the porousness of boundaries and plasticity

of definitions in Russian society does not necessarily challenge recent research on discrete social formations and experiences. Rather, it shows that
socioeconomic structures and relationships, appearing as *soslovie* subculture or class identity when viewed from the vantage point of a single, identifiable category, status, or group, can look very different when examined
across a broad range of social classifications from the perspective of ever-
shifting interstitial categories.

The discussion that follows is based upon a wide range of legislative,
archival, literary, memoir, and journalistic sources. Chapter 1 examines existing scholarship in order to identify the historiographical "typology" of
the *raznochintsy* and to define the problematics of the phenomenon. Chapter 2 analyzes the formation of social definitions and the dynamics of state
policy by focusing upon the legal parameters of the *raznochintsy*, with emphasis on the creation and re-creation of legal definitions in response to
state needs, public reception, and socioeconomic development. Chapter 3
considers the administrative application of legal formulas, with an eye to
the broader problem of defining social groups. It analyzes the origins of
the *raznochintsy* in the registration policies of the first and second revisions,
as well as its subsequent portrayals in administrative statistics of the late
eighteenth and early to mid-nineteenth centuries. Chapter 4 discusses the
creation of new *raznochintsy* in the processes of state building and spontaneous socioeconomic development. Chapter 5 moves from the develop-
mental sources of *raznochintsy* to social and cultural consequences and implications, exploring societal representations of *raznochintsy* in literature,
memoirs, and journalism. Chapter 6 then analyzes patterns of legal and
sociocultural self-definition, including the concept of the intelligentsia, the
problem of the "missing bourgeoisie," and the emergence of the professions. By relating these prominent historiographical themes to the phenomenon of the *raznochintsy*, it provides an alternative perspective on Russia's "absent" middle.

Given the diffuse nature of the *raznochintsy* and their presence in a variety of contexts, it is impossible to identify a closed body of institutional or
geographical sources that can serve as the primary basis of study. In official
documents the category appeared most frequently in the early and mid-
eighteenth century, a time when authorities were grappling with issues of
social registration and when institutions of central administration were not
fully developed. The category also occurred in European Russia and in
borderlands such as the Volga regions and Siberia that were being incorporated into the imperial framework. By the end of the eighteenth century
elaboration of state law and organizations both required and enabled
greater consistency in defining and applying social categories. Reform of
the Senate in the reign of Catherine the Great, followed by the creation of
ministries and the State Council under Alexander I, resulted in more coherent and systematic legal definitions and administrative practices, which

rendered the category *raznochintsy* less necessary for official purposes. Except for the instructions to the Legislative Commission of 1767–1768, societal representations of the *raznochintsy* were primarily a nineteenth-century phenomenon associated with the emergence of a self-sufficient, educated public. Cultural definitions emphasizing the role of *raznochintsy* as educated commoners thus joined and corresponded to the more precise administrative applications.

It is important not to exaggerate chronological distinctions or those between official and societal usages, for meanings recur, repeat, and overlap throughout the imperial period. Just as there is no single definition of the category *raznochintsy*, so, too, there is no clear chronology of development. The lack of chronological regularity and the need to pinpoint the phenomenon of the *raznochintsy* from a variety of perspectives and sources create difficult problems of organization and exposition. The documentation—which includes laws, Senate and State Council protocols, church and governmental statistics, local judicial-administrative and registration decisions, individual and group petitions, literature, memoirs, and journalistic essays—is official and unofficial, governmental and societal, institutional and cultural, European Russian and regional. That the sources are so dispersed, divergent, and fragmentary fully corresponds to the malleable, irregular parameters of the category *raznochintsy* and to the dynamism of the concept as it evolved from a predominantly legal-administrative-social designation into a sociocultural one—without, however, shedding its traditional aspects. Forever elusive, the *raznochintsy* are historically, and for the purposes of archival research, everywhere at hand and nowhere in particular.

Although the interpretation of the *raznochintsy* presented here finds solid confirmation in the history of the late nineteenth century, the category itself disappeared from the legal record in the postemancipation period. Traditional usages continued to appear in official and societal sources, but by the time of rapid industrialization, beginning in the 1880s, the notion of the *raznochintsy* was most readily identified with the history and mythology of the radical intelligentsia and revolutionary movement. To understand the social and administrative significance of the category in the late imperial period would require a corresponding examination of overall socioeconomic development, which is well beyond the scope of this study. The phenomenon examined here and its relationship to the larger problem of social categorization is limited primarily to preemancipation and preindustrial Russian society. The implications of the findings clearly are not. A need therefore exists for comparable study of the late imperial period; in particular, historians of the revolutionary era should consider what the traditional fragmentation of Russian society suggests about the acute sociopolitical conflicts of the early twentieth century.

*R*esearch for this book was supported in part by a grant from the International Research and Exchanges Board (IREX), with funds provided by the National Endowment for the Humanities, the U.S. Information Agency, and the U.S. Department of State. None of these organizations is responsible for the views expressed. Additional support was provided by the Research, Scholarship, and Creative Activity Program of the California State University and by a Faculty Development Mini-Grant and sabbatical leave from California State Polytechnic University, Pomona.

I am particularly indebted to the administrators and staff of the Russian archives and libraries where research for this study was conducted: the Russian State Archive of Ancient Acts (RGADA) in Moscow; the Russian State Military Historical Archive (RGVIA), also in Moscow; the Central State Historical Archive of the City of Moscow (TsGIAgM); the State Archive of the Russian Federation (GARF, formerly, TsGAOR) in Moscow; the Russian State Historical Archive (RGIA) in St. Petersburg; and the Russian State Library (RGB, formerly, the Lenin Library) in Moscow. I am also grateful to Russian colleagues who helped me to locate essential archival materials: Svetlana Romanovna Dolgova, Leonid Romanovich Veintraub, Marina Viktorovna Sidorova, and Galina Alekseevna Ippolitova. Additional materials were obtained from the New York Public Library, the Slavic Reference Service of the University of Illinois, and the Interlibrary Loan Department of California State Polytechnic University, Pomona, where Sue Benney and her staff worked tirelessly and effectively. Without the assistance of these institutions and individuals, this book could not have been written. Chapter 2 contains material from an article that appeared as "Problematics of Status Definition in Imperial Russia: The *Raznočincy*," in *Jahrbücher für Geschichte Osteuropas* [40 (1992): 319–39], and is reprinted here with the permission of the editors.

I thank my former teacher, Marc Raeff, for his generosity, honesty, and expectations. He was the first person to read a complete draft of this book, and his comments were crucial in helping me to revise it for publication. Hans Rogger graciously read the very earliest versions of some chapters and the entire draft at a later stage. His comments also have enriched this study significantly. Gregory L. Freeze and Gary Marker provided detailed and exceedingly thoughtful comments and criticisms, some of which have been incorporated here. Christoph Schmidt commented forcefully on an earlier draft, and Alan Kimball shared his own work in progress. I am grateful to Mary Lincoln of Northern Illinois University Press for her efficiency, professionalism, and commitment to this project. I also thank Linda Hart for assisting with the tables.

My parents, Rita and Sol Kimerling, have contributed more than their fair share to this endeavor. Not only has my mother read and reread arcane academic text without the least suggestion of boredom, but both my parents have repeatedly—with enthusiasm and visible pleasure—cared for their grandchildren so that I could run off to libraries and archives. Finally, this work was not completed without personal cost to my family. I can only marvel at the serenity and generosity of my husband, Gary. I thank him and our children—Eric, Carla, and Valerie—for their love, support, energy, and independence.

Structures of Society

Historiography and Problematics

WELL BEFORE THE ADVENT of "the new social history" in the decades following World War I, Russian scholars had developed two distinct, yet fully compatible, approaches to understanding the complex social arrangements of imperial Russia. Early in the nineteenth century the statist school of historiography focused upon institutions, instrumentalities of rule, and legal definitions in order to understand social relations and structures. By the later nineteenth century a socioeconomic approach had produced a plethora of monographs that examined the most important organizations and groups in society from a populist, Marxist, or liberal perspective. Following the rich prerevolutionary historiography, more recent studies also focus on either legal-institutional or socioeconomic issues. To some extent the distinction is chronological, reflecting the new socioeconomic classes that, with the capitalization and industrialization of the Russian economy, began to replace the juridically defined social categories called *sosloviia* (sing., *soslovie*). The sparse scholarship that directly examines the overall evolution of imperial social categories illustrates the dynamics involved and the need for closer attention to terminology.

Discussions of the relationship between governmental policy and social development rightly draw attention to the structure of *sosloviia*, juridically defined social categories distinguished by tax and service obligations and to a lesser extent by rights and privileges. Any inclusive study of Russian society must take into account this formal framework, beginning with the Law Code *(ulozhenie)* of 1649 and ending with the abolition of *sosloviia* distinctions by the Bolshevik government in November 1917. The first systematic effort to explain the concept of *soslovie* was that of V. O. Kliuchevskii, who viewed it as a legal term defining a series of political institutions *(uchrezhdeniia)*, independent of economic, intellectual, moral, or physical circumstances.[1] Kliuchevskii's main contribution was to focus attention on the negative quality of social differentiation. Inequality of obligations always corresponded to inequality of rights, but not vice versa; thus lighter obligations represented a negative "right" in relation to other groups.

In his truly compelling and largely successful analysis of "the *soslovie* paradigm," Gregory L. Freeze is quick to distinguish *soslovie* (status group) from another frequently used, though more exclusively legal designation, *sostoianie* (social category).[2] Freeze shows that in contrast to the relatively consistent application of the category *sostoianie,* the concept of *soslovie* evolved through a variety of flexible and nuanced usages beginning in the later eighteenth century, when it defined a gathering, assembly, or "social collectivity" lacking formal organization. By the end of the century it had come to designate a formal social organization with a distinct body of members. Only in the first decades of the nineteenth century did *soslovie* refer to a "constituted body" with an identifiable culture, legal status, and social identity.[3] While Freeze may overstate the corporative structure of social groups in the nineteenth century, he makes clear the flexibility, diversity, and complexity of *soslovie* definitions; the adaptability of the *soslovie* structure to economic and social development; and the multiplicity and proliferation of formal categories throughout the imperial period. In addition, he reminds us of the need to distinguish between legal representations and social facts.

Marc Raeff and Christoph Schmidt correctly counter the inclination to equate the *sosloviia* of Russia with the *Berufsstände* of Central Europe. Both men emphasize that the *sostoianiia-sosloviia* did not represent legally constituted bodies of persons with equal rights, eighteenth- and nineteenth-century Russian usages notwithstanding.[4] Richard Pipes echoes this view in modified form, attributing the apparent weakness of society before the state's power (comparable to Raeff's lack of constituted bodies) to the patrimonial or proprietary principle of Russian political authority.[5] Despite differences in interpretation these scholars place a shared emphasis on official policy and state-determined definitions as the basis for understanding Russia's complex social structure.

Historians of the postreform period are better positioned to incorporate socioeconomic explanations, but they, too, cannot ignore the legally determined *soslovie* definitions in analyzing the revolutionary situations of the late imperial period. Thus Leopold Haimson points to a growing discrepancy between legal definitions and socioeconomic realities as the basis for the shifting and fluid social identities that, in his view, account for the disintegration of society into a state of acute social conflict.[6] Other historians repeatedly identify the persistence of *soslovie* mentalities to explain Russia's failure to follow the model of Western European liberal, bourgeois development. Alfred J. Rieber sees the lack of political unity and the strength of regional and ethnic loyalties as evidence of the Russian merchants' failure to develop a mature class consciousness.[7] Another example of the incomplete transformation from *soslovie* to class is the peasant-worker described in so many studies of the Russian revolutions. More recently, historians of the educated classes describe a widespread search for professional and social bonds in a modern civil society—an impulse that dissolves into political and social fragmentation in the revolutionary situations of the early twentieth century.[8] Here, too, there is an assumption that the alleged rigidity and persistence of traditional *soslovie* fissures, combined with the commercial-industrial transformation of the late nineteenth century, underlay the crisis of social identities, which then helps to explain the unraveling of the old order. What is not recognized, however, is the extent to which those persistent *soslovie* boundaries were never fully erected.

Whether one emphasizes formal definitions, socioeconomic relationships, or some combination of the two, there are key issues of social and cultural development that remain problematic. First, neither the legal nor the socioeconomic approach adequately defines the structure of Russian society, or the lack thereof, in the age of serfdom (roughly 1649–1861). Historians traditionally draw attention to the discrepancy between formal categories and socioeconomic facts, but they still have not modified in a significant way the framework of Muscovite *chin,* imperial *soslovie,* and late imperial class. At the very least, there is a need to refine the noble landlord-peasant serf paradigm, which has not been fully examined and which may require significant modification.[9] Comprehensive study of the *raznochintsy* (people of various ranks, diverse origins) not only suggests the varieties of master-serf arrangements but also raises serious questions about the extent to which the nobility was delimited from other groups in society.

Second, inquiries into the relationship between state policy and social development repeatedly point to the absence of corporative bodies in Muscovite and imperial Russia to explain the nobility's failure to impose limits on autocratic authority and to highlight the difficulties experienced by the *Polizeistaat* in its efforts to reform and transform society.[10] But they do not fully explore the implications of this lack of structures and institutions for the formation of social and cultural identities.[11] Nor do they account for the dramatic, seemingly telescoped spurts of development associated with periods of reform from above. How is it that the professions, the literati, and the revolutionary intelligentsia emerged so quickly in the 1860s to dominate Russian cultural life? In light of research that reveals striking limits to autocratic power, it is imperative to reconsider the image of societal weakness and passivity *prior* to the postemancipation era.

Third, the formation of the intelligentsia and professions, their interrelationship, and their position in the larger social structure remain highly problematic. Although the subject of much serious study, because of its complexity and ambiguity, the phenomenon of the intelligentsia is still insufficiently understood. Investigation of the professions, on the other hand, has only barely begun, despite its importance to any analysis of the intelligentsia. Careful study of the *raznochintsy* illuminates the origins, contours, and particularly the sociocultural identities of the intelligentsia and professions. In addition, it helps to explain the prevalence of voluntarism, utopianism, and notions of classlessness in a wide range of societal and official groups during both the imperial and early Soviet periods.[12] Historians of late imperial Russia have yet to characterize adequately the social disintegration that played so prominent a role in the revolutionary situations of the early twentieth century. Although they correctly identify societal fragmentation as a basic reason for the acute, unmediated social conflict that swept the Bolsheviks into power, they erroneously treat it as a new phenomenon engendered by the dislocations of rapid industrialization. Thus they fail to recognize that social status in imperial Russia traditionally was ambiguous and indeterminate.

There are only a handful of very narrow studies that directly examine the phenomenon of the *raznochintsy*. Most discussions of this category take the form of peripheral comments in larger studies of towns, the bureaucracy, education, the revolutionary movement, or some other, more readily identifiable topic. In his very valuable and brief discussion of the *raznochintsy*, Christopher Becker relates the development of the concept to the larger process of estate formation during the eighteenth century.[13] At first an "et cetera" legal designation etymologically linked with the Muscovite *chin*, the term *raznochintsy* by the nineteenth century referred to a specific, relatively stable group of people outside the large estates—a transformation that occurred as a consequence of the regularization of ennoblement through service, embodied by the Table of Ranks. Becker goes on to identify an educational usage, also dating back to the mid-eighteenth century, that labeled non-noble students in state schools as *raznochintsy*. This usage was broadened in the nineteenth century, when literary, sociological, and historical texts referred to educated commoners as *raznochintsy*. By the twentieth century the term applied to déclassé or, to use Lenin's term, "bourgeois-democratic" intellectuals *(intelligenty)*, and it is this usage that has carried over into much contemporary historiography. Becker's analysis still provides a useful introduction to a very complex historical phenomenon; more important, it correctly insists upon treating the *raznochintsy* as a concept rather than as a social stratum.

More recent Soviet scholarship also examines the *raznochintsy* as a legal and social category in an effort to trace the formation of a concrete stratum *(sloi)* in society. The most extensive study published to date is that of G. N. Vul'fson, who supplies a range of information based on legislative, demographic, literary, and journalistic sources.[14] Vul'fson stresses the lack of any precise legal or even official definition of the *raznochintsy*, treating them essentially as the educated non-nobles who as early as the first half of the eighteenth century constituted a "democratic intelligentsia."[15] While Vul'fson's essay contains much useful data, his presentation often is confused, his sources are not always adequately identified, and his insistence on the democratic ideology of educated *raznochintsy* is plainly in error.

In a more successful treatment, I. B. Sidorova correctly draws attention to the confusion surrounding the category *raznochintsy* among Soviet historians.[16] Thus she attempts to provide a precise listing of *raznochinnye* subgroups, while acknowledging that there is no single definition. The subgroups included are hereditary *raznochintsy*, children of merchants and clergy who do not continue in the occupations of their fathers, unranked civil servants and personal nobles, lower-class townspeople *(meshchane)* and peasants who attain certain (unspecified) educational qualifications, retired soldiers, and for the eighteenth century, single householders *(odnodvortsy)* and other traditional categories of lesser servicemen *(starykh sluzheb sluzhilye liudi)* that eventually are absorbed into the taxpaying lower classes. Similarly, in her analysis of instructions *(nakazy)* to Catherine the Great's Legislative Commission (1767), Sidorova limits herself to statements by persons identified as *raznochintsy* and does not examine the many depictions of *raznochintsy* found in noble, single-householder, and merchant instructions. Both Vul'fson and Sidorova describe a process whereby the *raznochintsy* became a free, untaxed social stratum *(sloi)* by the end of the eighteenth century and, as such, evolved into the nineteenth-century "bourgeois-democratic" intelligentsia of Leninist conception. Despite the value of these studies, they are so very narrow in scope and intent that the full significance of the phenomenon of the *raznochintsy* is lost.

A careful reading of the voluminous secondary literature indicates that the *raznochintsy* originated in three aspects of Russian life: in governmental manipulation of social categories to meet the needs of the army and bureaucracy and to consolidate the empire; in economic structure and spontaneous societal development; and in the subjective, voluntaristic, and often essentially cultural nature of social definitions and identities. Within these areas of policy and development numerous conceptions and subcategories of *raznochintsy* evolved. The question immediately arises: Were these subcategories merely conceptions or did the conceptions mirror social subcategories?

It is important to stress at the outset that the category *raznochintsy* could be hereditary or transitional, taxed or untaxed, urban or rural, formal or informal. Thus definitions tended to overlap and often were contradictory. The discussion that follows will review in a brief, highly schematic manner the different types of *raznochintsy* that appear in the secondary sources.[17] Later chapters will then modify in detail the simplified types presented here. The most obvious source of *raznochintsy* and one that impacted on many other areas of Russian life was state service. Here one meets retired soldiers struggling to reintegrate themselves into civilian society and low-ranking officials or unranked administrative employees—the underground men of Ostrovskii, Dostoevskii, and Gogol.[18] While in service, soldiers belonged to the military domain *(voennoe vedomstvo);* once retired, they were free men, in most cases exempt from the capitation (poll tax) and other state and feudal obligations, though without a regular source of income.

They were entitled to engage in petty trades, acquire a plot on state lands, or return to their community of origin. The limited information presented in existing accounts suggests that, in general, retired soldiers found reentry into civilian society difficult. Although many returned to farming the family allotment, their free, tax-exempt status did not endear them to the landlord or taxpaying community.[19]

There is much more extensive information about *raznochintsy* in the bureaucracy. Both Soviet and Western scholarship focus on the development of the imperial bureaucracy as a distinct stratum *(osobaia prosloika)* in Russian society, clearly delimited from the landowning nobility.[20] While far from consistent in their definitions, studies of the bureaucracy tend to relate the *raznochintsy* to two discrete phenomena: sources of recruitment for the civil service and patterns of promotion within it. In this context it is possible to define the *raznochintsy* very broadly as non-noble officials with rank or as administrative employees below the Table of Ranks who were not registered in the poll tax population. Some authors distinguish *raznochintsy* from the sons of graded non-noble civil servants, while others also include the bureaucratic or "new nobility" in their definition. Both usages contradict the laws that regulated state service, though the inclusion of the service nobility is consistent with usages by nobles who considered themselves superior on the basis of lineage or culture.

In both military and civil service the *raznochintsy* benefited from the possibilities for promotion and mobility. As an upwardly mobile group the service *raznochintsy* occupied a transitional status, so that it is possible to characterize them as déclassé. But mobility was not necessarily upward; children of junior officers born before their father's promotion to officer rank *(ober-ofitserskie deti)* and children of personal nobles did not attain the privileges of their parents by hereditary right. Potentially, they constituted a downwardly mobile group, though one that was well positioned to rise through service and that fully expected to achieve nobility.[21]

In the early nineteenth century the growing importance of education to a successful career in the military or civil service also facilitated the rise of *raznochintsy* with special skills. At the same time, more stringent educational requirements reinforced barriers that blocked the promotion of those who were poorly trained.[22] Education thus benefited some groups of *raznochintsy,* just as it benefited some groups of nobles. It did not in and of itself guarantee social democratization of the officer corps or the bureaucratic elite, though significant advances in that direction had actually occurred by the twentieth century. The combined impact of the 1722 Table of Ranks, the new educational requirements of the early nineteenth century, and the sheer growth in the size of the bureaucracy created ever larger numbers of individual *raznochintsy* and subgroups of *raznochintsy.* Even if hereditary nobles continued to dominate the highest military and civil posts, their ranks were constantly being replenished from below. Regardless of political and cultural co-optation, the Russian nobility remained a porous social class throughout the imperial period.

The role of the *raznochintsy* in service was closely related to developments in education; in both areas existing subgroups of *raznochintsy* met specific needs of government and society. Concurrently, the growth and increasing complexity of the bureaucracy and the spread of education spawned new categories of *raznochintsy*. In some instances service and the acquisition of special skills constituted a single process. Before the reign of Catherine the Great there was no comprehensive effort to establish a system of state-sponsored primary schools, and even after her educational reforms the effective impact was limited to urban areas. It was not until the 1870s that significant progress in the spread of elementary public education to rural areas occurred.[23] Peter the Great's cipher schools, which aimed to provide a basic education for persons of all social categories (except serfs and single householders) opened in a few cities beginning in 1714–1715. By 1744 they had merged with the garrison schools for lack of resources and pupils.[24] For the better part of the eighteenth century both the government and the general population took a practical view of education; that is, formal education was desirable only to the extent that it met the specific needs of the government for trained personnel or of society for particular occupational skills.

The expansion of state schools in the eighteenth century thus followed the pre-Petrine pattern of specialized "professional" education, which now became more explicitly tied to prescribed social categories. Administrative departments and institutions opened schools or organized classes (as had the foreign affairs *prikaz* of the seventeenth century) to train the cadres needed to perform the duties of specific branches of government. In most cases the schools provided basic primary and religious instruction along with specialized and technical courses. As a result, Russia experienced a significant expansion of education in a wide range of military, administrative, church, medical, artisanal, artistic, and scientific or academic establishments. Still, there was no coherent, comprehensive system of education, but rather a fragmented, particularistic conglomeration of schools formed ad hoc in response to concrete needs or dreams. It was, however, a relatively open "system"; as such, it preserved another Muscovite pattern, that of state-sponsored education for commoners. Thus as early as the mid-eighteenth century the notion of the *raznochintsy* as educated commoners had appeared.

It is this category of *raznochintsy* that figures most prominently in the secondary literature. The centrality accorded the *raznochintsy* in studies of education emerges in three areas of investigation: (1) access to education, according to the laws regulating social status; (2) the relationship between social origin and the development of a revolutionary movement in the 1860s and 1870s; and (3) the role of educated commoners in the formation of the intelligentsia (whether defined as the radical *raznochinskaia* intelligentsia or more broadly as persons occupied with mental labor). In each of these arenas the *raznochintsy* came from a variety of statuses and backgrounds, including the vast unprivileged population subject to the capitation—a category that was created by the fiscal policies of Peter the Great and distinguished from the untaxed elites. They were bound together by a common occupation or educational experience, by their non-noble origins, or by shared attitudes and activities that stemmed from ideological commitments. The notion of *raznochintsy* as educated commoners included a broad range of administrators, technical specialists, proto- and semiprofessionals, professionals, scholars, artists, writers, and performers. Educated *raznochintsy* occupied positions at all levels of state service, though the majority were in low-ranking or unranked posts; others worked privately, perhaps even illegally. Comparable to the educated *raznochintsy* in skills and functions, members of the serf intelligentsia met the administrative, economic, and cultural needs of their noble landlords. A few educated serfs attained their freedom and consequently might enter one of the formally defined categories of *raznochintsy;* this transition could occur through state service, economic success, or a master's generosity. Eventually, the educated *raznochintsy* and the serf intelligentsia merged with the professions and the broader category of mental laborers.[25]

Throughout the imperial period social origin determined access to education (the type of school and curriculum) and the life chances (privileges, obligations, and career opportunities) that accrued. Still, with the exception of a few elite, primarily military schools for nobles, and until 1867–1869 the seminaries and ecclesiastical academies for the sons of priests, the vast majority of state schools contained a contingent of *raznochintsy* or could be characterized as *raznochinnye* institutions from the socially mixed composition of their student bodies. Because the *soslovie*/professional principle, first identified with the educational reforms of Peter the Great, tended to associate distinct social categories with specific occupations and functions, educational institutions were designed to train a given group of people for a prescribed service obligation. As a result, a legally defined category might dominate a given type of school or field of study. Medicine, engineering, and the arts, for example, were considered appropriate subjects for *raznochintsy*, whereas jurisprudence and the military sciences were directed toward nobles.[26] In addition, there were special schools for the sons of soldiers, unranked civil servants, clergy, and laborers in state factories and workshops. But the educational distinctions and the social boundaries they helped to define were never absolute, except for the exclusion of serfs, so that even the most basic delineation between noble and nonnoble was not necessarily maintained. In the garrison schools for soldiers' children, sons of poor nobles, officers, and the lowliest privates regularly studied together;[27] indeed, very few academic institutions were exclusively noble. As was the case all across Europe, the growing demand for formally educated personnel created new social and occupational opportunities for persons of diverse origins. Whatever restrictions or discriminations existed (and they tended to fluctuate), the number of educated commoners expanded continually.

Recognition of the growing pool of educated and semieducated Russians throughout the imperial period invariably leads to questions about the origins of the professions, the intelligentsia, and the revolutionary movement. However conceived, studies of these developments generally tend to overlap.[28] The terminology itself is so confused and contradictory that it will take more than one effort to formulate the appropriate distinctions, especially with regard to the intelligentsia.[29] The tendency to conflate the professions and the intelligentsia and to treat both as inherently oppositionist is primarily a Soviet phenomenon. But Western historians also are inclined to view the development of professional identities as a process that involved separation from state service and the formation of a political opposition. This follows directly from the fact that most studies of the professions take as their starting point the establishment of a state school to train specialists in a particular field.[30] Thus the historiography does not address the appearance of professional activities outside of state institutions before the 1860s, a process that surely is crucial to explaining the rapid development of the reform era.

The *raznochintsy* are most often discussed in order to characterize the radical intelligentsia of the 1860s and to explain the emergence of an underground revolutionary movement, particularly among university students.[31] Because of ideological constraints, Soviet historians are likely to associate radicalism with lower-class origins and so to search for evidence of progressive, oppositionist, or even revolutionary views among prominent eighteenth-century intellectuals who happened to be of non-noble origin. While recognizing the diversity and differentiation within the intelligentsia, these scholars still assume that educated commoners were naturally inclined toward opposition.[32] The search for latent revolutionaries is also evident in works that examine the role of *raznochintsy* (here defined as low-level service personnel, including artisans and retired soldiers) in peasant disturbances.[33] Such discussions are useful in countering the fixation with elite radicalism in the 1860s, but they do not challenge the basic argument that the emergence of the revolutionary intelligentsia or "the new people" of the 1860s resulted from the "arrival of the *raznochintsy*."

The alleged radicalism of the *raznochintsy* is by far the most familiar aspect of the phenomenon; it can also be the most misleading. Daniel R. Brower and Michael Confino correctly challenge the view that the presence of significant numbers of *raznochintsy* underlay the radicalization of the educated elite in the 1860s.[34] At the same time, Brower assumes that the phenomenon of the *raznochintsy* (and of the intelligentsia as a whole, for that matter) requires a sociological explanation. Confino also is inclined to represent the *raznochintsy* as a social entity by maintaining the distinction between noble and non-noble.[35] Once again, the notion of the *raznochintsy* (sing., *raznochinets*) as a social stratum or subgroup offers too narrow a perspective.

Almost unconsciously taking its cue from N. K. Mikhailovskii, the secondary literature points to another type of *raznochinets* whose very presence makes any purely sociological conception untenable, namely, the "repentant noble."[36] The repentant noble by definition is assumed to be déclassé, either because he was forced through impoverishment to earn a living by intellectual or professional labor (and hence became a *raznochinets* in the sociological sense) or because he achieved psychological alienation from his class of origin by adopting the appropriate attitudes, consciousness, or ideology (and hence belonged to the revolutionary *raznochinskaia* intelligentsia). In the second case the repentant noble was a *raznochinets* on the basis of culture and conscious choice, not on the basis of lower-class or non-noble origins that somehow inexplicably inclined the individual toward political opposition. The quintessential example of a cultural *raznochinets* was D. I. Pisarev, whereas N. G. Chernyshevskii and N. A. Dobroliubov met the necessary sociological criteria. As this study will show (and as Becker already has indicated), the first mistake of past discussions is to treat the *raznochintsy* as a social entity with identifiable (even if variable) boundaries. The second mistake, which follows from the first, is to use this fundamentally problematic social category to explain what is essentially a cultural phenomenon, namely, the emergence of the intelligentsia as a self-defined, self-proclaimed social subculture.

The tendency to deal with the phenomenon of the *raznochintsy* in sociological terms persists in histories of Russian towns, even when the *raznochintsy* do not appear as members of a distinct stratum in society but rather as persons occupying a temporary, transitional status.[37] In most studies of towns the *raznochintsy* represent a specific category in statistical reconstructions of the urban population.[38] Rarely is the category defined, and when it is, the cursory definition is not based on any general understanding of the terminology; rather, it derives from one or two official usages that are not necessarily applied with adequate attention to chronological accuracy.[39] Most historians ignore the problem of definition, presumably because they do not see it as central to their subject, yet the term *raznochintsy* appears in source after source, on page after page. In defense of the urban histories, it is important to note that the governmental and church sources containing the population data also fail to define the term adequately.[40]

Urban studies invariably also touch upon the *raznochintsy* in connection with official population counts. Associated with the formal taxpaying community *(posad)* in the late seventeenth century, and particularly with the introduction of the capitation in the Petrine era, the *raznochintsy* emerge as persons who were not members of the registered, service-bearing urban community *(posadskaia obshchina, gorodskoe obshchestvo, gorodskoe grazh-danstvo)* but who nonetheless resided permanently or temporarily in the towns and earned their living in urban trades that increasingly were supposed to be the monopoly of other specified categories.[41] Again, it is not clear who exactly belonged in this category ("trading peasants" sometimes are included), especially because as early as the mid-seventeenth century legal status did not necessarily correspond to occupation.[42] Moreover, throughout the imperial period there was considerable mobility into and out of the juridically defined social categories. The poll tax reform, and until the 1860s all subsequent regulations governing the towns, attempted to address the discrepancy between formal status and socioeconomic fact, to no avail. Whereas the urban community sought to restrict the presence of outsiders (here called *raznochintsy*), the government sought to register any unattached persons in a formal social category and preferably one subject to conscription and the capitation. Hence urban historians tend to define the *raznochintsy* of the eighteenth century as townspeople outside the formal taxpaying community, and those of the nineteenth century as persons without a formal social status (*bessoslovnye*) who did not pay taxes (*nepodatnye*).[43] As will be shown throughout this study, neither definition is adequate.

Despite confusion that is perhaps inevitable and certainly justifiable, given their intent, the urban historians nevertheless identify—not always consciously—two very important types of *raznochintsy*. First, they point to the existence of a hereditary *raznochinnyi* status comparable to that of other *soslovie* categories, large and small. Second, and most important, they suggest the notion of *raznochintsy* as outsiders.[44] This notion recurs in official and unofficial usages throughout the imperial period and sometimes is operative in the concept of the *raznochintsy* as educated commoners. As the remainder of this study will make clear, the idea of the *raznochintsy* as outsiders probably represents the most widespread and consistent application of the term, although the definition of an outsider was extremely unstable and variable.[45]

The notion of outsider status is particularly important for understanding the expansion and consolidation of the Russian empire. John P. LeDonne does much to illuminate the administrative aspects of this process in his study of local government in the borderlands during the reign of Catherine the Great.[46] LeDonne's work and that of Andreas Kappeler illustrate very nicely the intermingling of Russian and non-Russian laws, cultures, and elites. But these studies are unique in seeking broadly to explore how foreigners and minorities were assimilated into the general population and, in cases where assimilation did not occur, how Russian legal categories were applied to specific non-Russian individuals, communities, and social structures.[47] Although the sources usually identify minorities and foreigners separately and so do not normally include them in the category of *raznochintsy* (individual nationalities often are referred to as a *soslovie* or *sostoianie*), their position in Russian society was comparable in two important respects. First, assimilation or integration occurred formally through service and education and informally through economic activities and marriage. Second, whether assimilated or not, they comprised an outsider category.

Minorities and foreigners might enter one of the juridically defined Russian statuses, acquiring the privileges and obligations thereof. Otherwise, they continued to live under some special individual designation or within the particularistic legal framework of a distinct, officially recognized non-Russian community. That significant numbers of retired Jewish soldiers lived in St. Petersburg in the 1860s—Jews normally were restricted to a geographical area called the Pale of Settlement—suggests that integration into Russian categories through service and education did occur. Yet after a lifetime of military obligation, these veterans still were identified by their Jewish origins.[48] Even when a person's formal status did not become Russified, economic or occupational integration could occur.[49] The contradictory official policies that encouraged Russification, while preserving countless legal particularisms, could only antagonize minority groups and individuals, whether they resisted or sought assimilation; such policies also undermined, at least in a formal sense, the integration of those who did become Russified. Although the dynamics of these relationships are poorly understood and only partially documented, they are important in explaining the disintegration not only of the Russian empire but of the Soviet Union as well. Like their tsarist predecessors, the Soviet authorities pursued repressive policies of political and administrative integration, while recognizing and hence helping to maintain social and cultural particularisms.

The importance of imperial expansion in the development of Russian society suggests that even if one accepts the notion of the *raznochintsy* as a stratum, the nature and evolution of the group still would vary from region to region. Thus M. M. Gromyko defines the *raznochintsy* as a "*soslovie* group" of eighteenth-century Siberia formed primarily from retired military servicemen who intermingled with a variety of migrant and local elements. These Siberian *raznochintsy* generally earned a living as farmers (a few became merchants) and occupied a status equivalent to state peasants.[50] Eighteenth-century legislation identified a similar stratum in the frontier city of Astrakhan, where the *raznochintsy* also included runaway peasants, whose presence was tolerated because of the need for Russian settlement.[51] These and other regional variations in the development and definition of the *raznochintsy* indicate that, at most, they can be treated as a social entity only within the narrow confines of particular local conditions and preferably in conjunction with the history of the empire.

What general observations about the phenomenon of the *raz-nochintsy* can one derive from the morass of secondary literature? In a subject area where even the definition of the topic is ambiguous, one thing is certain: no single definition or formulation can be adequate. Yet, despite the wide range of approaches to the *raznochintsy* represented in the works of several generations of historians, there is a common thread that binds them—the tendency to treat the *raznochintsy* as a sociological phenomenon, either by presenting them as a discrete stratum in society (particularly urban society) or by attempting to explain the cultural aspects of the subject (for example, the birth of the radical *raznochinskaia* intelligentsia) in social terms. In the chapters that follow, this study will not ignore the social realities reflected in statistics, legislation, and administrative sources; on the contrary, the official institutional definitions of the *raznochintsy* are central to this endeavor. One cannot begin to understand the full significance of the phenomenon, how the *raznochintsy* defined themselves, how they in turn were defined by other groups in society and also in journalism and literature, without reference to the official categories. The interaction between formal and informal definitions is particularly important for understanding the dynamics of social relations and the formation of social and cultural identities.

Clearly, one must address the question of social structure, but this does not mean one must treat the *raznochintsy* as a fixed and unvarying social entity. Daniel Brower tellingly exposes the inadequacy of structural analyses that focus on *soslovie* and class for understanding urban change in late imperial Russia. He stresses instead the importance of formal and informal associations: clubs, mutual aid societies, professional organizations, and even official temperance societies and police unions.[52] Brower views the development of these associations as evidence of significant change precisely because at mid-century social relations had been isolated around families and neighborhoods.[53] Other historians also depict cultural societies in the early 1860s (The Society for Aid to Needy Writers and Scholars, literacy committees, and the Society of Lovers of Chess) and professional organizations at the turn of the century as expressions of a nascent civil society.[54] In both examples cultural and professional activities quickly became politicized as educated elites responded unfavorably to specific governmental policies and to police repression. Close examination of the *raznochintsy* suggests the need to move even farther from identifiable and familiar structures, networks, organizations, and associations—whether formal or informal, voluntary or obligatory, social or cultural. For it is unclear whether the nineteenth-century search for new forms of public identity, self-expression, and social and professional organization actually represented the emergence of a civil society. Like so much of the social and cultural terminology of imperial Russia, the meaning of such concepts as *obshchestvo* and *obshchestvennost'* has yet to undergo systematic investigation.

Whichever concept one examines, the *raznochintsy*, the intelligentsia, *ob-shchestvo* (liberal educated society), or *obshchestvennost'* (public service), to name only a few of the possibilities, emphasis must be placed on the word "concept." Thus the first step toward a serious understanding of the *raz-nochintsy* is to analyze the vocabulary and categorizations, both official (as represented in legislation and administrative practice) and customary (as represented in societal usages that include memoirs, literature, and period-icals). By treating the formation of social and cultural identities as a central factor in the development of social relations, one can eliminate the prob-lematic distinction between the "objective" and the "subjective" that plagues structural analyses and that cannot account for autonomous pro-cesses of self-definition or "self-fashioning."[55] Literary critics and intellec-tual historians often draw attention to the interactions and tensions that characterize the production, reception, interpretation or translation, and consequent reproduction of texts. The genealogy of the concept *raznochin-tsy*—expressed in official, societal, and scholarly representations—can thus be said to constitute "a reality as real as the concreteness of the relations within a society."[56] In other words, the social "imaginary" of the *raznochin-tsy* becomes a discrete social reality.[57] Clifford Geertz notes that explana-tion involves an exercise in "connecting action to its sense rather than behavior to its determinants."[58] The primary purpose here is not to explore the social foundations of such cultural phenomena as the *raznochintsy* but to make sense of the sociocultural terminology and the identities it repre-sented, however and by whomever they may have been defined.

This study addresses a range of interpretive themes, well established in the historiography, that require reconsideration in light of the case study of the *raznochintsy*. Some scholars may question how the study of a social category that is numerically so insignificant can touch upon and sometimes alter interpretations of such diverse topics as the nobility, the intelligentsia, the middle classes, the professions, the Great Reforms, economic develop-ment, and even serfdom. But it is grossly misleading to confine our under-standing of the *raznochintsy* to a statistically defined social category. The diffuse historiographical treatments of the *raznochintsy*—the very fact that the group appears in such a variety of works—highlight their importance to a broad spectrum of major historical problems; indeed, issues that seem unrelated can become interconnected in the phenomenon of the *raznochintsy*. We must therefore regard the *raznochintsy* not simply as a con-crete social element but as a dynamic concept in a process by which Rus-sians defined themselves and the contours of their society.

To that end, this study seeks to represent the *raznochintsy* as a social and cultural paradigm. The purpose, at least at this point, is not to supersede the established paradigms of existing historiography. The sources, texts, and social terminology that serve as the foundation of this work cannot sustain any notion of a predominant or inclusive "model." To understand the language and discernible realities of imperial Russian society, it is absolutely crucial to consider context and contiguity in all their unstable and incomplete particularity. Indeed, the essential lesson of the "*raznochinnyi paradigm*" relates neither to the numbers of identifiable *raznochintsy* nor to the frequency of the terminology, both of which can be regarded as statistically insignificant. Rather, it is manifest in the shifting contextual and contiguous spaces that the *raznochintsy* occupied and through which the category touched virtually every element of Russian society. It is therefore impossible to grasp the meaning of the concept *raznochintsy* without also reformulating or refining numerous clichés of Russian social history.

Chapter 2

The Legal Framework

IN ORDER TO UNDERSTAND a society lacking the principle of equality before the law, any analysis of its social structure must first consider the legal definitions underlying formal status, for although formal status did not always correspond to social and economic facts, it did reflect state policy. In imperial Russia most laws were not merely statutes setting forth juridical norms but administrative decrees that revealed the dynamics of policy formulation and social control. These laws cannot tell us how legal definitions were received and modified in private, nongovernmental usage, yet they do illuminate official responses to conditions in society that thwarted satisfactory implementation of social policy.

In the Russian empire formal social status derived from state-imposed legal definitions, not from traditional rights and privileges dating back to the era of European feudalism and institutionalized in corporative bodies or recognized as customary law. This did not mean that customary practices lacked a role in the evolution of institutions and laws; any close reading of imperial legislation reveals a dialogic process between legal definitions and socioeconomic realities that involved policymakers, administrators, communities, and individuals. The precise nature of this process still awaits comprehensive study. There is, for example, little understanding of the relationship between governmental regulation and the development of the peasant commune; the legislation regulating conscription makes clear that state law followed some (but not all) traditional peasant practices.[1] Indeed, there was no comprehensive legislation regulating conscription before 1830. It is equally clear, however, that peasant practices and priorities were not necessarily equivalent to—and in many instances actually violated—the official rules. The production of formal legal definitions may have originated in and been imposed from the highest rungs of political authority, but the legal formulations themselves still reflected societal reaction and customary practices.

In imperial Russia formal social status included three basic components:

heredity or birth (defined according to the status of one's father or husband), education (defined according to officially recognized courses of study), and occupation (defined according to heredity, education, and economic, service, or professional functions).[2] Each component carried with it a set of life chances or opportunities, including tax and service obligations, rights and privileges, and access to education, service, and its rewards; each component also brought subordination to an administrative authority or domain *(vedomstvo)*, so that it is perhaps more appropriate to speak of a person's belonging to an administrative-social designation than to a social category or group.[3] It was possible, then, for an individual to occupy a multiplicity of formal statuses. The best-known example was the ascribed *(pripisannyi)* or trading *(torguiushchii)* peasant of the serf era who legally resided in a town and paid taxes on favorable terms both as a peasant and as a formal member of the urban community *(posad;* later, *gorodskoe obshchestvo)*. Although such "peasants" were registered in the *posad,* they were not full members, and they might even remain under the authority of a landlord.[4] In a word, it was possible to be both a serf and a member of the *posad;* again, the formal status of a trading peasant reflected administrative rather than socioeconomic boundaries. Similarly, noncommissioned officers enjoyed special rights and performed required service duties, yet precisely because they came from a range of social statuses, their life and career chances also varied.[5] In retirement, for example, their right to occupy specified posts in the civil service depended not upon their service record but upon their status at birth.

The intermingling of formal statuses, categorizations, and definitions created a society in which no overriding principle or set of principles consistently determined social organization. Alfred J. Rieber's notion of a sedimentary society assumes a consistency within systemic, overlapping layers of social organization, each with its own characteristic set of features (Muscovite *chiny,* imperial *sosloviia,* and late imperial *klassy* or "classes").[6] The idea of coexisting sediments of social formations that originated in distinct periods and conditions of Russian history effectively suggests the complexity of the social structure. It may even explain the multiple statuses occupied by some groups and individuals, but it is far too neat and schematic to account for the inconsistency and ambiguity that so pervades official definitions of the *raznochintsy.* One might reply that it is the very inconsistency and ambiguity of definition that distinguished the *raznochintsy* from other groups in society, yet a close examination of legal usages of the term indicates that *all* social categories and types of categories intermingled and overlapped.

USAGES AND MEANINGS

The term *raznochintsy* appeared in legislative and administrative documents beginning with the reign of Peter the Great and ending with the era of the Great Reforms and Counterreforms. The legal sources do not provide a precise, self-contained definition; rather, they reveal a variety of amorphous, seemingly inconsistent usages, which at first glance suggest the impossibility of examining the *raznochintsy* as a distinct group in society. As the term itself indicates, the *raznochintsy* came from a variety of statuses and occupations; there was no single category of *raznochintsy* but rather numerous *raznochinnye* subgroups distinguished by social origin, occupation, and even formal legal rights. Further complicating the picture was the lack of correspondence between formal status and occupation—a situation that was commonplace in Russian social history.[7] Try as they might, policymakers could never confine that dynamic conglomeration of human beings called "society" to officially prescribed socioeconomic functions.

When examining the legal and administrative sources, it is important first to determine how the word *raznochintsy* was defined in a given context. In some instances it referred to a specific social category or cluster of categories; in others it served as a vague umbrella term. Thus a 1718 decree identified *raznochintsy* as a lower-class group that was neither peasant *(poseliane)* nor registered in the taxpaying urban community *(posadskie)*.[8] Similarly, a 1720 law levying a tax for construction of the Ladoga canal distinguished *raznochintsy* from peasants, merchants, single householders *(odnodvortsy)*, and natives who paid tribute *(iasachnye liudi)*.[9] Even more open-ended was legislation from 1736 that applied the term to a variety of taxed and untaxed groups employed as laborers in factories producing military supplies. One section of this law clearly separated the *raznochintsy* from soldiers' children, peasants, landless peasants *(bobyli)*, coachmen *(iamshchiki)*, craftsmen *(masterovye liudi)*, purchased slaves *(kuplennye)*, foreigners, and merchants; another, however, equated the term with several peasant categories being distinguished from merchants.[10] This inconsistency in usage occurred repeatedly. A decree of 1746 identified *raznochintsy* as a non-noble group that paid the capitation, including in its ranks Cossacks, junior clerks in the civil service *(pod'iachie)*, soldiers' children, and registered members of the taxpaying urban community *(posadskie)*. At the same time, the decree treated *raznochintsy* as a separate group, distinct from the others mentioned.[11] A ruling of 1756 that permitted seminarians to enroll in the Medical Surgical Academy also suggested the hereditary status of some *raznochintsy* when it referred to the shortage of students who were either foreigners *(inozemtsy)* or children of *raznochintsy (raznochinskie deti)*.[12]

Eighteenth- and early nineteenth-century legislation concerning the right to own serfs also presented the *raznochintsy* as an identifiable category, distinct from merchants, townspeople, members of craft guilds *(tsekhovye)*, peasants, coachmen *(iamshchiki)*, the lower service classes or petty servicemen *(arkhiereiskie slugi, deti boiarskie)*, Cossacks, Jews, Tatars, and other non-Orthodox persons *(inovertsy)*.[13] Similarly, in a law of 1775 *raznochintsy* represented a distinct category of taxpayers under the authority of the Astrakhan city magistracy. Because the population of Astrakhan contained significant numbers of migrants, it is not surprising that the *raznochintsy*, who included many runaway peasants, formed a distinct stratum. Government policy permitted runaways to remain in the area to encourage Russian settlement, which suggests a relationship between the phenomenon of the *raznochintsy* and the need to consolidate the empire. Still, the tax status of the persons comprising this "stratum" could vary: depending on occupation, some *raznochintsy* were equivalent to merchants and others to state peasants.[14] The law repeatedly treated the *raznochintsy* as a separate social category distinguished from nobles, peasants, and registered residents of the urban community (i.e., merchants, townspeople, and members of craft guilds).[15] At the same time, the malleable composition of the category explains why the *raznochintsy* often were defined negatively by exclusion. Thus one learns which groups were not classified as *raznochintsy* but gains no clear sense of exactly who was assigned to the category.

The earliest positive identification occurred in a 1724 decree specifically defining *raznochintsy* as low-ranking civil servants, administrative employees in government offices, and employees of the Court and stables (i.e., *sekretari* and *pod'iachie* down to the position of *podkantseliarist* and *podlye sluzhiteli dvortsovye i koniushennye*).[16] That same year another decree added retired dragoons, soldiers, and sailors, who did not pay the capitation; it also indicated that the *raznochintsy* included urban inhabitants who were not merchants but who nonetheless might be registered in craft guilds or in the formal taxpaying community *(posad)*.[17] This relatively precise definition continued to appear in the nineteenth century, though texts identifying specific groups of *raznochintsy* sometimes still contained an open-ended listing that concluded with "and others." Thus the 1800 bankruptcy regulation defined *raznochintsy* as "lower Court [*pridvornye*], state, and retired military servicemen, and others" who lacked the trading rights of merchants but who were permitted to borrow and lend money on the same basis as nobles and officials with rank *(chinovniki)*.[18] The 1857 edition of the Digest of Laws *(Svod zakonov)*, where one would hope to find an exact definition, echoed the accumulated legal confusion, first identifying *raznochintsy* as urban inhabitants, though not bona fide "citizens" *(grazhdane)* of the towns, and then listing exactly the categories found in the 1800 bankruptcy regulation.[19] The inclusion of retired soldiers in the category reinforced the lower-class, yet free and semiprivileged, status of its members. In addition, although these texts identified specific groups as *raznochintsy*, they also left the definition open by employing the term generically in the sense of "various other ranks, categories, groups."

The absence of a precise legal delimitation of *raznochinnye* subcategories was consistent with an even more ambiguous usage that employed negative social definitions and identifications. In numerous texts the term *raznochintsy* indicated outsider status of any type; that is, it applied to persons who were not formal members of the community *(obshchestvo)* or category in question. The very first legal reference to *raznochintsy*, in a decree of 1701 about judicial suits involving the ecclesiastical ranks, defined the *raznochintsy* negatively as persons who were not under the authority of the ecclesiastical domain *(Patriarshii dukhovnyi prikaz)*.[20] During the eighteenth century urban inhabitants who were not registered as merchants or members of the taxpaying community came under the rubric of *raznochintsy*.[21] Other eighteenth- and nineteenth-century laws applied the term to all non-noble groups who did not enjoy the right to own serfs.[22] Similarly, legislation from 1755 established Moscow University "for nobles and *raznochintsy*" with two preparatory gymnasia, "one for nobles, and the other for *raznochintsy*, except serfs";[23] here the law also suggested that *raznochintsy* were simply non-nobles.[24] Further confusing the picture, some eighteenth-century decrees even called peasants, in contradistinction to merchants, *raznochintsy*.[25] Finally, in the mid-nineteenth century, the Digest of Laws also made reference to *raznochintsy* who did not belong formally to any community *(obshchestvo);* such persons, unless they had relatives to support them, were to be entrusted to the social welfare boards *(prikazy obshchestvennogo prizreniia)* created by Catherinian legislation.[26]

Clearly, there was never an exact enumeration of the categories comprising the *raznochintsy*. The legal examples summarized here could be multiplied many times. Use of the term varied depending on the policy goals at issue, and thus frequently seemed to lack an objective basis. Although in some of the earliest legislation the *raznochintsy* included a range of Muscovite categories that were disappearing in formal law, there was no consistency even in this relatively narrow application. The category *raznochintsy* as an umbrella for archaic Muscovite terms represented only one aspect of a much broader phenomenon. Like the concept of the intelligentsia, the *raznochintsy* cannot be defined adequately without reference to the context of a specific usage.[27] In addition, legislation concerning ownership of serfs showed that over time the government continued to apply the label *raznochintsy* as an umbrella term—with, however, a variety of meanings.

TAXATION AND SUBORDINATION TO ADMINISTRATIVE DOMAINS

Early state efforts to identify *raznochintsy* grew out of the need to subordinate diverse groups in society to administrative domains *(vedomstva)* in order to facilitate tax collection, impose service obligations, and govern in the broad regulatory sense of the *Polizeistaat*.[28] Historians have long appreciated the central importance of the capitation in defining Russia's social structure and so have identified Peter the Great's poll tax reform as a significant step in the development of imperial social definitions. Beginning in the mid-seventeenth century, the numerous Muscovite ranks *(chiny)* began to agglomerate into larger groups called *sostoianiia* (sing., *sostoianie*) or *sosloviia* (sing., *soslovie*).[29] Introduction of the capitation accelerated this process by superimposing new social definitions on the functional Muscovite ranks, by establishing a clear criterion for separating the privileged few from the unprivileged many, and by impelling the government to attempt more comprehensive and accurate registration of potential taxpayers.[30] Legislation from the early eighteenth century identified *raznochintsy* as a lower-class, taxed category in both urban and rural society. The government acknowledged the separateness of *raznochintsy,* even if they lived within a taxpaying urban community *(posad,* as opposed to an untaxed *sloboda)* or belonged to a craft guild *(tsekh),* and while it did not regard them as formal members of the community, it still intended to tax them as such.[31] Indeed, *raznochintsy* could be included in the poll tax registers even if they did not belong to an urban community *(posad)* or a craft guild;[32] at the same time, groups such as retired soldiers and state employees, also identified as *raznochintsy,* in most circumstances remained untaxed.

The service obligations of the *raznochintsy* repeatedly identified them as a lower-class group. A decree of 1755 showed that rural *raznochintsy* in Siberia fulfilled the same tax and conscription obligations as state peasants. Here the term applied to residents who were neither state peasants nor coachmen *(iamshchiki).*[33] Earlier legislation affecting *raznochintsy* in Vologda also mentioned their obligation to perform state work, though it exempted officially certified craftsmen *(masterovye)* whose skills were needed elsewhere.[34] Finally, rules of promotion in military and civil service clearly equated the *raznochintsy* with peasants. Not only were the *raznochintsy* distinguished from nobles but also from the "volunteers" *(vol'noopredeliaiushchiesia)* whose rights in service placed them between the noble elite and the population subject to the capitation.[35] The legal-fiscal status of the *raznochintsy* in the eighteenth and nineteenth centuries left little doubt that the government regarded them as a lower-class group.[36]

Laws implementing the capitation identified several categories of *raznochintsy:* former indentured servants *(kabal'nye liudi)* who had served landlords, persons who lived on untaxed lands in Moscow and worked as hired laborers (including peasants who might already be registered to landlords), and factory workers who were the children of soldiers or low-ranking Court employees. All of these groups were to be registered to the urban community or peasantry, or be sent to the army.[37] The difficult process of defining which *raznochintsy* were subject to the capitation continued into the second half of the eighteenth century. Decrees of 1732, 1737, 1743, and 1744 ordered local authorities to ascribe to the urban community or guilds or send to the army any suitable *raznochintsy* who were not registered in the tax rolls.[38] The 1732 law provided the number, status, and location of such persons. These included low-ranking civil and military servicemen and their children who were not actively serving or whose numbers exceeded the statutory limits; (non-noble) officers' children; indentured servants and indentured minors *(kabal'nye maloletnie)* once they reached age fifteen; children of the almshouse poor *(bogodelennye nishchie);* executioners and their children; single householders, petty service gentry *(gorodovye dvoriane),* lancers *(kopeishchiki),* and cavalrymen *(reitary),*[39] craftsmen, apprentices, and laborers in factories, fortresses, and sawmills; immigrant Polish peasants; stone masons *(kamenshchiki)* and their children; Siberian furriers *(skorniaki);* workers at the state mint *(monetnyi dvor);* and runaway monastery peasants.

The law also instructed local officials to ascertain whether some persons had not been ascribed to the wrong category and thus omitted from the tax rolls in error. These might include individuals and their children registered in a variety of statuses: nobles; cavalrymen; retired lower military ranks and those with temporary leaves; retired craftsmen *(masterovye)* and their children; factory workers who were soldiers' children, registered members of the urban community, or peasants; minors whose age and rank were unknown; newborn children; employees of the Court; and petty servicemen of the church *(arkhiereiskie deti boiarskie).* Finally, noting that employees of the Moscow state printing house *(tipografiia)* and their children were ascribed, the Senate ordered officials to check the status of persons working in the armory and other workshops *(masterskaia i oruzheinaia palaty).* The 1732 decree strikingly revealed the confusion surrounding implementation of the capitation. The government sought to include in the tax rolls as many persons as possible and particularly to ferret out those who had been overlooked; at the same time, some categories of *raznochintsy* remained officially exempt, thereby undermining the seemingly precise meaning of the capitation in defining social status.[40]

Instructions for conducting a new revision, issued in 1743, showed that the problem of ascribing *raznochintsy* continued.[41] Here the term applied to a variety of categories that the government intended to register, except for merchants and peasants; the individual groups identified along with unspecified *raznochintsy* as subject to ascription included single householders, Tatars, and tributary natives *(iasachnye).* The law called all of these categories *raznochintsy* when distinguishing them from merchants and peasants.[42] In addition, it required that all unattached elements—that is, *raznochintsy,* persons of illegitimate birth, and freed peasants—who worked in trade or craft production in St. Petersburg or at state construction projects, such as the Kronstadt and Ladoga canals, be registered to a landlord, craft guild *(tsekh),* or urban community, or be sent to the army.[43] Those deemed unsuitable for service or community membership were settled in the strategic frontier town of Orenburg, at state factories, and if unable to work, in almshouses. Before taking action, however, authorities were to investigate whether any of the *raznochintsy* were actually runaway peasants or petty servicemen *(sluzhilye liudi)* who should be returned to their original place of residence. By applying the term to runaways, the instructions not only suggested the possible origins of some *raznochintsy* but also revealed the impossibility of confining the general population to a legally prescribed social-administrative framework. The dynamic commercial and handicraft needs and opportunities of Russian society, including the possibilities for employment in state enterprises, undermined the legal formalities that were so necessary for effective control.

A Senate decree of 1747 indicated another reason for the state's failure to realize its goal that "not a single person remain without a formal status [*polozhenie*]."[44] Taxpaying urban communities and craft guilds under the administration of a city magistracy or municipal council *(ratusha)* refused to admit *raznochintsy* who were too poor or disabled to shoulder their share of the tax burden. For this reason urban *raznochintsy* in Smolensk, Kazan, and Nizhnii Novgorod provinces, while ascribed in the poll tax registers, did not fall under the administration of local town governments. In Smolensk they came under the bureaus of the government, province, and district *(gubernskaia i voevodskaia kantseliarii)*, and in Kazan and Nizhnii Novgorod they were not registered to any domain *(komanda)*.[45] In this conflict between the central government and the localities, one finds clear support for traditional assumptions about the harmful economic effects of fiscal policy. Although the law made no such suggestion, it is conceivable that local communities simply expelled economically weak individuals, thereby perpetuating the creation of new *raznochintsy*.[46] Whatever the economic factors involved, it was clear that at mid-century the process of administrative subordination was far from complete.

On the eve of the Legislative Commission, the church and army continued to spawn unattached social elements that state authorities considered part of the poll tax population.[47] These included a variety of church, military, and Cossack ranks and their children who either were not in active service or had not served the statutory term. In most cases retired soldiers and any children born to them while in active service would have been excluded.[48] One last source of *raznochintsy* identified in the 1767 decree was foreigners whose economic activities brought them to Russia; those who converted to Orthodoxy (though not their children) remained exempt from the capitation, while all others were assessed at the same rate as townspeople *(meshchanskii oklad)*.[49] In its efforts to consolidate the empire the government also increased the number of *raznochintsy* by permitting runaway peasants to register in that status.[50] The contradictory goals of official policy thus helped to maintain the malleable social boundaries, which in turn served well the administrative needs of an expanding empire.

The important point here is not to attempt the impossible task of identifying every minor social category that some document included within the *raznochintsy* but to show that throughout the eighteenth century and well into the nineteenth, the government was engaged in a complex effort to determine which groups in society would be subject to the capitation and

which would remain exempt. As the process of registration evolved, officials referred to a wide range of unattached or unregistered social elements
as *raznochintsy*. The vast majority of Russians readily fell into the taxpaying
population, but the persistent problem of unattached persons revealed the
relatively fluid, indeterminate character of status definitions throughout
the imperial period. Characteristically, the *raznochintsy* included both taxed
and untaxed elements. Nor were the goals of ascription strictly fiscal; of
equal importance was the desire to subordinate specific groups in society to
administrative domains *(vedomstva;* sing., *vedomstvo)*. The issue of *vedomstvo*
subordination was vital, for it was the only means to ensure real government of the nonserf population. The *raznochintsy*—at one point directly
identified as persons under the authority of another domain—always were
problematic in that regard because their *vedomstvo* subordination could
vary and was sometimes unclear or undefined.[51]

PRODUCTIVE DEVELOPMENT AND LEGAL DELIMITATION

A major source of confusion in the definition of social categories
was the tension already mentioned between the state's legal-fiscal policies
and society's economic development. Whereas taxation and registration
policies tended to delimit boundaries, economic development and the government's own educational needs effectively blurred them. The confusion
was fully reflected in the assumed, but not always real, exclusivity of noble
rights. Like the capitation, the distinction between noble and non-noble
was a crucial factor determining social position, yet insecurity of status
among ordinary nobles is frequently attested. The sources abound in cases
of individuals who failed to gain official recognition of their claims to noble
privilege.[52] Less well known is the converse situation, where persons who
previously had paid the poll tax managed to enroll illegally in the ranks of
nobility, thereby gaining exemption. Thus a Senate decree of 1746 instructed the Siberian provincial administration to return to poll tax status
a variety of *raznochintsy* who wrongfully had attained noble (i.e., *dvoriane*
and *deti boiarskie)* status by order of the governor.[53] Here the problem of
the *raznochintsy* revealed just how porous the boundaries between formal
social categories remained.

Related to the vagaries of noble privilege—but more important as an
indication of the need to distinguish productive development from fiscal
policy—was the persistent practice of commoners' exploiting serf labor.
From 1730 on, house serfs, monastery servitors and employees *(slugi),* and
peasants were forbidden to acquire immovable property.[54] After 1739 service personnel (officers, dragoons, soldiers, petty officials, etc.) who did
not own estates lost the right to acquire "free persons" *(vol'nye liudi),*
though they still were permitted to possess serfs. Next a law of 1746 retroac-
tively prohibited the purchase of serfs with or without land by employees

and servicemen of the high clergy and monasteries *(arkhiereiskie i monastyr-skie slugi)*, boiars' servitors *(boiarskie liudi)*, and peasants; by persons registered as merchants or in craft guilds; and by Cossacks, coachmen, and various *raznochintsy*, who were ascribed in the poll tax registers.[55] According to reports submitted to the Senate, a wide range of non-noble groups had purchased serfs and registered them in 1723 during the first revision, in some cases obtaining entire villages and private estates.[56] Those who were now considered ineligible to own serfs included employees and servitors of the high clergy and monasteries, petty servicemen *(deti boiarskie)*, and *raznochintsy*, who were themselves part of the poll tax population and therefore not recognized as nobles, as well as Cossacks, coachmen, merchants, registered members of the urban taxpaying community, state farriers *(kazennye kuznetsy)*, and junior clerks in the civil service *(pod'iachie)*. The serfs in question were former exiles *(ssyl'nye)*, retired soldiers, and other lower-class servicemen settled on vacant lands *(gorodovye raznochintsy)*, and state peasants or private serfs sold by their masters. Whatever their origins, these serfs were to be re-registered as *raznochintsy*, formal members of the urban community, members of craft guilds, state peasants, private serfs, or factory laborers. By mid-century the tendency toward legal elimination of non-noble serf ownership was clear but far from complete.

Only in the second half of the century did these prohibitions become firmly established. Legislation from 1754 and 1758 clearly forbade non-nobles to purchase or possess populated estates. A law of 1758 also specified that non-noble military personnel and civil servants were no longer permitted to purchase individual serfs, although they could retain serfs already in their possession, as long as the prescribed taxes were paid on time. Otherwise the serfs would be turned over to landlords.[57] Instructions to the Legislative Commission submitted by merchants, low-ranking civil servants, and unranked administrative employees sought to rescind the recent restrictions and showed that the authorities indeed had applied them both to individual serfs and entire villages.[58] Finally, legislation of 1762 forbidding the purchase of serfs by factory owners and Catherine the Great's Charter to the Nobility represented additional steps toward enforcement of exclusive noble privileges, including the right to own serfs.[59] Nevertheless, as late as 1828—well after the 1812 general prohibition on the sale of peasants without land—the Senate again needed to clarify the point, stating that the prohibitions of 1758 encompassed individual serfs without land, as well as entire villages.[60] Certainly by the end of the eighteenth century, as state law and institutions became more systematized, the multiplicity of Muscovite ranks that so hampered official efforts to delineate social boundaries legally was becoming less of a problem, at least in relation to serfs and nobles. Tighter definitions had reduced the number of subcategories in terms of formal rights and obligations, yet throughout society and particularly at the middle levels, the lines separating categories remained highly fluid. Noble status in many cases continued to be subjectively and arbitrarily defined. Thus, in population counts from the first half of the nineteenth century, the St. Petersburg police failed to distinguish nobles from non-noble civil servants with rank *(chinovniki);*[61] at a time when the law was restricting ennoblement through service, they included all civil servants with rank in the noble category.[62]

The government's commitment to satisfying its fiscal needs, so strikingly expressed in the tax provisions of the 1758 decree, indicated that the "right" to own serfs was no less a convenient administrative mechanism than an exclusive noble privilege. As late as 1847—that is, virtually on the eve of emancipation—the central authorities still found it necessary to issue legislation regulating the status of illegally held "serfs" and fining their *raznochinnye* (i.e., non-noble) "owners." The *"raznochintsy* and others" who illegally possessed serfs included merchants, townspeople, personal nobles, petty officials *(prikazno-sluzhiteli),* and sacristans *(tserkovniki).* These "serfs" could petition local authorities for their freedom, while their "masters" faced fines. Once emancipated, the "serfs" and their families became state peasants, if they possessed land, or they entered an urban category subject to the capitation.[63] Increasingly harsh punitive measures revealed the stubborn persistence of the problem. An 1845 revision of the penal code prescribed that in addition to the fines already enacted, ineligible serfowners would not be compensated for the loss of "property" and might even face prison terms of from three to six months. Moreover, persons who falsely identified themselves as nobles would also be punished for perjury to the full extent of the law.[64] Two years later it became still easier for persons seeking freedom from ineligible masters to submit the necessary petitions.[65] Clearly, the government was intent on depriving all nonnobles of serf labor, but in treating what was essentially an economic phenomenon as a legal-fiscal matter, state policy failed to eliminate the abuses.

Indeed, the government's own policies directly contributed to the illegal practices. The legislation revealed several reasons for the continuing exploitation of servile labor by non-nobles. As was so often the case, the fiscal straits of the state undermined its intended goals. According to an 1836 decree, personal nobles and others who did not enjoy the right to own serfs but who had acquired serfs through inheritance were compensated for their loss upon the emancipation of their serfs.[66] The persons freed in these cases had to pay additional taxes to cover the cost of compensation—a disingenuous policy that later would be repeated in the redemption payments of the emancipation settlement. It is impossible to know the extent to which this obligation discouraged individuals from petitioning for their freedom. Some certainly sought and obtained emancipation, but overall the levy may have proved a deterrent. Not surprisingly, the government was more committed to solving its fiscal problems than to protecting noble rights.

Non-noble possession of servile labor also derived from official policies that at once promoted and limited social mobility. In his Table of Ranks, Peter the Great explicitly tied ennoblement to service rank. Throughout the imperial period people of lower-class origin enjoyed at least the theoretical possibility of attaining formal social mobility in military or civil service. Growing military and administrative needs required greater numbers of specially skilled, technically trained protoprofessional cadres, beyond those provided by the traditional educated elite. State schools attempted to provide the necessary personnel; by the first half of the nineteenth century, education played an increasingly prescribed role in determining social status—a role reflected in the entrance requirements and rules of promotion for military and civil service.

At the same time that the government sought to encourage performance with the promise of social mobility, it also became concerned about the influx of commoners into the noble elite and so took action to limit ennoblement.[67] The extension of personal noble status to larger numbers of people served this purpose. In the eighteenth and early nineteenth centuries persons who reached rank eight in civil service and rank fourteen in military service attained hereditary noble status. After 1785 (and possibly earlier) those below rank eight in civil service became personal nobles; that is, they, but not their children, enjoyed the rights of nobility, including ownership of serfs and estates. From 1845 on, hereditary noble status was not granted until rank five in civil service and only at rank eight in military service, thus increasing the number of personal nobles and their offspring.[68] The status of personal noble also became less privileged. According to legislation from 1814, personal nobles were forbidden to acquire serfs in the future, though allowed to retain those already in their possession. Their children, who had not themselves achieved noble rank and who belonged to the class of *raznochintsy*, were required to sell any peasants or domestic serfs they might have inherited either from hereditary or personal nobles.[69] Clearly, the complex state-determined processes of social mobility at work here contributed to the phenomenon of illegal serf ownership.

By the late 1830s even nobles who unwittingly acquired serfs previously in the hands of illegal owners were not permitted to retain possession.[70] This ruling resulted from a complicated and protracted investigation involving a townsman who had purchased a populated estate in the name of a nobleman.[71] The townsman's son had inherited the estate, but some of the peasants had gone to his sister, who had married a noble, and a few had been sold to other noble and non-noble individuals. The case revealed corruption and collusion among local officials, noble landowners, and upwardly mobile non-nobles. Equally important, it showed the extent to which wealth and commercial transactions challenged the legal-fiscal policies of the state, thereby undermining formal social boundaries. Thus a prosperous townsman capable of purchasing a populated estate also could hope to marry his daughter to a local nobleman.[72]

The phenomenon of illegal serf ownership by non-nobles makes particularly clear the need to distinguish productive development from the economic aspects of state fiscal policy. Economic trends, including noble impoverishment, provided a firm foundation for illegal exploitation of servile labor. Legislation from the eighteenth century showed that well after the administrative mechanisms were firmly in place, a free-floating population of laborers continued to escape formal registration. In conditions of labor scarcity, this group—which included runaways and persons with expired passports—fulfilled specific economic needs or even fell into illegal servitude through indebtedness. The government generally sought to uncover fugitives, but its main concern was to ensure payment of taxes.[73] The phenomenon of serf traders and laborers released by their communities to seek employment is well known; less apparent is the extent to which nobles themselves were involved in these illegal economic relationships. In 1816 a discussion in the State Council revealed that a host of *raznochinnye* elements—including *raznochintsy*,[74] merchants, townspeople, members of craft guilds, religious minorities *(inovertsy)*, Jews, and Tatars—acquired "Christian serfs" from nobles in exchange for loans. The State Council was concerned that *raznochintsy* not use such devices to obtain privileges reserved for the nobility.[75] Consequently, regulations issued the following year forbade nobles to mortgage serfs without land or to conclude financial agreements involving servile labor with the *raznochintsy* who administered their estates. The law did permit serfs to reside with *raznochintsy* on a temporary basis for education or training, though agreements reached on different terms prior to the new regulations were to be terminated.[76] The government tolerated non-noble exploitation of servile labor for narrowly defined purposes, as long as such exploitation did not evolve into permanent ownership.

Legislation from 1823 and 1824, which further tightened the 1816 rules, suggested that the authorities really aimed to eliminate virtually all uses of servile labor by *raznochintsy*—a goal consistent with other measures taken in the reign of Alexander I to limit serfdom more generally. The 1823 law required local authorities to review contracts between nobles and *raznochintsy* (i.e., persons lacking noble rights) for the use of servile labor; it permitted the employment of serfs as wage laborers on the basis of existing regulations or as paid apprentices to registered members of craft guilds. Under no circumstances could *raznochintsy* purchase serfs or exploit their labor without payment. The new law—while admitting that, despite all prohibitions, petty officials *(prikazno-sluzhiteli)* and sacristans *(tserkovniki)* continued to acquire peasants from nobles—represented yet another attempt to eliminate unlawful access to serf labor.[77] Going still further, the legislation of

1824 allowed "*raznochintsy* and other persons who lacked noble rights" to employ serfs "only for education and training."[78]

Subsequent decrees from 1825, 1828, 1840, and even 1847 indicated that illegal use of serf labor persisted. Not only did serfs pass between noble and *raznochinnye* masters/employers, but the *raznochintsy* possessed serfs on a hereditary basis in the name of nobles or exploited their labor free of charge through the generosity of noble relatives and acquaintances.[79] At the same time that official policy sought to tighten *soslovie* boundaries by limiting ennoblement, individual nobles continued to conclude private (and illegal) economic arrangements that undermined their exclusivity. Clearly, among ordinary nobles economic benefit or need took precedence over formal privileges. Serfs who participated in the national market could bring cash or skills to the estate economy. For the "*raznochintsy* and other persons lacking noble rights," access to servile labor represented an important source of manpower in conditions of scarcity that made it expensive to hire wage earners. Thus, in their instructions to the Legislative Commission, merchants and low-level bureaucrats clamored for the right to own even a few serfs; the "free" labor was crucial, they argued, if they were to fulfill their service and occupational obligations adequately.

Just as economic relationships revealed the gap between legal-fiscal categories and societal development, occupational diversity also tended to blur social distinctions, even in an age of serfdom. One need only examine the limited legislation dealing directly with *raznochintsy* to see the impossibility of defining the group economically. Despite their formal lower-class status, the occupational opportunities and actual levels of economic well-being of the *raznochintsy* varied enormously. Some depended on unskilled labor (*chernaia rabota*) or even begging for their sustenance, though those who lacked employment or relatives to support them were supposed to be sent to the army, factories, or church almshouses.[80] Others who possessed the requisite skills and resources became townspeople or sailors on shipping vessels.[81] Not surprisingly, local communities were reluctant to register impoverished individuals incapable of bearing the heavy tax and service obligations. By contrast, the central government, always fearful of losing potential taxpayers, generally sought to ascribe *raznochintsy* who were not already registered to landlords in the urban community where they had found gainful, though often also illegal, employment.[82] In so doing it sought to reconcile legal-fiscal definitions with economic realities.

Since the mid-seventeenth century, state law had linked occupation to formal social category; the purpose, revealed in legislation and subsequently in the urban instructions to the Legislative Commission, was at once fiscal and regulatory. As early as 1699, for example, the government limited specified areas of trade and handicraft production to merchants or registered members of the taxpaying urban community (*posadskie*).[83] Because the inhabitants of towns who were not formal residents often avoided taxes and service duties, they gained unfair economic advantage.[84] Thus the government sought to restrict their occupational activities and also facilitate enrollment in legitimate social categories. Beginning in the 1720s, authorities in St. Petersburg imposed residential and property restrictions based on social origins. A law of 1724 forbade low-ranking officials and employees of the navy and admiralty, identified as *raznochintsy*, to own homes on Admiralty Island; instead, they were to build only on Vasil'evskii Island.[85] Similarly, in 1735 the Senate ordered the creation of a new marketplace for St. Petersburg *raznochintsy*, segregating their shops from those of merchants and limiting their business to products the merchants did not carry. *Raznochintsy* were permitted to engage in merchant trades only if no merchants were so occupied.[86] The tendency toward greater occupational segregation continued. In 1754 St. Petersburg merchants obtained the exclusive right to transport goods between the capital and Kronstadt; foreigners, merchants from other cities, *raznochintsy*, and peasants were required to sell to them any shipping vessels they owned.[87] In contrast to these narrowly applied restrictions, the urban instructions to the Legislative Commission overwhelmingly indicated that nonmerchants continued to encroach on merchant trades *(torgi)*. Once again, economic development penetrated formal legal boundaries.

Catherine the Great's 1785 Charter to the Towns represented a capstone formulation of occupational restrictions based on social category,[88] although economic conditions and even official needs again undermined the desired symmetry. Despite the well-known competition between merchants and serf traders, which continued until emancipation, the two groups cooperated in commerce.[89] For persons who could not hope to achieve real social mobility in the form of ennoblement, legal and economic privileges represented a beneficial alternative. Thus the charter permitted a new category, distinguished citizens *(imenitye grazhdane)*, to participate in the once exclusively merchant trades.[90] According to the 1800 bankruptcy regulation, *raznochintsy* were allowed to borrow and lend money on the same basis as nobles and officials with rank *(chinovniki)*, and hence represented a relatively privileged group. *Raznochintsy* (defined here as retired low-ranking military servicemen and civil servants), their widows, and the wives and unmarried daughters of soldiers on active duty clearly needed sustainable sources of income.[91] Consequently, legislation from 1824 permitted the widows of *raznochintsy* and soldiers' wives and daughters to engage in trades designated for registered members of the urban community (i.e., *meshchane* or *posadskie);* they could sell or produce any product, though as shopkeepers they were restricted to goods they and family members manufactured with the assistance of no more than three laborers.[92] Clearly, there was no absolute commitment to occupational segregation based on social origin, particularly when the formal community failed to provide equivalent economic services or when social welfare needs arose.

Regardless of official intentions, it would not have been possible for the underinstitutionalized autocracy to enforce occupational restrictions on every petty trader. Moreover, the government's main concern was not individual economic encroachments but the possibility that outsiders who were not formal members of the local community might escape administrative controls, and hence avoid tax and service obligations. Whereas the central authorities sought to ascribe "outsiders" to the communities where they lived and worked, local administrators preferred to see the restrictions on persons who did not fulfill public duties strictly enforced. The last thing a community wanted was the additional tax burden that unnecessary members, unable to contribute their share, might bring. Legislation from 1832 addressed this conflict by making it easier for state peasants and free persons of any status to register in an urban category, while at the same time releasing the formal community from responsibility for the new members' taxes for five years.[93] When actual ascription was not achieved, the authorities still required *raznochintsy*, and even nobles who owned immovable property in the towns, to pay taxes and perform service on the same basis as "real city residents" (i.e., registered merchants, townspeople, and members of craft guilds).[94] The driving force behind ascription and occupational segregation remained administrative.

There is abundant documentation of the widespread economic, social, and geographical mobility that gave to imperial Russian society its dynamic, fluid, and infinitely colorful character.[95] At virtually all levels of society, economic relationships violated formal social boundaries. The lower-class entrepreneurs who moved with such ease across the vast, diverse reaches of the empire; the unregistered traders, artisans, and laborers who were so visible in the towns; the urban "citizens" who lived illegally in rural villages (and whose presence the peasants opposed); and the economic relationships (legal and illegal) that brought together nobles, merchants, peasants, and *raznochintsy*—all revealed a society where social boundaries were easily crossed and where nobles of elite or lowly birth need not worry about derogation.[96] Ownership of serfs did not necessarily indicate noble status, registered merchants did not necessarily engage in trade, and peasants were not necessarily farmers. According to official statistics from 1802–1803, the artisanal class in the town of Kremenchug included nobles, *raznochintsy*, townspeople, merchants, and Jews.[97] Even within that most regulated of hierarchies, the bureaucracy itself, there was no clear delineation of functions between the different levels of personnel and authority; here, too, the lack of correspondence between rank *(chin)* and office *(dolzhnost')* was indicative of porous boundaries.[98] Whether one examines economic relationships, formal categories, or the rules of service, it is impossible to characterize the social delimitations of imperial Russia as immobile and rigidly fixed. On the contrary, the absence of firm boundaries and the underlying lack of structure produced a society where social definition, whether high or low, was fundamentally indeterminate.

The formal boundaries (not to mention the informal relationships) distinguishing groups in Russian society were often vague and changeable. Variability in legal definitions resulted primarily from state policies that sought to subordinate all groups and individuals to prescribed administrative domains; because policy did not develop in a bureaucratic vacuum, the government repeatedly felt compelled to manipulate and adjust definitions in response to concrete economic and social conditions. Spontaneous, uncontrolled, and unregulated socioeconomic development made the formulation of legal norms a largely ad hoc affair. During the eighteenth century policymakers sought to define social boundaries by combining and manipulating the traditional Muscovite and newer Petrine categories. The process was confused and protracted. It was difficult to apply the Petrine categories by dictate; given the continued underinstitutionalization of society, the primary goal of administrative subordination remained elusive.

By the last decades of Catherine the Great's reign, much of the Muscovite social terminology had disappeared. Still, vestiges of traditional groupings remained, some having been renamed, and a new proliferation of subcategories was underway—a proliferation related to the expansion of the national (empirewide) economy, higher education, the army, and the bureaucracy. The Charter to the Towns did not mention the *raznochintsy*, though subsequent decrees continued to employ the term to represent both a specific category and clusters of categories. Legislation from the first half of the nineteenth century repeatedly evoked the *raznochintsy* to distinguish nobles from non-nobles, a usage that by the 1830s also appeared in literary and journalistic sources.[99] Similarly, St. Petersburg city regulations of 1846 and 1860 defined *raznochintsy* as scholars, artists, performers, and others who were not personal nobles or honored citizens but whose hereditary rights were equivalent to those categories.[100] The "*raznochintsy* as non-nobles" was actually a form of the "*raznochintsy* as outsiders" usage; while the non-noble meaning dated back to the mid-eighteenth century, its more frequent appearance in the early nineteenth century reflected governmental efforts to maintain the social formulas so painstakingly worked out over the previous century. Official policy may have exhibited a greater commitment to maintaining social barriers, but because of the state's own technical needs and because of society's own productive development, the prereform autocracy was no more successful in this regard than its eighteenth-century predecessor.

PROBLEMATICS OF SOCIAL DEFINITION

Legal definitions of the *raznochintsy* suggest several conclusions about the status and significance of these groups. Although in some cases the *raznochintsy* consituted a minor hereditary category, of which there were many in imperial Russia, they are best understood in negative terms relative to other social groupings. More than a transitional status, the category of *raznochintsy* as outsiders emerged in a particular context and generally referred to non-nobles or to local inhabitants who were not registered as formal members of a given community or social group. In the latter case the legal definitions clearly developed in conjunction with administrative designations, a practice that continued traditional Muscovite patterns.[101] Thus, while the category soldiers' children *(soldatskie deti)* always was defined in terms of the rights and obligations of children born to fathers in active service, the actual composition of the group encompassed a larger body of persons who collectively came under the jurisdiction of the military domain *(voennoe vedomstvo)*. Within (and sometimes even outside) the military domain, there were subcommands and consequently subcategories of soldiers' children, identified by their specialized training and functions, which then brought accompanying obligations and privileges different from those of the larger group.[102] In Russian society as a whole the *raznochintsy* embodied a similar structural dynamic. In whatever context the *raznochintsy* as outsiders appeared, they represented persons who lived beyond the particular administrative-social boundary in question.

It is possible to treat the eighteenth century, at least up to the promulgation of Catherine the Great's charters, as a transitional period during which the numerous Muscovite ranks *(chiny)* agglomerated into the larger, though still internally differentiated, social categories *(sostoianiia* or *soslov-iia)* of the imperial period. The term *raznochintsy* originated in this transitional process, wherein the new imperial categories were superimposed upon the traditional Muscovite ranks, which did not transfer automatically into the more recent groupings.[103] The open-endedness of this transformation would explain why the term *raznochintsy* referred to a specific social category and yet was also used generically in the sense of outsiders or "and others." Indeed, the transition to imperial categories was never fully accomplished. The state's need for educated personnel to man a growing military and administrative apparatus continually introduced new dynamics of social definition and a new proliferation of categories and subcategories, reminiscent in their particularism of the older Muscovite ranks. The specific usages of the term *raznochintsy* reflected this confusing social mosaic; more important, they suggest the need to consider the functional nature of social definitions and identities in imperial Russia as one crucial aspect of that society's fragmentation. By focusing on the functional element, which resulted from both socioeconomic development and state policy, one can further explain not only the insecurity of social status in Russia but also the voluntaristic, and hence subjective, evolution of social and cultural identities, including that of the intelligentsia.

*I*n his classic history, *The Empire of the Tsars and the Russians*, Anatole Leroy-Beaulieu relates the following conversation: " 'In our country,' one of the principal compilers [authors] of the Emancipation Act, Prince V. Tcherkassky, once said to me, 'the distinctions of classes have never existed but on the surface. From the Varangians of Rurik to Peter the Great and Catherine II, the nobility has been only a thin and superficial allusion. On scratching the soil, you find the old Slavic hardpan smooth and even.' "[104]

To interpret this statement correctly, it is necessary to avoid a socioeconomic definition of class. When Prince Tcherkassky spoke of "the distinctions of classes," he was referring to the fundamental insecurity of elite status that made social distinctions ambiguous and changeable and to the underlying importance of culture, as opposed to economic inequities, in defining social identities. The contradictory and variable legal statuses of the *raznochintsy* strongly suggest that Russian society lacked the structures and firm boundaries normally attributed to a social "system." Studies of urban-rural migration and of movement in and out of social categories also support this conclusion. The uncertain status of retired soldiers further illustrates the point. Large numbers of these men returned to their original homes, but administrative-social reintegration was difficult precisely because of their special legal status. Legal particularisms created an insecurity of status that undermined social boundaries by making it necessary for veterans to depend on their families without recognition as full members of the community. In short, multiple juridical definitions, porous social boundaries, and insecurity of status were compatible and mutually reinforcing.

If one views the legal definitions not simply as policy imposed from above but also as a process of production and reproduction in response to societal reaction and socioeconomic development, then the ambiguity and uncertainty of social distinctions become particularly clear. Historians repeatedly draw attention to the absence in Russian society of institutions that could challenge the authority of the tsar. Scholars attribute the absence of such institutions, and the ultimate failure to develop a true civic society on the Western European model, to the weakness of social groups and to repressive policies that stifled all private initiative, even when that initiative sought to address a recognized public need. At the same time, scholarship also shows that regardless of repression and autocratic pretensions, real state power was limited. How, then, can one explain both the weakness of society and the weakness of the state? The answer lies in the extreme fragmentation and particularism of Russian society—a fragmentation that official policy probably promoted, even as it tried and failed to overcome it. The legal confusion and the socioeconomic differentiation so apparent in definitions of the *raznochintsy* both reflected and reinforced the social fragmentation. Even Harold Perkin's notion of preindustrial England as a society of vertical (as opposed to horizontal) connections of dependency and patronage seems far too orderly and symmetrical to fit the Russian case.[105]

The imperial government's response to the lack of social structure was to regulate, reform, and solve problems through administrative means. The result was not to impose rigid structures but to prevent structures and institutions from ever crystallizing, precisely because of the constant interference and intervention that aimed to establish the elusive structure. This dynamic contrasts sharply with the situation in the German home towns of the eighteenth century, where the lack of any precise legal diagram of a town produced stable institutions that formed as "patterns of civic behavior" and that were discernible in actual events and social relations.[106] In Russia, society's response to the lack of structure and the insecurity it spawned was to clamor for formal definition, and hence for recognition of a status, function, or public role. Again, the purpose was not to defend rigid *soslovie* barriers that did not actually exist but to carve out a position, a mooring in society, that could provide some measure of security and predictability.[107] The failure to achieve a clear definition of social categories (either official or societal) helps to explain the continued importance of the tsarist myth and of personalized authority relationships in binding the social fabric.[108] An individual's place in society and the polity was conceived more in terms of personal relationships, including that with the ruler, than in terms of group membership (as the *soslovie* framework would suggest).

It is difficult to imagine any framework of social relations that would have universal validity throughout the Russian empire; even the noble-serf paradigm cannot account for the diversity and dynamism of societal relationships. As Alfred Rieber suggests, it is necessary to think in terms of multiple frameworks.[109] The historical processes that generated these conditions date back at least to the fifteenth century, when the gathering of the Russian lands created the unstable, socially fragmented Muscovite polity. The accumulation of regions, cultures, and socioeconomic structures continued with the formation and expansion of the Russian empire, again producing a fragmented, protean social "structure." In the absence of a suitable sociological model for defining imperial social categories, one can turn to the patterns of definition and self-definition revealed in administrative practices and the articulation of sociocultural identities. By examining the social terminology of imperial Russia, one can hope to learn something about how groups in society created and re-created themselves and their relationships to others. Historians describe a similar process in another of Europe's diverse preindustrial empires. In colonial Mexico subjective social terminology developed in a context where the Spanish Crown sought to govern by imposing legally defined categories; where groups in society redefined and remolded these categories for their own purposes; where formal social barriers either were ignored or never fully erected; and where races and cultures mingled, clashed, and combined.[110]

Administrative Applications and the Origins of *Raznochintsy*

Free persons and *raznochintsy* comprise a class about
which it is difficult to say anything definite.

Karl German, 1819

NOWHERE WAS THE CLOSE RELATIONSHIP between imperial social categories and fiscal-administrative policy more evident than in official applications of the category *raznochintsy*. And nowhere was the impossibility of formulating definitions that adequately contained society's spontaneous productive development more glaringly exposed. Muscovite law had employed the notion of "persons of various ranks" *(raznykh chinov liudi)*, but the *raznochintsy* as a collective entity originated in official efforts to register the population in legally defined social categories—categories designed to impose taxation and bring each and every individual under the authority of an appropriate administrative domain. This process began already with the Law Code of 1649, though the government did not make a concerted effort to achieve full registration until the capitation was introduced at the end of Peter the Great's reign. Like the laws upon which they were based, administrative interpretations of the *raznochintsy* confirm the absence of any uniform definition. At the same time, the very range of usages and categorizations sheds light on important dynamics of social definition. By carefully examining the specific contexts in which the category *raznochintsy* appeared, one can begin to understand the complex interplay of registration policies, state and military service, imperial expansion, and spontaneous societal development in the formation of social categories.

The formal category *raznochintsy* appeared most frequently in governmental documents of the early and mid-eighteenth century; at the end of the century and particularly in the first half of the nineteenth century, its importance as an official social designation declined. As statute law and state organizations were elaborated, greater regularity in defining and applying social categories became possible, and the category *raznochintsy* became less useful as an administrative tool. After emancipation in 1861 the concept disappeared entirely from legal sources; it survived in administrative statistics, but its meanings became increasingly informal and cultural. Administrative definitions of the *raznochintsy* shed light on two crucial aspects of Russian social development: the delimitation of groups subject to the capitation and the emergence of the educated classes. In the first half of the eighteenth century the category played an important role in the formation of the poll tax population. One cannot begin to understand the *sostoianie-soslovie* structure of imperial Russia without reference to the difficult process of assigning individuals, groups, and communities to the appropriate administrative domains. Similarly, by the first half of the nineteenth century official statistics associated the *raznochintsy* with semieducated, semispecialized, semiprofessional elites. In both contexts the category was transitional: at first it included Muscovite social elements that were undergoing redefinition, and later, "modern" social elements that would alter existing structures and generate new categorizations and identities.

There was no general census of the Russian empire until 1897. Before that date official statistics served narrow administrative needs and tended to be fragmentary, particularistic, and uneven in quality.[1] In most cases the available data are suitable only for purposes of illustration, not for sustained quantitative analysis. Still, if one explores the statistical materials as text rather than actual fact, they contribute significantly to historical understanding.[2] The preceding chapter shows the extent to which legal definitions of the *raznochintsy* constituted a "fictive" (in the sense of created) construction. This chapter will examine administrative applications of the category in order to explore further the notion that official documents are representations rather than transparent reflections of concrete historical circumstances. The purpose is not to determine the exact demographic dimensions of the phenomenon of the *raznochintsy;* to do so would require numerous microstudies of communities and institutions in the French tradition of *histoire totale.* Precisely because the statistical data can be no more indicative of social facts than either statute law or legal-administrative documents, the goal here is to examine how local officials applied the concept of the *raznochintsy,* thereby illuminating more fundamental dynamics of social categorization.

SOCIAL REGISTRATION AND DELIMITATION

Census data provide the most extensive, though still problematic, source for analyzing the general population of the Russian empire. Muscovite and early Petrine censuses had counted households subject to taxation.

Toward the end of Peter the Great's reign introduction of the capitation required periodic enumerations of all taxable males. In addition to these revisions *(revizii)* there were administrative records that counted persons actually present (assuming they registered with local authorities, and many did not), as well as parish-based church registers of confessions, marriages, and births.[3] Aside from the organization and maintenance of a bureaucracy and standing army, the central task of government in the first half of the eighteenth century was to register the population in official social categories and particularly to identify persons who were subject to the capitation and conscription. After the second revision (1743–1747) the initial process of registration was completed, but the close relationship between formal social definitions and the health of the state treasury continued to occupy the highest levels of government until emancipation in 1861.

The revisions expressed very clearly the administrative and fiscal concerns that drove official formulation of social categories. Data from the first revision, collected in 1718–1727 and summarized in a general table of 1738, included both taxed and untaxed groups; as a population count, it was therefore more complete than later revisions. The category *raznochintsy* appeared but was not consistently defined; groups that legal definitions included in the category at least by 1724, such as retired soldiers, were listed separately. While one must allow for a time lag between legal pronouncements and administrative implementation, it is clear that the census takers, regardless of whom they assigned to the category, recognized more than one group of *raznochintsy*. According to data presented by V. M. Kabuzan, the *raznochintsy* were not civil servants *(prikaznye liudi, pod'iachie)* or retired military servicemen; they and peasants could be registered in the urban community *(posad)*, but officials still distinguished them from full members (referred to as *kupechestvo* or merchants). They were also distinct from townspeople *(meshchane)* and members of craft guilds *(tsekhovye);* from the various categories of private, state, and church peasants; from church hierarchs and petty service nobles of Muscovite origin; from single householders, ecclesiastical ranks *(tserkovniki* and *popy)*, factory workers, artisans and laborers *(rabotnye liudi)*, minors *(nedorosli)*, foreigners, Christian and non-Christian minorities, Cossacks, and coachmen.[4]

. Local reports from the 1720s and 1730s had delimited the *raznochintsy* with less clarity than the table of 1738, revealing their importance as a transitional group from Muscovite to Petrine categories. Like the legal definitions of the early eighteenth century, these sources identified *raznochintsy* in a variety of ways: as taxed and untaxed, as rural and urban, as an umbrella term for subcategories of lesser servicemen (military, state, and ecclesiastical), as ecclesiastical offspring who lacked an active position, as persons with no clearly delimited place in Russian society (new converts, foreigners, and the poor who depended on church assistance), as a separate social category, as servitors in the Ukrainian frontier force *(landmilitsiia)*, together with single householders, and as a group that could be classified with peasants and domestic serfs.[5] The mosaic of *raznochinnye* subcategories reflected the full complexity of Peter the Great's poll tax reform, especially the redefinition of social categories. When *raznochintsy* and their children joined active Petrine service groups, they remained untaxed, but when the authorities identified them as merchants, artisans, peasants, and factory workers, they were registered accordingly and tended to become lower-class taxpayers. The role of *raznochintsy* and single householders in manning the Ukrainian frontier force offered the clearest illustration of this distinction. A vestige of Muscovite militia formations, the Ukrainian frontier force was not incorporated into the new standing army. Moreover, the special status of single householders, like that of Cossacks, revealed the persistence of pre-Petrine military social structures well into the nineteenth century.[6]

Along with the obvious goal of increasing the number of taxpayers, the registration of *raznochintsy* in the first revision revealed two other factors driving the formation of Petrine social categories: governmental efforts first to equate formal status with societal function and then to subordinate each status grouping to the appropriate administrative domain *(vedomstvo)*. Regardless of origins, *raznochintsy* of all types were assigned to Petrine categories on the basis of occupation and service function. Farmers became state peasants (and were referred to as such), traders and artisans became registered members of the urban community *(posad)*, and those who were suitable for military service became soldiers. Still, the lack of correspondence between social category, occupation, and administrative domain persisted; *raznochintsy* and peasants who resided in towns and paid the capitation did not necessarily belong to the formal urban community or come under the authority of the magistracy.[7] Consistent with the functional ranks of Muscovy and rooted in the Law Code of 1649, Petrine social categories did not represent a radical departure. Nor did Petrine legislation seek to replicate the estates of Central Europe or the orders of old regime France; rather, it attempted to redefine Muscovite categories only to the extent required to eliminate discrepancies between formal status and societal function. Similar reforms occurred in the reign of Catherine the Great and again in the 1820s under the direction of Minister of Finance E. F. Kankrin, but in each case spontaneous development prevented the realization of a firm correspondence between social category and function.

At the time of the second revision, administrative disputes over the relationship of *raznochintsy* to the urban community revealed that while the central government sought to identify and ascribe every potential taxpayer, local authorities had no desire to increase the size and hence the financial burden of their subordinate populations. The fiscal-administrative concerns of the government at once created and sought to eliminate the phenomenon of the *raznochintsy*. In the 1740s full registration of persons subject to the capitation still was not achieved; adjustments went beyond those

Table 1   Subcategories of *Raznochintsy* *

Year	1722–1725	1727	1736
Location	**Azov government**	**Nizhnii Novgorod province**	**Moscow government**
Categories	archpriests, priests, and deacons	petty Muscovite servicemen	musketeers
	sacristans	soldiers	Cossacks
	junior deacons	musketeers	dragoons and soldiers
	retired soldiers, dragoons, and	gunners/cannon founders	gunners/cannon founders
	sailors	gatekeepers	state and church police troops
	senior officers and their children	children of sacristans who	soldiers' children and children
	coachmen	are not in service	of ploughing soldiers
	chancery clerks	children of chancery clerks	chancery clerks
	state servicemen	who are not in service	registered townspeople
	single householders	Cossacks	*(posadskie liudi)*
	converts	persons of unknown birth	ecclesiastical ranks
	inhabitants of Cossack villages	"and others"	state farriers
	almshouse poor		gatekeepers
	state police troops		forest watchmen
	foreigners: Poles, Swedes,		potters, brick and tile makers
	Kurlanders, Cherkasses, Saxons		Court fishermen
	craftsmen at botanical gardens		Court botanists
	apprentices to vineyard keepers		police officers and watchmen
	stable men		stonemasons
	state farriers and carpenters		archpriests, priests, and deacons
	indentured servants		sacristans
	domestic serfs of landless officers		monastery employees
	Turkic nobles and Tatars		falconiers
			landowners *(pomeshchiki)*
			single householders and
			cavalrymen
			Poles
			ploughing soldiers
			state servicemen
			petty Muscovite service nobles
			petty Muscovite servicemen,
			retired dragoons and soldiers,
			and sailors
			runaways and persons of
			unknown rank *(chin)*

*   The *raznochintsy* from Nizhnii Novgorod province are identified as taxed; those from Azov and Moscow governments, as untaxed. Note also that local lists are not consistent in identifying subcategories of *raznochintsy*. This table includes all the possibilities.

Source: RGADA, f. 248, kn. 695; 1163, ch. 1–2; 1117

required to account for population losses from flight, conscription, and deaths. Correspondence between the Main Magistracy *(Glavnyi magistrat)* and its local offices frequently identified *raznochintsy* as urban residents who were not registered in the formal taxpaying community. The *raznochintsy* could be state or church peasants, freed serfs, retired military servicemen and their children, the children of state and ecclesiastical ranks, foreigners, or persons of uncertain origins. They also might own homes, perform the service duties of registered townspeople, and pay the capitation; in some cases they actually had been registered in the urban community. Still, from the fiscal-administrative viewpoint of the magistracies, the *raznochintsy* occupied one of two anomalous positions. If they were economically established in trade, manufacturing, or crafts, then according to existing laws they should be formally registered in the towns as merchants or artisans. Those who lacked the means to pay taxes and perform local service should not come under the authority of the magistracy and hence were forbidden to engage in urban trades or own immovable property located on taxed city lands.[8] Based on the 1649 Law Code and subsequent laws, authorities assigned these persons to military service or to private, church, or state villages.

Magistracies and local communities repeatedly welcomed new members judged to be economically and morally worthy; either local authorities or the individuals seeking formal membership could initiate the process of registration. Towns sometimes needed population, and individuals sought to regularize or change their formal status.[9] At the same time, not all desirable individuals were granted membership. In 1749 the Senate excluded a "noble's son" *(dvorianskii syn)* from the poll tax registers of Tsaritsyn, not on the basis of birth, but because in 1734 he had been appointed a copyist in state service. As a serviceman, he (and his son) should not have been registered in the urban community. Ironically, the procedures for registration demanded that an individual be economically established (and hence illegally involved in urban trades) before requesting membership in a given community. The "noble" copyist-turned-merchant thus claimed to possess capital of between three and five hundred rubles, which, however, was officially registered to a retired Cossack.[10] According to the law, *raznochintsy* who gained admission to the *posad* were supposed to possess a minimum capital of five hundred rubles in a recognized enterprise. If their need to register did not result from geographical relocation, then in order to meet the economic qualifications for membership, they must have engaged in illegal trade.[11]

Petitions from "residents of various ranks" requesting recognition as merchants or craftsmen and orders requiring local magistracies to compile lists of *raznochintsy* who lived on city lands revealed the continuing failure to achieve full compliance with the laws on registration.[12] The inclusion of peasants in virtually all discussions of urban *raznochintsy* who either had escaped registration altogether or traded in the towns illegally provided particularly striking evidence of Russia's porous social boundaries. Ironically, the administrative policies that were designed to protect the fiscal interests of the state also played a significant role in preventing full registration. During the second revision the Main Magistracy and its affiliates repeatedly clashed with the provincial authorities responsible for general registration, who were eager to assign persons of illegitimate or uncertain origins to a category subject to the capitation. Urban communities, represented by the magistracies, were just as determined to prevent the registration of individuals deemed economically or morally inadequate.[13] The collective responsiblity of communities for paying taxes and the individual accountability of local officials required the exclusion of any persons who might be unable to carry their share of the burden.

In defining Petrine social categories, responsibility for tax collection became as much an issue as a liability for the capitation. The crucial problem was not necessarily avoidance of taxation but delimitation of fiscal-administrative authority. Although some *raznochintsy* had escaped registration in the first revision, local records repeatedly identified them as persons who paid the capitation and performed service duties; only those who remained in active service or enjoyed exemptions for prior service legally avoided these levies. Collecting the taxes was another matter. Here the *raznochintsy* remained problematic because their position in the structure of administrative domains was unclear. Local officials found it difficult to collect taxes and enforce restrictions on trade precisely because *raznochintsy* often lived in cities but did not come under the authority of the magistracy; administrative disputes repeatedly arose over who was responsible for collecting the taxes. A chronic lack of accurate information further exacerbated the problem. Many *raznochintsy* had disappeared since the first revision; many were new arrivals *(prishlye)* who easily could have been deserters from other communities. Conflicts became especially pronounced when impoverished *raznochintsy* were registered to an urban community without its approval and local officials were held responsible for tax arrears. On at least two occasions the Main Magistracy asked the Senate to intervene because its local officials had been placed under guard for refusing to collect taxes from persons who in their view came under the authority of provincial administrators. Nor did the Main Magistracy always take the side of its affiliates.[14] The law clearly assigned *raznochintsy* to the provincial domain, but real populations were not always so easily distinguished.[15]

In the second half of the eighteenth century *raznochintsy* already subject to the capitation, former state servicemen, and the children of ecclesiastical ranks continued to join the urban taxpaying community. As in the past, the appropriate administrative domain was supposed to release these petitioners before they could be registered in a new category, and the Main

Magistracy was required to certify that they possessed the minimum capital.[16] In practice, local officials and individuals seeking registration continued to ignore the legal niceties. As late as 1795 there still were families that had escaped registration entirely and others that had never lived in their assigned locality.[17] Illegal trade also remained a problem, and changes in formal status continued to generate disputes between individuals, communities, and competing administrative domains.[18] Nevertheless, the institutional mechanisms needed to implement the law clearly were in place and functioned much more effectively than in the first half of the century; overall, authorities were more successful in tracing the origins of individuals who sought legally or illegally to cross social boundaries.

The less frequent appearance of the category *raznochintsy* in administrative records of the Catherinean era reflected the more stable social categorizations of European Russia. The situation in Siberia, still very much a borderland prior to the provincial reforms of 1775–1785, was quite different. The reforms represented a major step toward integrating the area into the imperial framework, but Siberia and its myriad peoples still retained distinctive characteristics.[19] References to *raznochintsy* in Siberian administrative sources reflected the more fluid social boundaries there. Prior to the reforms the *raznochintsy* comprised a sizeable and identifiable category of urban and rural taxpayers who could be registered as farmers, factory workers, artisans, or merchants.[20] Reports sent to the Ilimsk provincial administration *(voevodskaia kantseliariia)* in 1765 equated local *raznochintsy* with peasants who paid taxes in money and kind and who served as drovers.[21] In their instructions to the Legislative Commission (1767), *raznochintsy* from the city of Iakutsk identified themselves as retired Cossacks, exiles, and former tributary natives who had been raised by Russians; although registered taxpayers, they were not permitted to trade on the same basis as formal members of the urban community.[22] The *raznochintsy* of Irkutsk included exiles and lesser military servicemen who still were designated by Muscovite categories *(dvoriane, deti boiarskie, otstavnye kazaki);* they could be taxed or untaxed, and some remained in active service.[23]

Siberian officials drew attention to the problem of social delimitation when they attempted to distinguish *raznochintsy* who belonged in that category from those who should be registered as farmers. Reviewing data from Tobol'sk, the governor of Siberia, Denis Chicherin, concluded that there were far too many *raznochintsy* living in towns and working as artisans; in 1764 he proposed to resettle as many as three thousand families on vacant lands, where they could farm and support defense lines. Motivated by a desire to increase agricultural production (in Siberia provisions were expensive and in short supply) and populate Russia's southern borders, Chicherin described many urban *raznochintsy* as parasites who lacked a useful trade. But rather than settle them on the abundant lands available for agriculture, local magistracies encouraged registration in towns where they could employ the *raznochintsy* for personal services or as laborers for state works.

Senator and former governor of Siberia F. I. Soimonov took issue with Chicherin's characterization, arguing that the *raznochintsy*, whether or not they possessed an urban trade, performed important economic functions that were essential to the success of merchant enterprises; without their labor, which served both private and state needs, local merchants would be ruined. Both opinions could be traced to the painful discrepancy between Siberia's sparse population and its enormous military and administrative tasks, but this discussion was also significant for what it revealed about the confusion of social categories. In Siberia the designations merchant, artisan, and *raznochinets* bore no direct relationship either to occupation or residence; individuals officially registered in any of these categories could reside in a town or village and earn a living in trade, crafts, manufacturing, or agriculture.[24]

In Ilimsk a similar lack of delimitation between town and countryside also undermined the desired correspondence between social category and occupation. In 1768 the municipal council concluded that, among *raznochintsy* living in the town and subordinate villages, three hundred sixty-seven were actually *raznochintsy*, whereas more than thirteen hundred should be registered as farmers, sixty-three as merchants, and fifty-two as artisans. Except for vague references to old age and youth, there was no explanation of the criteria used to distinguish the *raznochintsy*. As happened so often in the legislation, *raznochintsy* were defined negatively by exclusion; that is, they were not farmers and they did not possess trades that would identify them as merchants or artisans.[25] Several years later, in 1773, authorities in nearby Iandinskii ostrog described an agricultural population of peasants, *raznochintsy*, and Cossacks who should have been paying the capitation and performing service on an equal basis. Instead, the so-called Cossacks fulfilled absolutely no service obligations. The Ilimsk governor *(voevoda)* proposed that all of these people be registered in agriculture and that their lands be redistributed according to the number of male souls, as was the practice in central Russia.[26] Conditions in Siberia clearly were extreme, but even in Russia proper the government was unable to eliminate the discrepancy between social definition and societal function. As late as 1852, legislation that sought to provide for the army's housing and provisioning needs permitted the commander of the Separate Siberian Corps to settle Kirghizes, *raznochintsy*, and retired Cossacks on vacant steppe lands.[27] The phenomenon of the *raznochintsy* remained, and the specific conditions that continually produced it revealed the ultimate failure to confine societal development within a bureaucratic framework.

In the first half of the nineteenth century the problem of social registration continued to occupy officials at the highest levels of government. Following the ministerial reforms undertaken in the reign of Alexander I, administrative regularity and centralized control improved significantly, and the problem of subordination to social-administrative domains receded. Of greater concern to officials, both high and low, was the health of the treasury. The Ministry of Finance now bore responsibility for registering the population and accounting for the payment of taxes. Disputes between administrative commands became less apparent than those between society and officialdom. Repeated legal pronouncements and a series of communications (dated 1828–1833) between local officials, the Ministries of Finance and Internal Affairs, and the Senate revealed the continuing importance of fiscal-administrative policy in the development of social categories.[28] In particular, the authorities addressed the question of whether free persons, required by law to enroll in a category subject to the capitation, could be registered to a community without its approval.

Inquiries sent to the Ministry of Finance by its provincial representatives revealed a diverse range of free persons who were unregistered: lesser Polish nobles *(szlachta)* who had failed to document their lineage; postmen, originally from the ecclesiastical domain, who had been released from postal service "for drunkenness and bad behavior"; escheated and freed serfs; former wards *(vospitanniki)* of state orphanages; foreigners; and a woman, allegedly from Hungary, who had lived in the Russian empire for eighteen years and given birth to two illegitimate children, both of whom were now grown but had never been registered. Although the persons identified had requested registration in specific towns or villages, none of the affected communities agreed to accept them. A few officials reiterated local objections to registering these people, arguing that they would become a burden because of their inability to pay taxes or perform service. Not surprisingly, Minister of Finance Kankrin dismissed these arguments and, with Senate approval, ruled that free persons obliged to enter a taxpaying category be enrolled in urban or rural communities even without local agreement.[29]

Kankrin then sweetened the bitter pill by applying to these cases a law of 1828 that granted five-year tax exemptions to freed serfs who registered in a category subject to the capitation. The few exceptions to this decision included foreigners who did not have sufficient capital to enroll in merchant guilds and who could become registered townspeople or state peasants only with the community's approval. In addition, postmen and other petty functionaries released from service for poor behavior were sent to the army or state factories or, if unfit for both, assigned to local welfare boards as laborers *(rabochie liudi)*. The only other circumstance that prevented the registration of unwanted individuals was land shortage in state villages. Clearly, fiscal-administrative policies, in particular procedures for registering the empire's population, played a central role not only in the formation of social categories but in the delineation and evolution of local communities as well.

NINETEENTH-CENTURY STATISTICAL INTERPRETATIONS

At the end of the eighteenth century local authorities no longer regarded the *raznochintsy* as a group subject to the capitation. The fourth and fifth revisions (1781–1782 and 1794–1795) did not include the category, though individuals may have been counted as members of an urban community or craft guild; census takers also continued to designate retired soldiers separately. The category *raznochintsy* reappeared in the sixth revision (1811) under the rubric of "persons who do not pay taxes," and subsequent statistics, compiled by the Ministry of Finance, continued to refer to a segment of the population that was exempt from the capitation.[30] The absence of *raznochintsy* in the poll tax enumerations did not indicate their disappearance from the population. A cursory review of administrative statistics from the early and mid-nineteenth century reveals both divergent definitions of the *raznochintsy* and the category's changing contours.

Two features of the eighteenth-century demographic data recurred: the negative definition of the *raznochintsy* by exclusion and the distinction between *raznochintsy* and retired soldiers, a distinction that suggested both the social-administrative separateness of retired soldiers and the pliable nature of the *raznochintsy*. Many administrators also distinguished *raznochintsy* from civil servants (with or without a *chin* in the Table of Ranks), while some combined them with one or another category of officials. Still others listed nobles and officials with rank together, regardless of whether the officials held a rank conferring hereditary nobility.[31] Table 2, based on data published in the official organ of the Ministry of Interior, indicates that there were significant differences in the interpretation and application of legal terminology even within a single ministry.[32] The reasons for this inconsistency lay beyond the administrative arbitrariness so frequently and justifiably decried by historians and contemporaries—in the ambiguous social definitions and indeterminate social boundaries of the time.

It is of particular interest here that local authorities generally distinguished *raznochintsy* from military and civil service categories; by contrast, some contemporaries, relying on official data, associated *raznochintsy* with unranked administrative personnel. One possible explanation for this confusion is that retired state employees and the children of state employees may have been included among the *raznochintsy*, but not persons in active service. If this was the case, then the unranked clerks were not always counted, a practice that also demands explanation.[33] Who, then, was included in the category *raznochintsy*? There is no easy answer to this question. The notion of *raznochintsy* as persons who were not registered to an official urban category is obviously too broad. Local authorities consistently listed peasants, who also were not formal members of the community, as a separate category in the enumerations. Indeed, the police and other provincial officials often did not know whom to include under the rubric of *raznochintsy*.[34]

Table 2   Social Categories Used in Urban Population Counts*

City	Samara	Simbirsk	Podol'sk	Torzhok	Kashin	Romanov-Borisoglebsk	Kremenchug
Province	Simbirsk	Simbirsk	Moscow	Tver	Tver	Iaroslav	Poltava
Year	1842	1846	1848	1850	1851	1852	1858

Categories

Samara (1842): nobility and civil servants with rank; clergy; merchants; townspeople and members of the *posad*

Simbirsk (1846): nobility; clergy; merchants; townspeople; *raznochintsy*; state peasants; serfs; veterans' unit; transport/communications unit; police and fire unit; cantonists; retired soldiers and those on indefinite leave; foreigners

Podol'sk (1848): nobility; clergy; honored citizens; merchants; *raznochintsy*; townspeople; state peasants; serfs; freed serfs; retired soldiers; soldiers' wives

Torzhok (1850): clergy; children of district clergy in schools; monks; nobility; administrative office employees; merchants; townspeople; lower [military] ranks; state peasants; serfs; coachmen

Kashin (1851): clergy; children of district clergy in schools; nobility; administrative office employees; merchants; townspeople; lower [military] ranks; state peasants; serfs; monastery employees

Romanov-Borisoglebsk (1852): hereditary nobility; personal nobility; white clergy; honored citizens; merchants; townspeople; members of craft guilds; state peasants; *belopashtsy*†; serfs; postal domain: postmen and coachmen; service personnel (*raznochintsy*); administrative office employees; medical students; church guards; veterans' unit; police and fire units; lower ranks on indefinite leave; retired soldiers and soldiers' wives; foreigners

Kremenchug (1858): nobility; clergy; merchants; townspeole; civil servants with rank (presumably non-noble) and administrative office employees; *raznochintsy*, senior officers' children, and administrative office employees (*prikazno-sluzhiteli*); single householders; foreigners; colonists; military settlers; cantonists excluded from the military domain soldiers' children; retired soldiers; soldiers on indefinite leave; lower ranks of various commands; teachers; students

---

* Note that population data for other cities and for entire districts (*uezdy*) and provinces (*gubernii*), also published in the *ZMVD*, reveal comparable categorizations.

† Peasants who farmed white (untaxed) lands.

Source: N. Volkov, "Statisticheskie i etnograficheskie zametki o Podol'skom uezde Moskovskoi gubernii," *ZMVD* (October 1850): 56–57; "Svedeniia o gorode Samare," (November 1850): 245–48; "Gorod Torzhok," *ZMVD* (April 1853): 72; "Gorod Kashin," *ZMVD* (December 1853): 180; "Gorod Romanov-Borisoglebsk," *ZMVD* (August 1853): 192–93; A. Tereshchenko, "Statisticheskoe opisanie goroda Kremenchuga, "*ZMVD 47* (March 1861) otdelenie 3, 10–11.

Population tables for 1858, published by the Central Statistical Committee of the Ministry of Internal Affairs, confirmed the absence of a uniform method among provincial statistical committees for counting *raznochintsy*. In a discussion of these data, A. Bushen defined the *raznochintsy* as "persons who occupy a transitional status and are required within a prescribed period to register in some *soslovie*"; he listed as examples wards of state orphanages, foundlings and persons of illegitimate birth, persons who had been captured by "Kirghizes and Asiatics," foreigners who became Russian subjects, Muslims and "pagans" who converted, "and others and others."[35] After providing this open-ended definition, Bushen went on to identify the social rubrics devised by the Central Statistical Committee: nobles (hereditary and personal) and officials with rank, clergy of all faiths, urban social categories *(sosloviia)*, rural social categories, military social categories, non-Christian minorities *(inorodtsy)*, *raznochintsy* or persons who do not belong to the designations already mentioned, and foreign subjects of the Russian empire. As before, the definition of *raznochintsy* remained sufficiently ambiguous to cast doubt on the overall reliability of these data. Thus Bushen noted that in some localities the category included temporary residents from other cities and persons for whom there was no information at hand, nor was there any indication as to how the Central Statistical Committee adjusted the local data in order to construct its category of *raznochintsy*.[36]

The quality of statistical sources improved greatly in the postemancipation period; the St. Petersburg city census of December 1869, which provided the most precise listing of *raznochinnye* subcategories among the data examined, is worth considering in detail. Like previous population counts and contrary to the Digest of Laws, the census distinguished *raznochintsy* from retired soldiers, but unlike the earlier sources, it specified exactly who were *raznochintsy*. The authorities in St. Petersburg identified no fewer than seventeen *raznochinnye* subcategories; most were included on the basis of education or specialized occupation *(zvanie)*, but the last subcategory also contained a group of people referred to as "simply *raznochintsy*." Interestingly, non-noble civil servants with rank *(chinovniki)* did not appear, an exclusion that was consistent with the occasional conflation of nobles and civil servants with rank and also with the distinction between hereditary and personal nobles in the 1869 census.[37] In 1846 and 1860 laws governing election procedures had identified five separate categories *(sosloviia)* of St. Petersburg voters: hereditary nobles; personal nobles, honored citizens, and *raznochintsy;* merchants; townspeople; and artisans.[38] As the categories enumerated in the census of 1869 showed, local officials did indeed view the *raznochintsy* as a segment of urban society,[39] but they in no way sought to conflate the diverse subcategories; they were perfectly comfortable with a multiplicity of designations and even maintained the minute distinctions when presenting the data on literacy. One could interpret this specificity as evidence of a commitment to preserving rigid social distinctions. It seems more likely, however, given the traditional inconsistency in applying formal definitions, that the distinctions were not necessarily viewed as a matter of great importance.

Another source of nineteenth-century data that sheds light on the concept of the *raznochintsy* depicts the university student population, which produced a steady stream of revolutionaries and renowned cultural figures. Here the term *raznochintsy* appeared with some regularity, though usages still varied and did not necessarily follow the legal formulations. Legislation dating back to the mid-eighteenth century identified *raznochintsy* as nonnoble students (exclusive of serfs, who were barred from the university and preparatory gymnasia). The ambiguity of this negative definition was not questioned before the second quarter of the nineteenth century, a time when formal social mobility and access to the rewards of service became increasingly tied to education. Thus in 1831 the Ministry of Education requested that the Senate define the term more precisely. Referred by the Heraldry Office to the bankruptcy regulation, which served as the basis for

Table 3 Population of St. Petersburg According to the Census of 10 December 1869*

Social Category (soslovie)	General Number of Residents	Children under Age Seven	% of Total Population
Hereditary nobility	54,398	5,957	8.3
Personal nobility	40,186	4.441	6.1
Black clergy	336		.05
White clergy	5,777	602	.9
Hereditary honored citizens	4,130	557	.645
Personal honored citizens	2,860	438	.45
Merchants	22,333	3,407	3.5
Townspeople	123,267	11,634	18.6
Members of craft guilds	17,678	2,361	2.759
Combat lower ranks	32,516		4.5
Noncombat lower ranks	6,447		.89
Soldiers on indefinite leave	11,335		1.6
Retired soldiers	15,333		2.1
Soldiers' families	66,495	11,634	10.758
Finns	17,205	1,430	2.6
Raznochintsy	17,771	3,606	2.9
Peasants	207,007	10,397	30.0
Foreigners	21,335	2,545	3.3
Persons whose *zvanie* is not indicated	798		.11
TOTALS	**667,207**	**59,009**	**100.062**

* The census was conducted by the Central Statistical Committee of the Ministry of Internal Affairs.

Source: *Sankt-Petersburg po perepisi 10 dekabria 1869 goda*, vypusk 1–3 (St. Petersburg, 1872), vypusk 1: 110–11.

the only definition to appear in the Digest of Laws, the ministry instructed its subordinates to include among *raznochintsy* children of non-noble copyists, unranked administrative personnel, and officials with rank nine or lower, as well as children of priests and ecclesiastical servitors who had been released from the church domain.[40]

In contrast to such broad legal and administrative prescriptions, educational data from the nineteenth century repeatedly distinguished the *raznochintsy* from other non-noble groups, including some the law assigned to that category. The following examples are indicative. Non-noble civil servants with rank could be paired with nobles (personal or hereditary) or with *raznochintsy*. Personal and hereditary nobles might or might not be distinguished. After 1845, when non-noble civil servants below rank nine were no longer considered personal nobles, those two categories might

Table 4   Subcategories of *Raznochintsy* According to the St. Petersburg Census of 10 December 1869

1	Agronomists, technicians, etc.: mechanics, land surveyors, price-fixers, draftsmen, topographers, certfied managers *(uchenye upravliaiushchie)* and their assistants.
2	Chemists, phamaceutical chemists *(provizory)*, etc.: pharmaceutical chemists *(farmatsevty)*, chemists' assistants, chemists in training, medical students, assistants of pharmaceutical chemists, veterinarians, medical attendants *(fel'dshera)*.
3	Freed serfs who have not been registered in a taxpaying category.
4	Domestic tutors, including governesses.
5	Wards of schools and institutions for orphans, the poor, and the disabled.
6	Administrative office employees below the Table of Ranks *(kantseliarskie sluzhiteli)*, including transport/communications conductors, employees of the horsebreeding domain, and postmasters *(stantsionnye smotriteli)*.
7	River and sea pilots, etc.: skippers and their assistants, navigators, and free sailors.
8	Artisans (masters, journeymen, and apprrentices), workers, and employees of various state enterprises (military, industrial, minting, paper, printing, etc.).
9	Persons of illegitimate birth, adopted and foster children, and foundlings.
10	Employees of the Court domain, including emloyees of the imperial stables, wards of the riding-master schools, and retired weighers.
11	Employees of the postal domain, including postmen *(pochtal'ony)* and their families.
12	Employees of state theaters, including some actors and their families.
13	Persons released from various administrative domains.
14	Natives of the former Russian-American holdings, including creoles *(kreoly)*.
15	Artists *(khudozhniki)*.
16	Coachmen.
17	Persons not included in the above categories because of uncertain *zvanie*, including persons calling themselves simply *raznochintsy (prosto-raznochintsy)*, convicts, vagrants, persons of unknown origin, military prisoners, musicians, families of notaries, nurses, families of exiles, students of some institutions who did not indicate their *zvanie*, pupils *(ucheniki)* of the Academy of Arts, and factory workers who did not indicate a *zvanie*.

Source: *Sankt-Peterburg po perepisi 10 dekabria 1869 goda*, vypusk 1: 116–117.

be conflated, and thus distinguished from hereditary nobles; more often, however, nobles and all civil servants with rank appeared as a single category, with the *raznochintsy* unequivocally separated from nobles, senior officers' children, ecclesiastical progeny, and children of non-noble civil servants with rank. It is particularly noteworthy that in the second half of the nineteenth century the *raznochintsy* sometimes were included in the lower urban classes along with townspeople and artisans, though they still might be listed as a separate category. Thus the statistical applications revealed that even after the definite emergence of the Russian intelligentsia, a development in which students from the *raznochintsy* played a prominent role, . the larger category of *raznochintsy* continued to represent a lower-class group, distinct from the educated elite.[41]

The formulation in law of social definitions, and their fragmented application by a variety of governmental agencies, served first and foremost to accommodate a range of diverse administrative purposes. Interpretations of the category *raznochintsy* revealed both the increasingly complex tasks of government and the ever greater intrusions of the bureaucracy into local life. Multiple usages derived from societal development and the specific functions and concerns of distinct administrative domains. In the eighteenth century the *raznochintsy* appeared most frequently, but not exclusively, as lower-class taxpayers or untaxed lesser servicemen; in the nineteenth century they represented a relatively more elite group of educated or semieducated specialists and low-level state servitors. The nineteenth-century usages were not new, and the lower-class definition did not disappear; rather, the change was one of degree, and it corresponded precisely to the dynamics of development that continually replenished the ranks of the *raznochintsy*. Originally an outgrowth of new Petrine definitions and institutions, particularly introduction of the capitation and the assignment of social categories to functional administrative domains, by the nineteenth century the creation of *raznochintsy* more directly reflected the consequences of state building and educational expansion. Administrative statistics thus contained no single definition or application of the category; moreover, the divergent definitions of *raznochintsy* inevitably altered the acknowledged boundaries of contiguous groups. It follows, then, that only by considering the context in which a specific formulation occurred can historians begin to understand the meaning and significance of any social categorization.

CHURCH DEFINITIONS

Yet another source of population data indicates the need to pay close attention to the context in which specific categorizations appeared. The church employed its own social designations, distinct from those of the secular state. Before 1841, when church records ceased to employ the category *raznochintsy*, the following rubrics applied:[42]

> Ecclesiastical: all categories of white clergy, including archpriests, priests, subdeacons, choristers, sacristans, psalm readers, and sextons.
>
> Military: generals, officers, noncommissioned officers, privates, soldiers, and sailors.
>
> *Raznochintsy:* nobles, petty servicemen/gentry, single householders, coachmen, "police" troops *(razsyl'shchiki)*, and monastery employees.[43]
>
> State servicemen *(prikaznye):* senior secretaries, secretaries, low-ranking civil servants, and unranked office employees *(protokolist, aktuarius, registrator, kantseliarist, podkantseliarist, kopiist)*.
>
> Registered members of the formal urban community *(posadskie)* and of craft guilds.
>
> Household serfs *(dvorovye liudi)*, including *szlachta* and other ranks (persons with homesteads?).[44]
>
> Peasants and landless peasants/squatters *(bobyli)*.

The church's idiosyncratic categorizations were consistent with state administrative practices both in the conflation of noble and non-noble categories and in the separateness of the military. Still, it is important not to approach the church data simply as those of another administrative domain. The church and the ecclesiastical personnel it governed did indeed comprise a distinct institutional domain, but the church also played a unique social and cultural role—a role that was reflected in local registers of confessions, marriages, and births. Without reference to this broader historical role, it is impossible to make sense of the social definitions employed by the church.

The church's categories, which clearly were based on occupation and the structure of administrative domains, comprised a combination of rubrics organized as vertical hierarchies of functional/service ranks (ecclesiastical, military, *raznochinnye*, state, and *posadskie*) or as horizontal strata (*posadskie, dvorovye,* and peasant). The designation *posadskie* could be either, since the notion of registered members of the taxpaying urban community failed to delineate merchants from lower-class townspeople and artisans. Local churchmen, like their secular counterparts, were never consistent in their use of formal categories, which makes sophisticated statistical analysis virtually impossible. Although the reforms of Catherine the Great produced a clearer delimitation of the horizontal strata within urban society, church definitions did not change, and their application to local society remained imprecise. Even so, a sampling of eighteenth- and nineteenth-century data from the Moscow ecclesiastical consistory provides more than the church's conception of the *raznochintsy;* it also illuminates their place in local society and raises more general questions about the formation and representation of social categories.

It is clear from the outset that the church's view of social organization did not correspond to the fiscal-administrative categories of the Petrine state. The church was responsible for preserving and administering the Orthodox faith and so naturally understood society in terms of parish and household. In the confessional records *(ispovednye vedomosti)* of local churches, priests listed parishioners by household *(dvor),* including the head of the household, family members, and any boarders. The social rubrics found in the confessional lists thus apply to the head of the household and his or her family, not necessarily to each individual resident. Even if the social origin of boarders also is indicated (e.g., soldier's wife, retired soldier, etc.), they still are counted as members of a *raznochinnyi* household and hence as *raznochintsy.* Implicit in the organization of these records is a conception of the local church and parish as a basic social unit and, more important, as the locus of community—something that is commonly recognized in the historiography of Western Europe, but inexplicably ignored in the Russian case.

The discussion that follows is based upon confessional registers from the churches of Zamoskvoretskii *sorok* (forty) in the city of Moscow for eight years between 1741 and 1856. No effort is made here to engage in sustained quantitative analysis or to attempt parish/family reconstitution; rather, the purpose is to consider how the church categorized society and to explain what that reveals about the underlying dynamics of social definition in imperial Russia. From these records it is possible to determine not only who was included in the category *raznochintsy* but whether *raznochintsy* were concentrated in particular parishes or more broadly distributed across a range of communities. Marriage and baptismal records yield more suggestive information concerning personal and family relationships. A few examples from the period 1770–1793 reveal whom *raznochintsy* married, who stood as witnesses at their weddings, and who became godparents to their children. Additional information from Moscow and Serpukhov districts *(uezdy),* Sergiev *posad,* and the city of Dmitrov (both in Moscow district) also sheds light on particular attributes of the *raznochintsy.*

Tables 5–8 indicate the subcategories of *raznochintsy* that appeared in confessional lists, as well as the proportion of *raznochintsy* in specific parishes. Although the records of individual churches contain many similarities, local priests were not entirely consistent in applying or defining the category *raznochintsy.* Repeatedly, occupational and social designations associated with *raznochintsy* in the records of one church are not so associated in those of another. Moreover, even if a church counted *raznochintsy* among its parishioners, it did not necessarily identify them individually or indicate who belonged to the category. The tables presented here thus include all

Table 5 Subcategories of *Raznochintsy*, Zamoskvoretskii sorok, Moscow

Year	1741	1751	1754	1772	1791	1797	1814
Categories	princes	nobles	nobles	nobles	coachmen	coachmen	unranked state servicemen (*prikaznye*)
	nobles	courtiers	watchmen	factory artisans and apprentices	farriers	state farriers	
	cathedral guards	members of craft guilds	state farriers	former monastery employees (now economic peasants)	factory workers		
	monastery employees and servicemen	state farriers	factory workers, artisans, and apprentices	watchmen	persons living on public assistance (almshouse poor)		
	chancery clerks	almshouse poor	almshouse poor	cathedral bell ringers			
	textile factory workers	coiners	Court kvass makers	peasants			
	petty Muscovite service nobles	factory workers and apprentices	petty state servicemen	state printing house workers			
	coachmen	state bakers	university students	coiners			
	police troops	state engravers	state turners/lathe operators	textile factory workers			
	almshouse poor	monastery peasants	coachmen	state gilders (*zolotari*)			
	state farriers	serfs	police troops	engravers at Moscow state printing house			
	coiners	state watchmen	peasants				
	factory workers, artisans, and apprentices	retired ensign	coiners				
	members of craft guilds	petty state servicemen	state engravers				
	state engravers	coachmen	Senate typesetters				
		furriers	Court stonemasons				
		knackers (*zhivodernye*)	tailors				
			medical assistants (*fel'dshera*)				
			single householders				
			furriers				
			petty Muscovite service nobles				
			factory managers/clerks				

Source: TsGIAgM, f. 203, op. 747, dd. 45, 173, 245, 422, 623, 707, 872, 1712.

possible subcategories of *raznochintsy* explicitly designated as such in the sources.

Echoing legal and state administrative usages, church officials presented the *raznochintsy* as a transitional grouping from Muscovite to Petrine categories. Lesser Muscovite ranks of noble and non-noble servicemen were included, as were traditional nonecclesiastical monastery employees and servitors, destined after 1762 to become economic/state peasants.[45] In the parish Kosma i Damian v Kadashakh in 1754 the category contained nobles' children, factory workers, and petty Muscovite servicemen *(raznykh sluzheb sluzhiteli)*. The large number of *raznochintsy* in at least two parishes of Sergiev *posad* (Voznesenie Gospodnia and Voskresenie Khristova) in 1761 resulted from the presence of monastery servicemen, and even as late as

Table 6   Subcategories of *Raznochintsy*, 1737–1790

Serpukhov district, 1737	monastery employees
	state farriers
	stable men
	petty state servicemen
Radonezhskaia desiatina, Moscow district, 1761 (Sergiev *posad*)	domestic serfs and yardmen
	church watchmen
	monastery servitors
	"*raznochintsy* and parasites"
Serpukhov district, 1769	state farriers
City of Dmitrov, 1790	physicians *(lekari)*, teachers in "normal" schools, and *raznochintsy*

Source: TsGIAgM, f. 203, op. 747, dd. 7, 293, 392, 603, 614.

1772 the registers of Vse Skorbiashie parish equated *raznochintsy* with another broad Muscovite label "persons of various ranks" *(raznykh chinov liudi)*. Church usage thus reflected the origins of the *raznochintsy* in the redefining of social categories engendered by Petrine tax policies and efforts to subordinate society to administrative domains. One reason for the high proportion of *raznochintsy* in some parishes was confusion about the delimitation of social boundaries. In 1791 the parishes Chernigovskie Chudotvortsy and Petr i Pavl na Kaluzhskoi both combined *raznochintsy* with household serfs *(dvorovye)*, whereas a few years earlier other parishes had identified them with nobles or peasants.[46] Finally, some registers with large numbers of *raznochintsy* did not identify subcategories, so that it is impossible to explain their preponderance. In any of these examples, irregularities of definition may account for the statistical fluctuations.

State building in the form of administrative, military, and economic institutions also produced a significant contingent of *raznochintsy*. In 1769 three parishes of Serpukhov district (Prorok Iliia na Posade, Preobrazhenie Gospodnia, and Uspenie Bogoroditsy) contained unusually large numbers of *raznochintsy*, who in each case constituted a specialized occupational group of state and artillery farriers. Contrary to the laws but consistent with administrative practices, the church generally distinguished *raznochintsy* from ranked and unranked military servicemen and civil servants no

Table 7   Concentration of *Raznochinitsy*, Zamoskvoretskii sorok, Moscow *

Year	1741		1754	
Parish Church	Parishioners	*Raznochintsy*	Parishioners	*Raznochintsy*
Nikolai Chudotvorets v Kuznetskoi slobode	288	30 (1.0)		
Paraskeva Piatnitsa na Piatnitskoi ulitse	716	126 (17.6)		
Soshestvie Sv. Dukha v Tolmachakh	322	25 (7.8)		
Georgii v landove	517	96 (18.6)		
Kosma i Damian v Kadashakh			946	570 (60.3)
Rizopolozhenie v Donskom			1,784	946 (53.0)
Vse Skorbiashie Radosti v Kolomenskoi iamskoi slobode (Skorobiashenskaia)			737	458 (62.0)
Nikolai Chudotvorets na Pupyshakh			469	32 (6.8)
Nikolai Chudotvorets v Golutnine			445	73 (16.4)
Voznesenie za Serpukhovskimi vorotami			732	130 (17.8)
Voskresenie v Monetshikakh			454	72 (15.9)
Sofiia na Naberezhnykh Sadovnikakh				
Voskresenie v Plennitsakh				
Spas Preobrazheniia na Bolvanovke				
Kliment papy Rimskogo				
Mikhail Arkhangel v Ovchinnikakh				
Chernigovskie Chudotvortsy				
Ioann-Voin na Iakimanke				
Voskresenie za Danilovon monastyrem				
Nikolai Chudotvorets ma Bersenevke				
Petr i Pavl na Kaluzhskoi †				
Uspenie v Kozhevnikakh				
Varlaam Khutynskogo na Bol'shoi Ortsynke				
Troitsa na Shabalovke				

* All data include male and female parishioners. Figure in parentheses indicates the percentage of *raznochinnye* parishioners.

† *Raznochintsy* and *dvorovye*.

Source: TsGIAgM, f. 203, op. 747, dd. 45, 173, 245, 422, 623, 707, 872, 1712.

higher than senior secretaries. In addition to nobles, this left in the category *raznochintsy* a range of state and Court lower ranks with particular artisanal and technical skills—skills that were necessary for state building, governing, and economic development.

Other church usages also had parallels in legal and state applications. The 1761 data from Sergiev *posad* listed many *raznochintsy* simply as *raznochintsy,* a usage that suggested a hereditary category in addition to the collective, umbrella term. Also important was the relatively large and for now inexplicable category "*raznochintsy* and parasites [*zakhrebetniki*]" found in the confessional register of the parish church Iliia Prorok (Sergiev *posad,* 1761). Here church sources echoed the secular notion of *raznochintsy* as

1772			1791			1797		
Parishioners	*Raznochintsy*		Parishioners	*Raznochintsy*		Parishioners	*Raznochintsy*	
350	6	(0.2)						
			561	89	(15.9)			
391	134	(34.3)						
			617	49	(7.9)			
						493	14	(2.8)
231	7	(3.0)						
186	28	(15.0)	154	61	(39.6)			
211	11	(5.2)	285	21	(7.4)			
181	14	(7.7)						
			435	12	(2.8)	434	8	(1.8)
			302	96	(31.8)			
			319	29	(9.0)			
			506	105	(21.0)			
			313	121	(38.7)	295	93	(32.0)
			662	412	(62.0)	738	22	(3.0)
			329	37	(11.2)			
						329	20	(6.0)
						498	10	(2.0)

outsiders. Finally, records from the city of Dmitrov in 1790 foreshadowed the more common nineteenth-century association of *raznochintsy* with educated elites. The confessional list from Uspenskii cathedral *(sobor)* thus identified "physicians, teachers in 'normal' schools and *raznochintsy*" as a single designation. Clearly, church definitions of the *raznochintsy* were no more precise than those found in state law or administration. Whether grouped with peasants, nobles, and protoprofessionals or with unranked government officials, factory workers, and artisans, the category remained porous and fluid. Once again, no single definition could suffice.

Despite important similarities between church and state categorizations, there were several crucial differences. Of particular importance was the

Table 8   Concentration of *Raznochintsy* *

Parish Church	Number of Parishioners	Number of *Raznochintsy* (%)	
Radonezhskaia desiatina, Moscow district, 1761 (Sergiev *posad*)			
Vvedenie Bozhiei Materi	763	53	(7)
Voznesenie Gospodnia	1,092	278	(26)
Iliia Prorok	1,289	352	(27)[†]
Voskresenie Khristova	2,152	1,971	(92)[‡]
Serpukhov district, 1769			
Nikolai Chudotvorets v Butkakh	354	12	(3.4)
Prorok Iliia na Posade	167	57	(34)[§]
Vozdvizhenie Kresta	246	25	(10)
Sretenie Gospodnia	885	30	(3.4)
Voznesenie Gospodnia	139	7	(5)
Voskresenie Khristova na Posade	418	59	(14)
Rozhdestvo Presviatoi Bogoroditsy	95	5	(5.3)
Preobrazhenie Gospodnia	281	146	(52)[§]
Nikol Belyi	330	12	(4)
Sviatye Zheny Mironosits	1,634	28	(2)
Uspenie Bogoroditsy	179	45	(25)[§]
Serpukhov district, 1789			
Sretenie, city of Serpukhov	1,498	33	(2.2)

* All data include male and female parishioners. Figure in parentheses indicates the percentage of *raznochinnye* parishioners.

[†] Figure includes "*raznochintsy* and parasites"

[‡] These *raznochintsy* were monastery employees and servitors.

[§] The *raznochintsy* in these parishes were state and artillery farriers, a special service category.

Source: TsGIAgM, f. 203, op. 747, dd. 7, 293, 392, 603.

church's inclusion of nobles who were not in military service in the category *raznochintsy*, a practice that suggests the primacy of occupation rather than birth in the formation of social definitions. Equally significant, both state and private factories (here primarily private textile mills) produced a visible group of *raznochintsy*. The confessional records repeatedly identified factory workers as *raznochintsy*, though provincial reports describing the same factories in 1791–1792 did not apply the category.[47] One final distinction also requires explanation. There can be little discussion of social structure or social relations without reference to the role of the *raznochintsy*, or of any other group for that matter, as parishioners. The confessional records reveal that *raznochintsy* were a continuing presence in virtually every parish examined. Even if local definitions were inconsistent and contradictory, the important point is that the category *raznochintsy* appeared, and hence a concept of the phenomenon existed. Nor were the *raznochintsy* segregated in isolated parishes. Generally few in number, they were from the local viewpoint neighbors, churchgoers, and members of the parish community.[48] It is precisely the role of *raznochintsy* as parishioners that raises questions about traditional representations of social categories and identities in imperial Russia. The church was far too important an institution for historians simply to dismiss its classification of *raznochintsy* as an anachronism.[49]

A brief discussion of the marriage and baptismal records from Zamoskvoretskii *sorok* illustrates the point. The priests who compiled these registers did not employ the general social rubrics found in the confessional lists; they did, however, identify individuals by the more minute occupational and functional designations that the confessional records grouped under the larger categories. By applying the *raznochinnye* subcategories found in the confessional records, it is possible to use the registers of marriages and births to establish personal relationships among individuals and categories of parishioners. The data presented in table 9 are based on marriages and christenings where at least one spouse or parent came from a social, occupational, or functional subcategory of *raznochintsy* identified in the confessional records. The social designations of spouses, witnesses, and godparents indicate the extent to which *raznochintsy* (and others) formed personal bonds with neighbors, fellow workers, and individuals of similar background. The purpose is not to measure marriages or associations that crossed social and parish boundaries, though such a study might be feasible. The present goal is much more modest: to illustrate the relationship of the allegedly transitional and disconnected *raznochintsy* to the local parish, neighborhood, and workplace.

In compiling table 9, the author found it impossible to avoid arbitrary ad hoc definitions comparable to those applied by contemporary legislators and administrators. Thus the category *raznochintsy* includes soldiers' wives and daughters, regardless of whether their husbands were retired or in active service. To separate all military ranks from the *raznochintsy,* as church and state administrative sources do, would be misleading; the marriage and baptismal records clearly show not only that the military ranks associated with *raznochinnye* elements but also that these elements were integrated into the parish community. Similar problems arose in connection with the daughters and wives of ecclesiastical ranks, included in table 9 among the non-*raznochinnye* subcategories. Many employees of state printing houses, a group regularly identified in church sources as *raznochintsy,* originated in the ecclesiastical domain and married daughters of priests and unordained churchmen.[50] In terms of personal relationships, these marriages represented a crossing of administrative, not social, boundaries. A similar anomaly occurred when two textile workers married; because the bride was a possessional serf, it was necessary to count the spouse as a non-*raznochinets.* Clearly, the differences between fiscal-administrative and parish conceptions of society prevented precise social delimitation. In addition, the very existence of wives, widows, and daughters thwarted the realization of regularized definitions.[51]

Table 9   Marriages and Christenings among
Raznochintsy of Zamoskvoretskii *sorok,* Moscow (1770–1793)

Number of Marriages [*]	39	
Spouses from:	a. Any *raznochinnyi* subcategory [†]	**59** (68%)
	b. Same *raznochinnyi* subcategory and/or place of work	**32** (37%)
	c. Non-*raznochinnyi* subcategory [‡]	**12** (37%)
Number of Witnesses [§]	45	
From:	a. Any *raznochinnyi* subcategory [†]	**25** (56%)
	b. Same *raznochinnyi* subcategory and/or place of work	**17** (38%)
	c. Non-*raznochinnyi* subcategory [‡]	**19** (42%)
Number of Christenings [#]	45	
Number of Godparents	87	
from:	a. Any *raznochinnyi* subcategory [†]	**59** (68%)
	b. Same *raznochinnyi* subcategory and/or place of work	**32** (37%)
	c. Non-*raznochinnyi* subcategory [‡]	**28** (32%)

[*] Data from 1770–1793.
[†] Following the legislation and confessional lists, *raznochinnye* subcategories include shop assistants, craftsmen, and workers at textile factories; craftsmen and workers at printing houses; coiners; state bookkeepers; coachmen; watchmen; land surveyors; unranked state administrative employees; low-ranking (presumably non-noble) civil servants; retired lower military ranks; soldiers' wives, widows, and daughters; bell ringers; monastery employees; domestic servants *(sluzhiteli);* freed serfs.
[‡] Non-*raznochinnye* categories include ecclesiastical ranks, their wives and daughters; officers, their wives and widows; merchants; townspeople; members of craft guilds; domestic serfs; peasants.
[§] If employers stood as witnesses, they were counted in categories b and c.
[#] Data from 1777, 1787, and 1793.

Source: TsGIAgM, f. 203, op. 745, dd. 1, 52, 85; f. 2121, op. 1, dd. 1, 504.

The personal relationships manifested in this sampling of marriage and baptismal records reveal that despite legal and administrative confusion, there was a relatively stable social reality to the phenomenon of the *razno-chintsy*. It was, however, a microreality rooted in daily life and localized around neighborhood, parish, and workplace. While most *raznochintsy* (69 percent) married persons of comparable definition and a third (33 per-cent) married individuals from the same subcategory or place of employ-ment, close to another third (31 percent) took spouses from non-*raznochin-nye* designations. The choices of godparents, generally an indicator of personal bonds, show similar results: 68, 37, and 32 percent, respectively. Witnesses to marriages represented the group most likely to include per-sons who were not from a *raznochinnyi* subcategory, though here, too, a clear majority were of similar definition. Overall, in addition to the sizeable majorities of spouses, godparents, and witnesses who came from compara-ble categories, there was also a fairly significant minority of non-*raznochin-nye* participants. Clearly, the social boundaries so meticulously worked out in state law and registration practices were much less apparent in daily life.

There is one final aspect of the church data that demands explanation. Why did the church eliminate the category *raznochintsy* after 1841, at the very moment it became significant in literature and journalism?[52] One pos-sible answer is provided by eighteenth-century parishes that did not in-clude the category in confessional lists. Between 1769 and 1814 some par-ish priests in Serpukhov district and the city of Moscow identified functional and occupational subcategories of *raznochintsy* in place of the general rubric: in 1769 "servicemen" *(sluzhiteli)* and farriers; in 1772 fac-tory workers *(fabrishnye)* and servicemen; in 1789 "musketeers (soldiers) registered in craft guilds"; and in 1814 employees of printing houses *(tipo-grafskie)* and factory workers.[53] The eventual disappearance of the *raznochin-nyi* rubric from ecclesiastical sources was consistent with the church's em-phasis on occupational designations. As subsequent chapters will establish, the *raznochintsy* cannot be defined in socioeconomic terms, particularly after the first quarter of the nineteenth century, when the category became increasingly cultural. The crucial point to emerge from the parish context is that individuals who legally and administratively belonged to *raznochinnye* subcategories were primarily identified by functional, occupational, and residential criteria. The more abstract concept of the *raznochintsy* cohered only in the interstices where local society met formal state institutions. The registers of the parish church, which was both a formal and an informal institution, thus exhibited both patterns of social classification.

CONCLUSION

Administrative categorizations and their applications in state and church statistics show that formal social definitions remained ambiguous,

Chapter 4

State Building,
Economic Development,
and the Creation of *Raznochintsy*

BEGINNING WITH THE REIGN of Peter the Great and continuing until the military reforms of the early 1870s, social development and state building, the process of constructing and maintaining instrumentalities of rule and imperial defense, were closely intertwined. Essential for the effective imposition of tax and service obligations on the general population, state building—and particularly the personnel requirements of state building—represented a significant source of *raznochinnye* subcategories. Closely related to the requirements and success of state building was productive development, which served as a second source of new *raznochintsy*. It is precisely in the economic sphere that the impossibility of defining the *raznochintsy* as a stratum or class was most striking. At the same time, the economic sources of *raznochintsy* are crucial to understanding the larger issue of social plasticity. Only by considering the relationship of the legal category *raznochintsy* to discrete economic phenomena—in this case, unlawful trade and the exploitation of serf labor by non-nobles—is it possible to explain the evolution of the terminology into social definition, delimitation, and identity, and hence into a dynamic aspect of social and cultural consciousness.

SOCIAL CONSEQUENCES OF MILITARY SERVICE

The same Petrine registration policies that provided the framework for collecting the capitation also served the manpower needs of the military. Russia's quasi-reserve standing army depended upon conscripts drafted primarily from the servile population of serfs, state and church peasants, and townspeople. Because conscription brought juridical emancipation, whether from the authority of the landlord or from the obligations imposed by rural and urban communities, it represented a fundamental change in the legal status of individual conscripts. At the same time, this newly acquired freedom was not implemented as long as a conscript remained in active service.[1] For his family and community of origin, the legal and socioeconomic consequences were more immediate: each conscript represented a lost laborer, taxpayer, father, husband, or child. Whatever the impact on a specific household, and experiences varied, the conscript's family and by extension the larger community remained liable for his share of the capitation until the next revision. Equally problematic, his wife, children, and elderly parents posed a potential welfare burden. Legally and practically, the conscript and his wife, if he had one, were at the moment of induction not "emancipated" but excluded from membership in their local community.

The loss of formal ties to a community meant that once a soldier was discharged from service, he entered the category of *raznochintsy*. Free from taxation and subordinate to the offices of provincial administration, retired soldiers occupied an ambiguous position in a social structure designed to achieve full registration of the entire population. Although it was hoped that the retired soldiers would settle permanently (i.e., register) in an urban or rural community, legally, they could move as they pleased or as the need to provide for themselves dictated, on the condition that they not fall into a life of crime or vagrancy.[2] Despite prescribed rights and privileges that identified them as members of a fiscal-administrative category, at the moment of retirement they were men without ties to any formally or informally constituted community. Nor, as had been the case when they entered military service, did they have immediate or guaranteed access to an occupation or other means of subsistence; the army released them with a small sum of money, barely enough to reach their destination, a passport, and the clothes on their back.[3] After a virtual lifetime of service and membership in a structured collective, they at last became truly free—free to return to family and friends, to establish themselves on a new and independent basis, to rely on church or public assistance, or to suffer loneliness and hunger. Actually, there were significant opportunities available to retired soldiers, but their poverty and generally sad plight remained a chronic social problem.[4]

Poverty and reintegration into civilian life were the most pressing problems faced by retired soldiers; whether one considers informal socioeconomic networks or formal fiscal-administrative categories, these problems tended to be mutually reinforcing. Already in the early eighteenth century, the introduction of the capitation raised questions about the legal and social categorization of soldiers. Despite their juridical freedom and formal social separateness, a significant number returned to their families and even to farming. For them and from the official viewpoint as well, return to the familial hearth provided the best means for reentering civilian life. For the soldier facing old age and sickness, it meant greater economic security and the comforts of family relationships. For the government, it meant reduced public expenditures; it forestalled vagrancy, begging, and presumably crime; and it facilitated resettlement, which in turn promised to augment the ranks of future farmers, taxpayers, and conscripts. Still, when a soldier returned to his village or town of origin, he was not a taxpayer, nor was he entitled to a share of allotment land; the military authorities thus released him to the care of relatives or former landlords, upon whom he depended for shelter and sustenance.[5]

If return to family and community proved impossible, the government encouraged retired servicemen to settle on vacant state lands. Until legislation of 1867 prescribed that conscripts remain members of the communities from which they were drafted, resettlement was the officially preferred solution to the problems of discharged soldiers.[6] Designed to promote "a settled way of life" *(osedlost')* and hence to eliminate idleness and increase the pool of potential taxpayers and conscripts, the policy of resettlement produced limited, and from the state's viewpoint inadequate, results. Because former soldiers were free to choose a place of residence, it was difficult to induce them to settle on empty lands in sparsely populated areas. At age fifty or sixty a retired soldier was not likely to embrace the life of a frontiersman, nor was a younger soldier, who would have been discharged only for physical reasons, a likely candidate. In addition, despite various exemptions from taxation and conscription, their former landlords, native villages, and urban communities were not necessarily eager to see retired servicemen, who did not pay the capitation and could easily become dependent on public assistance, return. In a very real sense, it was not only the long term of service but the very privileges and freedoms enjoyed by retired soldiers that deterred massive resettlement, even though any children born to them in retirement would be registered as full members of the taxpaying community.

Although the anomalous legal position of soldiers in service and retirement can easily be overdrawn, it is crucial to understanding the larger problem of social categorization. Armies, regardless of time and place, create welfare problems in civilian society; equally problematic is the need to integrate soldiers and their families into the larger social framework. These issues were particularly acute in Russia, where the formal status of wives and children derived from that of husbands and fathers, where the boundaries separating military from civilian society were irregular, and where the long term of service left dependents abandoned and vulnerable. Except for noblewomen, who did not face derogation as a result of marriage to commoners, the formal status of wives throughout Russian society corresponded to that of their husbands. Soldiers' wives thus became legally free at the time of a spouse's induction; as "free" women who no longer belonged to the landlord or the taxpaying community, they came under the jurisdiction of military authorities and technically could live with their husbands.

Lacking a place in their community of origin, soldiers' wives were free to obtain passports that allowed them to move in search of employment. They maintained a visible presence in towns, where they became involved in petty trade, prostitution, and the trafficking of unwanted children between foundling homes and the countryside; a few even owned artisanal workshops or commercial establishments.[7] Like other persons forced by economic pressures to seek the protection of employers, soldier's wives were vulnerable to unlawful enserfment.[8] The nineteen-year-old sergeant's widow, Martona, in M. D. Chulkov's *Comely Cook* explained the anomalous position of these unfortunates. Although Martona bore the title of sergeant's wife, she had no source of sustenance; her husband had been neither a noble nor a landowner. In describing her lack of preparation for the circumstances in which she found herself, Martona noted, "My misfortune seemed to me unbearable, for I knew nothing of human relationships and could not find for myself a place [*mesto*], and so I became free [*vol'noiu*] because they did not assign us to any position [*dolzhnost*]."[9] Martona's description is not entirely accurate; as a legally recognized widow, she could remarry and hence regain a position in society. For the soldier's wife who had no proof of her husband's death, the conditions of life were likely to be even more dreadful and uncertain.[10]

Not surprisingly, the same Petrine service categories that replenished the official ranks of the *raznochintsy* also produced significant numbers of illegitimate children. The uncertain status of children born to soldiers' wives illustrated with particular clarity the larger problem of illegitimate births—a problem that was especially complex in a society where social affiliation corresponded to that of the father at the moment of birth.[11] According to the law, any male child, legitimate or not, born to a woman after her husband entered active service, belonged to the military domain and was destined for a life of service. Although the law was quite clear as to what the legal-administrative status of these children should be, they and their mothers occupied a precarious social position—a position characterized by endless disputes between parents, landlords, and government.

Nobles, for example, frequently had illegitimate soldiers' children ascribed to them in the poll tax registers. If a landlord did in fact support one of these children, eighteenth- and nineteenth-century legislation permitted him to enserf the child. But landlords were responsible only in cases where parents or relatives could not provide subsistence. This distinction was virtually impossible to enforce, and the government admitted as much, ruling in a law of 1816 that any soldiers' children (legitimate or not) erroneously registered in the civil domain or to a landlord in the first six censuses should remain in their present status.[12] Decisions from the Arzamas district court (Nizhnii Novgorod province), dated from 1790 to 1838, indicate that wrongful registration continued.[13] The government, always interested in manpower for the army, sometimes managed to uncover the ruses of a landlord; the offender risked losing not only the soldiers' children who were claimed unlawfully but also the spouses and offspring of any who might have married.[14]

As so often in imperial Russia, exposure of abuses was sporadic and difficult. One suggestive case came to light only after a village belonging to Princess Golitsyna drafted both illegitimate sons of a soldier's wife. Unlike the first son, the second, when he was called to the levy, requested freedom from servile status on the grounds that his father was a soldier. The Arzamas district court agreed, noting that, as a soldier's son, he was automatically required to serve. Princess Golitsyna appealed the decision to the Senate, which confirmed it in 1808 and also fined her for submitting an inappropriate petition.[15] To be fair, one should note that soldiers' sons, assisted by their parents, often concealed their identity in order to avoid the army, as did their mothers in order to remarry. Thus a landlord did not necessarily know when the offspring of a serf and his bigamist wife were in fact illegitimate soldiers' children. To be sure, landlords also had an interest in forcing or abetting these unlawful marriages, especially of couples who already had produced children, though presumably they would have preferred to find women of servile status to marry their serfs.[16] Moreover, despite the clear intent of the law, sons of retired servicemen and unfit conscripts, who clearly did not belong to the military, were known to have been enrolled in garrison schools by mistake.[17] Even where the law was precise, as in the case of children born to retired soldiers, the social reality could remain ambiguous.

Moving from the specific, juridically defined categories of soldiers' wives and children to the general problem of illegitimacy, the sources reveal similar patterns of conflict between the government, landlords, parents, and children. In a society where social status was legally defined and where each person theoretically occupied a position within a framework of administrative or seigneurial domains, illegitimate births made it particularly difficult to preserve formal social definitions. Eighteenth-century legislation allowed persons who raised foundlings and illegitimate children also to enserf them, though early in the reign of Catherine the Great the government specifically forbade this form of enserfment by non-nobles. Still, as with unlawful enserfment in general, there was no clear pronouncement of these prohibitions before 1785, and the practice continued into the first half of the nineteenth century. The potential for disputes over the status of other illegitimate children was probably greater than for soldiers' children, who belonged either to the landlord-provider or the army. Peasant and urban communities could not lay claim to soldiers' children, even if they supported them. Other illegitimate children could, however, become a source of conflict between landlords, state villages, factories, and merchants, and unlike soldiers' children, who belonged only to one state domain, the military, other illegitimate children could be claimed by competing administrative domains.[18]

The social condition of soldiers and their families offers a concrete example of the administrative and human dimensions of formal categorization. Aside from the obvious problems of poverty and subsistence, the manpower needs of the army required constant changes in formal status, which in turn spawned new social categories and increased the uncertainties of social definition. This situation was not limited to the military domain; the personnel needs of the civil service and church created similar problems. Secular authorities regularly conscripted the excess progeny of clergy for service in the army, bureaucracy, and state schools. Some children of clergy requested and received discharges from the church domain because they lacked the skills or education needed for an ecclesiastical career; whereas most of these sought to enter state service, a few became state peasants, townspeople, and even merchants. Others were expelled from ecclesiastical service for behavioral problems.[19] Similar discharges and expulsions occurred among unranked administrative employees. In state service, shortage of personnel was more likely to be the norm than abundance and sometimes actually forestalled the dismissal of troublemakers.[20] The crucial point here is that service—whether military, administrative, or ecclesiastical—generated subcategories of *raznochintsy* or potential *raznochintsy* (including wives and offspring) who crossed social boundaries and changed formal statuses through a variety of legal and illegal channels.

One witnesses in the spawning of subcategories an important phenomenon that made precise definition of social boundaries impossible: the existence of multiple statuses within a single family. The legal position of a soldier's wife was entirely different from that of her spouse or children. Ecclesiastical families presented a similar picture: a daughter who married a peasant or unranked official; a son who received a secular education or pursued, not always voluntarily, a career in the military or civil service; a father or grandfather who was an ordained priest or a church employee. Urban families—whether registered as merchants, lesser townspeople, nobles, peasants, or civil servants—also could occupy multiple statuses; even an individual within a single family could be registered in more than one category.[21] If one wonders why there was no single definition of the *raznochintsy*, the simple answer is that *raznochintsy* occupied a multiplicity of statuses. While there is no definition of the *raznochintsy* that would include all members of military, administrative, or ecclesiastical families, there is no question that the progeny of these groups often became *raznochintsy* in a legal sense.

NOBLE DELIMITATION

Traditional scholarship portrays a clearly delimited noble elite that by the end of the Catherinean era had secured its privileges and control over the instrumentalities of rule, all the while remaining open to newly ennobled state servitors. This depiction is accurate for wealthy landowners and for nobles, regardless of origins, who made successful careers in civil or military service. It also applies to impoverished and not particularly well-educated nobles who could rely upon the patronage of highly placed relatives or friends to assist them in finding service positions that at the very least guaranteed a minimum income.[22] It does not, however, tell the entire story of the Russian nobility. Close examination of the category *raznochintsy* reveals that the uncertain and changeable status of interstitial groups was a more general phenomenon that also affected the noble elite. Indeed, the noble-serf paradigm, which until 1861 served as the foundation of the *soslovie* structure, was much more nebulous than is generally recognized. Studies of serf millionaires and trading peasants generally acknowledge the ambiguity, but the phenomenon of the *raznochintsy* provides equally compelling evidence that neither the formal status of noble nor that of serf was firmly fixed. This circumstance along with the better known plasticity of free, non-noble categories reflected a society where insecurity was ubiquitous and boundaries were forever shifting.[23]

Historians have long noted the concentration of serf ownership in the hands of a small minority of landowners and the correspondingly meager resources of the vast majority of provincial gentry, not to mention those without land who depended entirely on state service.[24] Beyond the impact of impoverishment, service, or even lack of education (the children of hereditary nobles were legally nobles regardless of these or any other attributes), there was the important phenomenon of unrequited claimants to nobility—claimants whose origins were not officially recognized and whose status therefore remained indeterminate. The precise size of this group is unknown, but its potential significance is illustrated by a few statistics. In 1820, a relatively uneventful year, the Inspectors' Department of the War Ministry reported that only 560 out of 1,000 petitioners were allowed to enter the army with noble rights.[25] Similarly, data compiled by the Ministry of Justice in 1845 indicated that 3,332 claimants to nobility were confirmed, whereas 3,215 were refused. The respective figures for 1846 were 3,320 and 3,013.[26]

Comparable to the ambiguities of social definition in general, questions about noble identity resulted from official registration policies, imperial expansion, and ennoblement through service—all central aspects of state building. Whether falsified, justified, or simply erroneous (distinctions not always easy to determine), formal claims to noble status were based either on ancestry or service. Ancestry was traditionally the most coveted and prestigious source of nobility, yet it remained problematic and often difficult to prove. The existence of special social categories whose members enjoyed the legally defined right to prove their noble origins revealed the full complexity and uncertainty of elite genealogies. Clearly, downward mobility played an important role in the development of the imperial ruling class already in the early stages of its formation and certainly well before the postemancipation period, when significant numbers of déclassé nobles joined the ranks of the intelligentsia and professions. Indeed, the Petrine reforms did as much to exclude traditional categories of servicemen from the elite as to open its ranks to new ones; in either case, social definitions were disrupted and boundaries blurred.

In the early nineteenth century entire groups, such as the single householders and after 1831 the landless Polish *szlachta,* retained the right to prove their noble ancestry. To regain these lost privileges, single householders had to document that the land grants received by their ancestors had been awarded specifically for noble service.[27] The single householders were readily identifiable as a social category because of their geographical concentration in areas that once had comprised the southern borderlands of the Russian state; throughout the prereform period they enjoyed special privileges in military service.[28] Their very existence shows that while many traditional Muscovite servicemen were absorbed into the Petrine categories of the eighteenth century, others retained a distinct or indeterminate status until after 1861, when the elimination of serfdom, the standing army, and eventually the capitation led to another fundamental restructuring of official social classifications.

In addition to entire categories of servicemen whose formal status lay in the interstices of the larger Petrine "framework," there also were individuals whose claims to noble ancestry had been rejected or overlooked and who consequently had been enrolled in the poll tax registers, usually during the first half of the eighteenth century.[29] Still others enjoyed indefinitely the right to prove their noble origins—a right that could be lost in the event of a judicial conviction.[30] The ambiguous status of these claimants resulted either from a family's inability to provide sufficient evidence of noble lineage or from an individual's failure to establish descent from a family recognized by the Heraldry Office. The often impossible task of documenting noble genealogies placed both unsatisfied claimants and honest officials in a frustrating predicament. The questions raised in these cases and the inability to answer them testified to the very real uncertainties of noble status, the fundamental commitment of officialdom to protecting noble rights, and the pervasive ambiguity of social definitions.

One case, forwarded to the Moscow provincial administration from Orel in 1792, glaringly revealed the difficulties encountered. The saga began when the city government of Elets attempted to confirm the status of a sergeant's son who possessed a passport indicating that his deceased father was noble. The Elets nobility had refused to recognize the petitioner's noble ancestry because of the lack of documentation, nor could his neighbors, single householders in a suburb of Elets where he owned a home, confirm his origins. The only evidence of nobility was the passport his father had received (apparently regarded as authentic) from the head of the Moscow city government, showing that he had entered service in Elets as a landless Russian nobleman.

Since no information was forthcoming from Moscow, the petitioner and his brother asked to be registered as merchants in Elets, where they apparently made a living in trade. Local merchants expressed their willingness to accept them, but not before their status could be clarified; because this requirement could not be met, the petitioners requested registration in the category of townspeople. Once again, officials in Elets postponed making any decision before the brothers' origins could be determined; the petitioners were, however, permitted to remain in their home indefinitely and earn a living as in the past. Obviously, the authorities were baffled—a not uncommon occurrence—and the claimants themselves did not press their case; twenty years later their formal status still could not be determined.[31] Most important, even in the absence of legal registration, full and spontaneous socioeconomic integration clearly was achieved.

A later case from the army—where the terms of service depended upon social origin but also where the greatest opportunities for upward mobility existed—further illustrates the uncertainties associated with genealogical claims. In 1855 a Private Pokramovich lost the right to prove his noble ancestry after being sentenced by a military court. Ironically, he was convicted of unruly conduct and disrespect toward superiors for reacting violently when a lance corporal and later his company commander addressed him with the familiar "thou" *(ty)*—a form of address that was entirely appropriate when speaking to one's peers or social inferiors. But Pokramovich considered the "rude treatment" he had suffered an insult and openly declared to his commanding officer: "You do not have the right to address me with the familiar thou." Although Pokramovich claimed descent from a noble family recognized by the Heraldry Office in 1788, the authorities did not find sufficient documentation of his father's ancestry—hence the conflict between official status and personal expectations that this blue-blooded private found so unbearable.[32]

A second group of claimants to nobility arose from uncertainty in applying Russian laws to the minority populations of areas such as the Polish lands, subjected to Russian rule in the reign of Catherine the Great.[33] Polish nobles, with their long historical memory and traditional political power, must have been particularly perturbed when forced to seek recognition of their ancestry from the Russian Heraldry Office. The case of F. Sheniavskii, a Polish private in the Russian army, was indicative. In 1850

Sheniavskii lost the right to prove his noble origins after being convicted of perjury and two desertions. As a putative noble, he was spared the corporal punishment that most privates received for similar crimes, but upon reassignment to the ranks, he was to serve under the same terms as any lower-class conscript from the poll tax population.[34]

The last category of aspiring nobles was spawned by Petrine reforms and particularly the Table of Ranks, which regularized ennoblement through service. For many individuals, the Table of Ranks and the continual growth of the army and bureaucracy created enormous opportunities for social advancement. The idea of a service nobility was nothing new, and the nobility of lineage was not displaced, yet the Table of Ranks, with its implied emphasis on merit and performance, did promote a broader definition of nobility—a definition that included a cultural component based on education and Westernization.[35] Not surprisingly, the upwardly mobile educated (or semieducated) service nobility were subject to the greatest uncertainty of elite status. The children of personal nobles, classified as *raznochintsy*, represented upward and downward mobility;[36] unlike the offspring of most social categories, they began life and career in a category below that of their fathers, with a resultant gap between their formal rights and individual expectations.

In his study of the bureaucratic census of 1754–1756, S. M. Troitskii describes the descendants of seventeenth-century chancery clerks who achieved hereditary nobility in the post-Petrine era. The case of D. S. Kop'ev was especially interesting. Born before his father attained hereditary nobility, Kop'ev could not be considered a noble; still, he referred to himself as such well before reaching a service rank that granted nobility.[37] While not at all typical—the vast majority of these civil servants never achieved noble rank—Kop'ev's self-definition suggests two possible conclusions. Either he did not understand, or actually found meaningless, the distinction between hereditary noble and non-noble in the graded ranks of the civil service. This view would be perfectly understandable; Kop'ev's father obviously remained the same parent while passing from "senior officer rank" *(ober-ofitserskii chin)* to hereditary nobility. Or it could be that he well understood his non-noble origins but, fully expecting to be elevated, called himself a noble. This, too, makes sense, given the successful career of his father and his own very promising possibilities. In either case, there was an expectation of ennoblement that was consistent with actual experience, though not yet with formal status. Perhaps more significant, Kop'ev's self-image also indicates that, even for non-nobles, informal status could be higher than the formal definitions would allow.

Other aspiring nobles were not so well positioned. Far less promising was the career of Nikolai Shapov, a former postman, who in 1819 was sent to the army as a private after striking a coachman. Shapov also described himself as a noble, the son of a staff physician *(shtab-lekar')* with the rank of collegiate assessor (rank eight). Only after he deserted from the army twice and then falsely accused two noncommissioned officers of cruelty did the authorities even investigate his father's status with the Heraldry, the documents in the military's possession having perished in a fire. As it turned out, Shapov's father was born into the ecclesiastical domain, attended Moscow University, and ended his career as a staff physician with rank nine, which did not confer hereditary noble status. Shapov, then, was the son of a personal noble and, regardless of when he was born, was not entitled to the privileges of nobility.[38] Again, one is struck by the confusion surrounding the status of this self-defined noble. Even if Shapov deliberately falsified his origins, which is entirely plausible in light of his troubled service career, the authorities were careful not to violate the rights of a potential blue blood. Only after Shapov committed multiple crimes, which prompted the military to conduct a detailed investigation, did the authorities conclude that he was not of noble origin.

The range of individual and group claimants to nobility and the significant number of persons who sought but failed to gain recognition of such claims reflected the general uncertainties of social identity. If these people rightfully belonged to the nobility, then their indeterminate status reflected the ease with which landless nobles fell into the poll tax population. Equally important, even if the grounds were contrived, the ability to press claims that the authorities took seriously suggests a lack of clear delineation between the general population and ordinary nobles. Officials certainly were concerned not to violate rights that might become legally recognized.[39] Although governmental efforts to delimit the nobility began with the introduction of the Table of Ranks in 1722, it took most of the eighteenth century just to define the legal parameters of noble status. Indeed, the two cornerstones of noble privilege—preferential treatment in service and the exclusive right to possess populated estates—did not become firmly established in law, not to mention administrative practice, until the second half of the eighteenth century.[40]

Not only were individuals subject to the capitation regularly admitted to state service as unranked office employees, but they also received appointments to graded positions that opened the door to ennoblement at rank eight.[41] Inveighing against the presumptions of civil servants who erroneously regarded themselves as noble, the Senate in 1759, 1760, and again in 1761 reminded officials of senior officer rank (ranks nine and below), who were commoners by birth, that according to the precise "representation" *(izobrazhenie)* of the Table of Ranks, "their children are not nobles [and] unlike nobles, they are not permitted to purchase or possess villages." Furthermore, because they did not "enjoy noble rights," according to a law of 9 February 1758, they had only six months to sell any estates already in their possession.[42] Clearly, among civil servants in ranks fourteen to nine, which did not confer nobility, it was difficult to maintain the distinction between hereditary nobles and commoners.

The failure before the 1760s to adhere to the prescriptions in the Table of Ranks eased the rise of commoners beyond what would have been possible had the table's provisions been strictly enforced. This occurred even though the table itself institutionalized ennoblement through service and so supposedly facilitated the promotion of men of talent into the ruling elite. In addition, because the 1762 emancipation of the nobility from obligatory service was in some measure an exclusion from the rewards of service, it also blurred the boundaries separating hereditary nobles from non-noble officials with rank. If the hereditary nobles were no longer required to serve, then they also were no longer entitled to an appointment.[43] Despite the preferential treatment that nobles continued to receive, the boundaries separating them from commoners remained blurred and porous—even in the hierarchical and relatively regulated context of the civil service. The very lack of delineation helps to explain how Russia's small ruling class was able to extend and maintain its power by consolidating personalized networks based on kinship and patronage.

Official efforts to delimit the nobility continued in the first half of the nineteenth century. Among the issues of social categorization examined by the Committee of 6 December 1826 were access to the nobility and the regulations governing promotion in service. The concerns of the committee subsequently were embodied in legislation from the 1840s, which attempted to restrict ennoblement by raising the rank at which elevation could occur. The category of honored citizen (created in 1832) was added to that of personal noble to accommodate civil servants and military officers whose ranks no longer conferred hereditary or personal nobility. The new rules thus avoided the potential danger, identified in the committee's deliberations by Count V. P. Kochubei, that the result of limiting the number of service nobles, both hereditary and personal, would be to create additional *raznochintsy,* who "would enter a category [*sostoianie*] which lacks any definition and which should not exist in the state."[44] Kochubei's objection illustrates very well the larger issue that informed discussions of ennoblement through service, specifically the need to define in law and administration the composition of Russian society, or in the words of the Moscow governor-general, Prince Golitsyn, the search for "the means to establish order and precision in the mechanism of the parts [*mekhanizm chastei*] that comprise the social composition of the Empire."[45]

The members of the Committee of 6 December 1826 correctly associated the phenomenon of service *raznochintsy* with the problem of delimiting the nobility; they implicitly understood that state building represented a threat to noble exclusivity because it extended and hence blurred the boundaries of the hereditary nobility. The lack of correspondence between service post and rank, the continual creation of new subcategories of *raz-nochintsy*, and the general difficulty of defining the middle layers of society—all of these circumstances contributed to the lack of clear delineation. The committee's desire to define formal status in terms of societal function was nothing new; neither were the problems of registering individuals and groups to juridically defined categories, nor the confusion caused by ambiguous legal definitions. But added to these traditional sources of social uncertainty, and the direct result of state building, were a range of manpower needs that created new categories of educated and semieducated personnel who, if not incorporated into the hereditary nobility, could only become personal nobles, honored citizens, or *raznochintsy*. The proliferation of new subcategories did not increase the numerical significance of the category *raznochintsy*, but it did underscore its complexity and that of social classifications in general.

From the mid-seventeenth century until emancipation in 1861, and for the peasantry well beyond that date, the autocracy attempted to legislate social structure and development in order to meet the ever-changing requirements of state building and to ensure that formal status corresponded to societal function. The linkage of formal definition to function injected elements of dynamism and instability into the delimitation of social categories; the result was a fluid social framework, where even the boundaries of the nobility could never be firmly fixed. Ultimately, and particularly after emancipation, the only way to preserve noble exclusivity and the status honor derived from it was to limit the enrollment of new nobles. State building made this difficult because the promise of ennoblement was the primary reward of service. The solution, which dated back at least to the reign of Catherine the Great, was to create additional sources of status honor embodied in the categories personal noble and honored citizen ("distinguished citizen" in Catherinean legislation). Formulated in connection with policies that aimed to delimit the hereditary nobility, these categories brought privileges most readily identified as noble: freedom from conscription, the capitation, and corporal punishment; preferential access to education and promotion in service; and, in the case of personal nobles, the coveted and short-lived right to purchase and possess populated estates, though not to pass them on to non-noble children. The effect of legislating status honor was not, however, to delineate the hereditary nobility more clearly; it was to assign "noble" privileges increasingly to non-noble groups on the basis of service or education, and hence to undermine noble exclusivity.

The evidence presented thus far in no way suggests that officially recognized nobles occupied an uncertain status, though they might be economically insecure and their service careers might be less than brilliant. It does suggest, however, that among those upwardly and downwardly mobile middle social groups (claimants to noble status, at least some of whom must have been legitimate; personal nobles; single householders; *raznochintsy*, however defined) formal status often was uncertain. Individual aspirations (or machinations?) frequently ended in disappointment; more important, the authorities themselves had difficulty determining who exactly was a noble. Whether one considers common soldiers or noble elites, the processes of state building, particularly the growing manpower needs of the army and bureaucracy, generated new categories of servicemen, altered the definitions of categories that already existed, and in general contributed a dynamic ambiguity to the delimitation of social groups.

THE MALLEABLE BONDS OF SERFDOM

The phenomenon of illegal serf ownership originated in the mid-eighteenth century, when the government first began to restrict non-noble access to servile labor. Its continued existence right up until emancipation testified to a lack of noble exclusivity, a more generalized uncertainty of status, and the deliberate violation of formal social boundaries at all levels of society. The issue of non-noble ownership of serfs is crucial to understanding the *soslovie* framework, for by the end of the eighteenth century the absolute right to possess populated estates had become a hallmark of nobility. Indeed, the noble response to emancipation—virtually wholesale opposition—tellingly revealed the importance attached to the privilege of owning serfs. In practice, the Russian nobility never realized exclusivity in the possession of servile labor, and in some cases individual nobles actually abetted violations of their own privileges. Individual motives tended to be economic, but the fluidity of Russian society created the conditions that permitted such abuses. The startling fact that emerges from the legal, judicial, and administrative sources dealing with unlawful enserfment is the ease with which individuals not only fell into illegal bondage but also escaped from lawful servitude.

The illicit ownership of serfs took two forms. First, persons who were forbidden by law to possess estates and serfs continued to acquire them, at least until the late 1840s. Second, nobles who enjoyed the right to own serfs, and non-nobles who did not, repeatedly subjected free persons to illegal enserfment. The circumstances leading to unlawful enserfment varied, but Russia's weak legal tradition and lax enforcement were major factors; ambiguities in the laws allowed individuals and local officials, knowingly or unknowingly, to conceal illegal relationships.[46] The records of the Arzamas district court (Nizhnii Novgorod province) indicate that by 1785, the year of Catherine the Great's Charter to the Nobility, the Senate strictly interpreted existing prohibitions against the possession of serfs by non-nobles and even denied ownership in cases where serfs or their descendants had been registered to a non-noble in the first, second, or third revisions. Thus the central government informed officials in Riazan province that in the future they were not to confirm purchases of serfs by non-nobles on the basis of registration in the first and second revisions.[47]

Local officials did not, however, immediately implement the Senate's instructions; in 1785 and 1788 the Arzamas court upheld the ownership of serfs by merchants based on registration in the first, second, and third revisions. In one case the court determined that a merchant's widow did indeed have the authority to emancipate a serf whose grandfather had been registered to her husband in the first revision. The serf's grandfather, father, and uncle also had been registered to the merchant in the second revision. By the third revision the serf's grandfather had died, but his father, uncle, and he himself were inscribed.[48] Again in 1788 the court exhibited a similar understanding of the law: when the grandson of a Swedish convert who had been registered to a merchant in the first revision requested emancipation, the court denied the petition and returned the grandson to his merchant master.[49] Similarly, a provincial report of 1796 revealed the presence in Nizhnii Novgorod of twenty-five domestic serfs who were registered to *raznochintsy* in the first, second, and third revisions; the largest number belonged to officials *(prikaznye)*, then merchants, townspeople, and coachmen.[50] Even as late as 1801 the Arzamas court registered the illegitimate son of a domestic servant to a merchant's wife, although the child's mother had begun her employment well after the appearance of strict prohibitions against the acquisition of serfs by non-nobles.[51]

Despite lax enforcement, especially in the eighteenth century, the Senate's stricter interpretation of the law increasingly affected local decisions, first at the provincial and then at the district level. In 1801 and 1802 the Nizhnii Novgorod provincial administration took action that led to the release of seventeen domestic serfs registered to merchants, townspeople, officials, and soldiers (collectively referred to as *raznochintsy*).[52] Again in 1808 the Arzamas district court forwarded to the Senate a complicated case in which one merchant acquired a serf family after another posed as the middleman in an ostensibly legitimate sale by a landlord. The local court recognized that these dealings were illegal but was uncertain about the status of the serfs. Nine years later, in 1817, the Senate ordered that they be sold within six months to someone entitled to own serfs.[53] Given the ambiguous formulations found in the laws, and given that it took the Senate nine years to return a decision, it is perhaps not surprising that more than two decades passed before the Arzamas district court began to interpret the Senate rulings from the 1780s accurately. One cannot rule out the possibility of corruption and deliberate misrepresentation of the law; local officials and courts, dominated by the nobility, repeatedly certified illegal sales and ignored peasant complaints against illegal masters.[54] At the same time, there also can be no doubt that provincial authorities frequently found it difficult to understand the laws they were supposed to enforce—a difficulty at least partly attributable to the lack of legal codification.

Even when officials understood the law and honestly sought to enforce it, there were other conditions that permitted illegal forms of serfdom. One problem, addressed in the legislation, involved economic relationships between nobles and *raznochintsy,* here defined as all free persons who did not enjoy the right to possess serfs. The most common abuse occurred when noble masters entrusted serfs to "middlemen" who were expected to sell them to legitimate buyers. In case after case these middlemen retained possession of the serfs, based on letters of credit *(veruiushchie pis'ma)* given to them by the nobles. Before 1816, serfowners were permitted to address these letters to the *raznochintsy* who were "hired" to conduct the sale; after that date, the letters could not bear the name of a person who did not enjoy rights of serf ownership. The new law gave the illegitimate owners one year to conclude any outstanding sales, after which the serfs would be set free, but even when officials prosecuted violations, a decade or more could pass before an illegally held serf was liberated.[55]

Enforcement remained difficult because *raznochintsy* and nobles alike stubbornly pursued the unlawful relationships.[56] Sometimes nobles themselves served as the "middlemen" between illicit serfowners in order to legitimize a deal.[57] Landlords also sold letters of credit for their runaway serfs (Gogol's "dead souls"), which "entrepreneurs" then used to sell substitute conscripts, who immediately deserted and could be resold.[58] In an unresolved case from 1799 a servant *(sluzhitel')* who claimed he had been freed by his noble master ended up being registered to a peasant family who planned to use him as a substitute conscript. According to his petition, the servant had requested registration as a merchant, but because he was illiterate and unfamiliar with administrative procedures, his former master had given the document certifying his release to an individual who was supposed to assist him.[59] The "document" may have been a letter of credit that the noble sold to a middleman, who then sold the supposedly freed servant as a conscript. Whatever the facts of this case, it reveals very clearly the dangers scholars encounter when using legal sources, which are not in and of themselves true.

It is well known that serf entrepreneurs acquired laborers in the name of their masters; similar arrangements also existed between *raznochintsy* (here, free non-nobles) and nobles. The difference was that neither the *raznochinnye* owners nor the serfs they possessed necessarily knew or had any subsequent dealings with the legal noble master. Indeed, several generations of serfs could be registered to nobles, while remaining de facto the property of the same *raznochinnyi* family.[60] In one particularly infamous case from Vitebsk province, the townsman Lev Koronovskii acquired twenty-six serfs as a gift from a local noblewoman in 1798; the gift received official sanction in a deed *(krepost')* registered in the name of another noble. The following year Koronovskii bought an estate with two hundred and sixty-five serfs from the same noblewoman, this time in the name of still another noble. When Koronovskii's daughter married a noble in 1810, she received part of the estate, including twenty-nine serfs, as a dowry along with a proxy *(doverennost')* indicating that the noble in whose name her father had bought the estate had transferred a portion to her as repayment on a debt. Koronovskii's son, also a registered townsman, inherited the balance of his father's estate. When Koronovskii's peasants learned that they actually belonged to another noble, they petitioned the district court. In 1817, after submitting four complaints and receiving no response, twenty-six of them appealed to higher authorities; only then did an investigation begin, which resulted in their transfer to state property. Koronovskii's son was deprived of his father's hard-earned property in 1827; Koronovskii's daughter, whose status as a noble serfowner had been secured through marriage, was allowed to retain her serfs.[61]

Yet another path to illegal enserfment arose when noble serfowners granted persons of any status the right to employ their serfs on a temporary basis. These temporary arrangements were in no way illegal, provided the serfs obtained passports from their masters and went to work for employers who paid them wages. It was quite another matter, however, for *raznochintsy* to possess serfs on the basis of illegal contracts or to borrow them at no cost from noble friends and relatives.[62] Sometimes the serf labor served as repayment on a loan, and sometimes also the *raznochinnye* masters acquired the right to sell them. According to one contract concluded in 1815, a captain entrusted three serfs to a sergeant's wife ostensibly to learn housekeeping; after five years she was entitled to keep them permanently or sell them. In return she promised not to charge interest on a debt of three thousand rubles owed to her by the captain. In 1821, finding that the sergeant's widow was not registered in a craft guild and hence did not have the right to train apprentices,[63] the State Council declared this agreement illegal and ordered that the serfs be freed. In similar cases *raznochinnye* employers did not necessarily attempt to establish legal ownership over serfs; still, the labor contracts might continue indefinitely.[64]

Greed provided only one source of illegal serfs; free persons also fell into servile status as a result of employment or economic distress, just as they had in the Muscovite period before serfdom was legally fixed by heredity. Historians of the army and working classes document relationships that were tantamount to indentured servitude. In connection with military service, these relationships resulted from the purchase of substitutes to fulfill conscription quotas; among the working classes, they arose from poverty and the opportunities for employment in towns.[65] Indeed, the history of illegal enserfment suggests that relationships comparable to indentured servitude were generalized throughout society. Thus the district governor *(voevoda)* of Solikamsk (Kazan province) reported that in 1763 "an unknown woman" had asked him to raise her son of six months; the governor agreed and subsequently had the boy inscribed as his serf on the basis of illegitimacy. When the boy came of age, he claimed to be the son of a townsman and requested registration in that category. He eventually succeeded in proving that he had been under his master's authority only five years and had been taken in not as a serf but as an "adopted son." In 1807 the Senate declared him free.[66]

Despite legal prohibitions and at least partial enforcement, poverty or simple employment could result in unlawful enserfment right up until emancipation. At the end of the eighteenth century, a young boy called Rodionov, the son of a free peasant from the Dorpat area, went to work for a local baron; from there he traveled to Nizhnii Novgorod, where he worked twenty-three years for a second noble. When this employer died, his heiress tried to prove that Rodionov was actually a serf. Because the name on the bill of sale she presented, while similar, did not match exactly, a local court emancipated Rodionov and his family in 1821. (By then he had married the serf of yet another noble.)[67] In a similar case a boy from the ecclesiastical domain went to work for a noblewoman because of his father's poverty. The boy began his employment in the mid-eighteenth century, subsequently was registered as a household serf, and then passed as an inheritance to his mistress's heiress. In 1822 a local court, finding that he was a free person who never should have been inscribed as a serf, liberated him and his children.[68] Finally, as late as 1859, the son of a townswoman *(meshchanka)* was returned to his mother after having been registered to a landlord as a foundling *(podkidysh)* in the ninth revision (1850). Again because of poverty, the mother had entrusted her son to the care of a serf—an arrangement that then resulted in the son's being ascribed to a noble master.[69]

Economic vitality could also lead to illegal enserfment, while permitting some individuals to escape legitimate servitude. Widespread geographical mobility, even among serfs, is well documented throughout the imperial period. Even if it did not represent an economic decision, then at the very least, movement was made possible by economic opportunity or necessity;[70] it could be legal or illegal, or a combination of both, as happened repeatedly in the business career of the serf entrepreneur Nikolai Shipov.[71] Local administrative records from the 1780s and 1790s reveal that among male and female runaways, some had lived in forests and peasant villages or found employment in factories and towns for as long as thirty years.[72] Runaways also frequently found themselves enserfed by local landowners and officials. One peasant, who had fled to Saratov in 1796, was taken in by a landlord, promised emancipation in seven years, and immediately put to work. Unfortunately, the landlord died before fulfilling his promise, and his widow refused to give up her serf. The runaway again fled, but this time he was caught and in 1809 returned to his original owner.[73] This extensive migration, well before the onset of industrialization, was one indicator of the dynamic social and economic conditions.

Even more suggestive was the ease with which runaways moved into and out of serf status. In 1784 authorities returned a woman from the category of single householders to her husband in Voronezh province. As early as 1751 the woman had fled or been abducted. (The source contradicts itself on this point.) She subsequently became the property of a landlord from Nizhnii Novgorod province and was married to one of his peasants; after being widowed, she was sold to another landlord who also had her married. In 1780—twenty-nine years after her initial departure—the woman petitioned the governor for her freedom and was sent back to her first husband along with their son.[74] In a similar incident a naval officer abducted the daughter of a townsman and deceived her into marrying his serf. An acquaintance had persuaded the girl, aged seventeen, that the officer intended to marry her; when she realized the truth of her situation, she fled. In 1800 she and her serf husband were freed and registered in the category of townspeople.[75]

A third case indicates that the crossing of social boundaries was not limited to "abducted" women or runaway wives.[76] In 1783 a runaway serf from Iaroslav province was registered as a townsman of Nizhnii Novgorod, where he married and had two sons. In 1786 he entrusted the older son of two years, Mikhail, to the care of a serf named Ulitin. A contractual agreement formalized the arrangements, stipulating that when Mikhail came of age, he be permitted to leave his benefactor. A year later the townsman delivered his second son, Petr, to the same serf. At that time a new agreement was not signed, but the serf supposedly promised to find the boy suitable employment with a merchant or townsman. Years later in Balakhna, Mikhail, now aged twenty, approached the mayor of Nizhnii Novgorod, explaining that he had been held in fetters by the owner of a local glass factory and only recently had been released after injuring himself. Because Mikhail identified himself as "a person belonging to the Nizhnii Novgorod magistracy," he was questioned by that office. (His mother had died in 1789, and his father had disappeared sometime before the fifth revision of 1794–1795.)

Mikhail reported that after becoming the charge of Ulitin, he had lived with one townsman and three merchants, worked as a guide for a blind man, again lived with Ulitin, who hired him out as an agricultural laborer in the summer, and then lived with another townsman, Kuznetsov, for nine years. Finally, in 1799, the factory owner, Lebedev, convinced Kuznetsov that Mikhail was his runaway serf and sent him to work in chains; there Mikhail remained for two months. Although three witnesses confirmed Mikhail's parentage, the case stalled because Lebedev produced evidence that he had purchased a serf of the same name in 1795. By 1802, however, the governor became convinced of Mikhail's honesty—a conclusion that was confirmed when the landlord who supposedly sold Mikhail to Lebedev "bought" him back and immediately "freed" him in 1803. Mikhail then appeared before the magistracy in Nizhnii Novgorod and was registered as a townsman. His brother, Petr, also became a townsman of Nizhnii Novgorod, after the authorities discovered that he had been registered to Ulitin's master as a foundling in the fifth revision.[77]

This case, for all its complications, well illustrates how readily a runaway serf could change his formal registration, how tenuous formal status could be, and how easily a labor contract could lead to illegal enserfment. Clearly, local officials were reluctant to challenge the claims of nobles, so that even after the governor dismissed these claims, the magistracy still did not take action until the two nobles effectively withdrew from the proceedings. For the historian, the "facts" of the situation are virtually unknowable. It is no surprise that abandoned and orphaned children, runaways, and the poor were vulnerable to unlawful enserfment; what is striking is the extent to which the ownership of serfs was not an exclusive noble privilege and the ease with which individuals changed or escaped their formal status—legally or illegally, voluntarily or involuntarily. It was this constant movement in Russian society—be it social, economic, juridical, or geographical—that bred a widespread insecurity of status and that produced the phenomenon of the *raznochintsy*.

Although by the end of the eighteenth century non-noble possession of serfs was clearly illegal, enforcement remained incomplete. Throughout the prereform period the phenomenon itself, and the legal proceedings to which it gave rise, required repeated examination in the Senate and State Council. Not until 1847 did lawmakers and administrators finally work out the legal formulas and procedures needed to decide suits brought by peasants seeking emancipation on grounds of illegal possession by *raznochinnye* masters.[78] Based on legislation from 1816 and 1823, these cases sometimes dragged on for more than a decade. Often they were initiated by peasants who, though currently in the hands of nobles, had at some time in the past lived with *raznochinnye* masters. When the available documentation showed that these peasants had been returned to noble owners only after a suit was begun, decisions were easily rendered. In other instances either nobles were not aware that their serfs had served *raznochintsy* in the past or they lost them through erroneous rulings by local authorities.[79] The laws allowing illegally possessed serfs to sue for their freedom—in itself a legal anomaly, given that serfs had no civic identity—generated so many petitions and caused so much confusion that in 1837 and 1840 the State Council forbade all such suits in cases where serfs currently resided with nobles. In the future, however, nobles who acquired serfs previously held by unlawful *raznochinnye* masters would lose their property and would have to document that they had no knowledge of these past abuses to obtain compensation.[80] Ironically, in seeking to eliminate non-noble ownership of serfs, the government in effect restricted the rights of nobles freely to dispose of their

property. Thus both socioeconomic realities and the problems of enforcement revealed that even in that most touted arena of noble privilege—the
possession of serfs—noble exclusivity was in many respects a legal and social fiction.

SOCIAL FLUIDITY AND
SPONTANEOUS ECONOMIC DEVELOPMENT

Legislative and administrative sources clearly indicate that the institutional framework within which Russians made a living, pursued an occupation, or conducted a trade could not contain spontaneous societal
development. Restrictions on trade and geographical movement neither
impeded development nor prevented individual economic success. Lawmakers constantly and to little avail sought to reconcile formal structures
and socioeconomic realities, but the amorphous legal definitions (not to
mention problems of enforcement) lacked the consistency needed either
to regulate or secure development. It was not that overregulation and the
alleged constraints of serfdom necessarily slowed the pace of economic
transformation but rather that organizational weakness, legal uncertainty,
and social fragmentation—all reinforced by authoritarian arbitrariness and
patronage politics—exacerbated personal insecurity, dissipated economic
resources, and hence reduced the productive impact of entrepreneurial
initiative and governmental stimuli.

Traditional scholarship focuses attention on the relationship between
state policy and economic development from the seventeenth century to
the present. Debate centers on the effects of official policies, particularly
whether state involvement (or indifference) hindered or stimulated progress toward a modern industrial economy. Historians of the eighteenth
century are inclined to stress the beneficial results of governmental measures during a period of productive growth, when Russia's industrial infrastructure did not differ significantly from that of other European powers.
Students of the nineteenth century are less sanguine and less in agreement
about both the overall patterns of economic development and the efficacy
of governmental measures. To be sure, the first half of the nineteenth century, a time of relative stagnation, culminated in a new awareness of Russia's backwardness as a result of the Crimean War, yet the government did
not commit itself to full-scale industrialization before the 1880s. Although
the impact of this commitment and of equally significant private efforts
remains a major source of controversy among economic and social historians, there is general agreement that a profound transformation was at least
under way by the end of the century.[81]

Beyond these large-scale productive processes there was significant mi-
crolevel activity—activity that could be extralegal, semilegal, or outright
illegal and that was motivated by petty greed, pressing need, or the honest

pursuit of profit. Because this activity took place outside the prescribed framework of economic relations, it is difficult to document; its impact on macroeconomic development is often impossible to measure. The concept of the *raznochintsy* frequently appeared in discussions of this small-scale search for economic survival or individual prosperity. As early as the reign of Peter the Great, official and societal sources identified an indistinct grouping of mainly (though not exclusively) urban residents who were not registered in the formal categories of town or rural district, and hence not subject to the standard forms of taxation. Often depicted as outsiders and referred to collectively as *raznochintsy,* these nonmembers of a given community or social category were highly visible in manufacturing and trade as factory owners, merchants, shopkeepers, artisans, and hired laborers. In the postemancipation period they even became owners of communal land and participants in the village assembly. Clearly, the *raznochintsy* did not represent a specific class or category that played a concrete, identifiable role in the organization of production, nor was there a single aspect of development that explains their economic significance. Rather, official and societal perceptions of their presence illuminated the relationship between legal status and occupation, as well as the economic dynamism of both urban society and serfdom.

Already in the Law Code of 1649 the government attempted to limit urban commerce to designated social categories by prescribing who could trade, what they could trade, and where. Numerous peasants and petty servicemen, collectively referred to as *"raznochintsy* nonmerchants," *(raznochintsy ne kupetskie liudi),* were forbidden to trade unless they registered in the urban taxpaying community, thereby becoming subject to local taxes and service obligations. Administrative records from the first half of the eighteenth century reveal the dynamism of illegal economic enterprise and the failure of local officials to enforce restrictions. The corruption and political patronage networks that sanctioned such abuses also permitted spontaneous socioeconomic development.[82] In the late 1740s, when the local city magistracy in Olonets attempted to enforce prohibitions on trade, the provincial administrative office *(voevodskaia kantseliariia)* refused to back these efforts with the appropriate decrees *(ukazy).*[83] Similarly, in 1748 the magistracy in the city of Dmitrov complained that *raznochintsy* and the local governor *(voevoda)* himself possessed "merchant lands" but did not pay the taxes required of registered townspeople.[84]

Throughout Russia, officials reported that despite the legal prohibitions, peasants and *raznochintsy* who did not register in the urban taxpaying community or perform local services continued to own homes, shops, warehouses, and stubble fields located on merchant lands. In the Blagoveshchenskaia suburb *(sloboda)* of Nizhnii Novgorod, 265 peasants and *raznochintsy* owned shops; by contrast, only 112 shops belonged to registered townspeople. In this case, at least, the peasants did perform service and pay taxes in the suburb, though their obligations were not the same as those of the townspeople.[85] In Pskov a wide range of peasants and *raznochintsy* illegally conducted business and maintained enterprises in their homes, which were regarded as unregistered places *(neukaznye mesta)*. Others lived and traded "in merchant homes on taxed lands" and even married merchants' widows and daughters but still did not register in the urban community. Thus Crown and monastery peasants, private serfs, priests and deacons, coachmen, gunners, administrative "police" *(kantseliarskie razsyl'shchiki)*, and "other persons of various ranks" possessed shops, flax- and hemp-scutching enterprises, and malt and leather factories.[86]

The fluid socioeconomic conditions of the early eighteenth century and the desire of local officials to register as many taxpayers as possible allowed runaways and persons of unknown origin to establish themselves legally and economically in a variety of urban categories. As noted in chapter 3, the economic criteria for admission to the registered urban community—capital worth five hundred rubles and the approval of local merchants/ officials—almost certainly required that an individual already possess an established business in a given locality before seeking membership. Given the prohibitions on local trade by unregistered urban residents, such individuals would not have become economically integrated had they not evaded those very restrictions.[87] Clearly, illegal trade in many cases constituted economic development and entrepreneurial success.

Even serfs sometimes managed to register in an urban community without the approval of their masters.[88] Others actually were registered in one city but lived and worked in another. During the second revision, authorities discovered a wood-carver who had trained and worked in Moscow for seven years and then journeyed to Shuia with a one-year passport. He remained there another seven years, married the daughter of a priest, and eventually moved on to Kineshma, where he lived with his wife and children for fifteen years—without, however, obtaining a new passport. Only in 1744 did the authorities return him to Moscow, where he had been registered in the first revision.[89] This personal history and many others like it indicate that labor mobility and flexible socioeconomic relationships, both of which facilitated illegal enserfment, also framed the existence of people in less vulnerable categories, in this case a trained artisan who formally belonged to a Moscow craft guild and maintained a stable family life.

In the Catherinean era illegal trade persisted, as did the prominent role of *raznochintsy*. In the instructions to the Legislative Commission virtually every social category that was not part of the urban citizenry under the authority of the magistracy appeared in one context or another as *raznochintsy;* even nobles were included on occasion.[90] Merchants, who at this time were distinguished from the general population of registered townspeople only by the amount of capital they possessed, consistently complained about unregistered peasants and *raznochintsy* who interfered in merchant trades or produced crafts outside the organized guilds. The term *raznochintsy* thus referred to a specific category of outsiders or to a variety of categories that did not enjoy "merchant rights" but nonetheless engaged in merchant trades: nobles, state officials, ecclesiastical ranks and churchmen, military servicemen (retired and active) and their wives, single householders, coachmen, "ploughing soldiers" (former *strel'tsy* and *pushkari*), peasants, farriers, artisans who were not members of craft organizations, ethnic and religious minorities, and merchants from other cities. As the instruction from Norskaia sloboda (Moscow government) explained, a *raznochinets* was a "free man" *(svobodnyi chelovek)*—free of tax and service obligations—who conducted his trade without interference or interruption and so was "useless not only to the town, but also to the state."[91]

A close reading of the instructions reveals that the economic activities of the outsiders were as broad and diverse as their social makeup. *Raznochintsy* from the countryside and towns owned retail stores, warehouses, storerooms, cellars, bakeries, offices, fishermen's cabins, inns, and eating houses. Their factories produced leather, soap, and tallow. Their extensive participation in trade and transport (even as shipowners) took them to a variety of regions, cities, and ports. Their wares included imports from Germany, Persia, and China; grain, fish, salt, honey, and beeswax; furs, silk, brocade, canvas, and cloth; hemp, indigo dye, and hops. It is clear from the nature and range of these activities that some *raznochintsy* were involved in substantial economic enterprises serving a national or regional market—enterprises that merchants emphatically distinguished from the small-scale production and sale of crafts and foodstuffs by individual families.

Some historians express skepticism about the real burden of taxation and service that merchants identified as the primary reason for their opposition to unfair competition from *raznochintsy*.[92] The skepticism seems justified; the urban instructions also complained that merchants hired *raznochintsy* as shop assistants and stewards or to transport goods. These arrangements deprived poor merchants and their sons of jobs, forcing them to work as peasants and laborers. More significant than the hiring of *raznochinnye* employees—*raznochintsy* could also be found among factory workers and unskilled laborers—merchants made loans and extended credit to outsiders.[93] They sold their merchant rights, signed promissory notes for persons who were forbidden to do so, and bought goods from *raznochintsy* and peasants instead of from other merchants. Whatever allegiance they might profess to the formal rights of merchant status, business was their first priority, and business—as practiced by nobles, merchants, *raznochintsy*, and peasants in imperial Russia—was dynamic, fluid, and indifferent to formal social boundaries. Not unlike the ownership of serfs by non-nobles, the involvement of *raznochintsy* (here, nonmerchants) in merchant trades revealed the extent to which the pursuit of profit evolved without regard for juridically defined rights and boundaries.

The continuing failure of city officials to enforce restrictions on trade was due in part to the splintered nature of administrative authority.[94] In many instances the legal particularism of social categories corresponded to fragmented judicial and administrative jurisdictions. Registered towns-people came under the office of the magistracy, *raznochintsy* under the district or provincial authorities, and factory workers under the Colleges of Mining and Manufacturing.[95] This atomized authority and Russia's weak legal tradition made it extremely difficult for merchants, tradesmen, and entrepreneurs to resolve economic disputes or recover losses—especially when the parties to a conflict came under different administrative domains. Catherine the Great's local reforms attempted to strengthen judicial institutions and provide mechanisms to bridge administrative divisions, but the results were disappointing. Illegal trade conducted by *raznochintsy*, peasants, and other outsiders continued unabated in both central Russia and the borderlands. Provincial governors and economic administrators repeatedly ignored and sometimes openly opposed the efforts of urban officials, under the authority of the Main Magistracy, to enforce restrictions.[96] The institutional framework for economic development remained glaringly inadequate to meet the needs of independent entrepreneurs who crossed virtually every socioeconomic boundary erected in law.

The illicit trade and movement of population that underlay the porous social boundaries of the eighteenth century persisted until the 1860s and 1870s when emancipation and the secondary reforms fundamentally altered the legal framework of society.[97] Prereform officials also identified *raznochintsy* as social-administrative outsiders involved in unlawful economic activities. Together with nobles, graded civil servants, and peasants, *raznochintsy* avoided urban taxes but continued to own shops and engage in merchant trades.[98] As homeowners and proprietors of manufacturing, artisanal, and commercial establishments, they also remained integrated into local communities.[99] Regulations of 1812 and 1824 attempted once again to eliminate unregistered traders and to increase state revenues by easing restrictions on enrollment in urban categories; the new rules effectively abandoned traditional pretenses, never realized in practice, that equated social categories with specific occupations and service functions. Instead, various categories of nobles, peasants, merchants, and townspeople purchased official certificates *(svidetel'stva)* permitting them to trade within prescribed limits; each category of urban resident and each type of certificate granted specific economic privileges. The purpose clearly was not to protect the interests of registered townspeople but to expedite the collection of fees; the result was a regulatory nightmare that actually institutionalized traditional violations of formal social boundaries. According to the intricate legal prescriptions, trading peasants could choose from six different certificates, each carrying specified economic rights.[100] Not surprisingly, the reforms did little to stem the tide of unregistered entrepreneurs and traders.

During the reign of Nicholas I, the career of the serf entrepreneur Nikolai Shipov strikingly revealed the social fluidity, legal uncertainty, and dissipation of capital and resources that proved so detrimental to long-term economic development.[101] Born a private serf in Nizhnii Novgorod province in 1802, Shipov was a prime example of the widespread geographical mobility that the formal structure of social categories explicitly denied.[102] He began his career in May 1813, when he accompanied his father, a wealthy sheep trader, on his annual trip to the Orenburg steppe. The Shipovs followed a route that encompassed Simbirsk, Ural'sk, Kazan, and Astrakhan on the Caspian Sea. They employed about twenty peasant laborers and traded with Cossacks, Siberian nomads (in this instance called Kirghizes), and Russian merchants; in addition, they paid "tribute" to local Cossack, Bashkir, Chuvash, and Kalmyk communities for permission to cross their lands free of attack. After transporting their livestock across the Volga river, they returned home by mid-October. Besides sheep, Nikolai and his father traded tallow, furs, leather, cotton and silk robes, and red calico in places like Rostov, Moscow, and the Makar'ev fair.

The economic effects of serfdom are abundantly clear in the story of the Shipov family. Their master, well aware of their business successes, repeatedly appointed Nikolai's father to administrative posts and sometimes demanded such high monetary dues that the elder Shipov had to borrow from merchants in order to pay. These exactions and those of bandits made it impossible to accumulate a secure reserve of capital, even if trade generally was profitable. Still, the Shipovs pressed on and remained "wealthy," despite the very real possibility of losing everything overnight. Along with repeated displays of economic resilience they also stubbornly sought freedom; efforts to purchase the emancipation of individual family members failed, but Nikolai eventually was successful. His saga began in 1830, when he left home with thirteen thousand rubles. On this occasion, after hearing that his father was seriously ill, he returned almost immediately. He was then deprived of his passport, but before his father's death, Nikolai managed to deposit merchandise with a relative and fifteen thousand rubles with a local merchant. A month later he received a new passport and resumed trade.

At the end of 1831 Nikolai and his wife again fled, and with the help of a "disappeared" relative and an Odessa merchant, they obtained a false passport (the first of three) that identified them as residents of Kishinev. After journeying to Moldavia and Constantinople, they returned to the Russian empire and rented a store in Piatigorsk. Shipov's wife and an employee tended the shop, and Shipov went to work in the Caucasus for a Cossack entrepreneur who filled state orders, leased a postal station, and worked in oil processing and trade. Arrested in 1837, after his employer discovered he was a runaway serf, Shipov again returned to his village, where he was unable to obtain another passport until 1842. Although he could not collect previous debts or recover property that had been left with associates, he managed to lease a glue factory in Kishinev for twelve hundred rubles—all of which he lost when his landlord again refused to renew his passport. Shipov found himself without a source of income—but more determined than ever to attain his freedom.

Finally, at the end of 1842, Shipov began the journey that led to his emancipation. He received a passport and traveled to the Caucasus, where serfs who were taken prisoner by mountain bands became free upon release from captivity. Working as a sutler for a Jewish merchant (who previously had worked for him), Shipov allowed himself to be taken captive. At last, in 1844, he achieved liberation after a Tatar deserter from the Russian army (who also had worked for him in Orenburg) helped him to escape. Shipov's wife and children then joined him in Kherson, where his son graduated from the gymnasium and became a teacher in a private school in Odessa. His wife found employment as a custodian at the same school, and Shipov worked as a sutler in the Caucasus and Bessarabia. Although at least two other peasants owned by the same noble were equally prosperous, Shipov's success as a serf entrepreneur was not at all typical. Still, his story reflected more generalized socioeconomic conditions: geographical mobility, socially and ethnically diverse associates, repeated financial disaster, frequent changes of occupation, and an underlying uncertainty of status.

As the life of Nikolai Shipov reveals, Russia maintained a partially fluid labor market alongside the constraints of serfdom. Equally important, Shipov's unstable career indicated that the failure of institutional structures to incorporate autonomous, dynamic activities such as his contributed significantly to a more general dissipation of human and economic resources. Depictions of the *raznochintsy* also suggested a lack of secure structures and an abundance of vital entrepreneurial initiative. The phenomenon of the *raznochintsy* actually reveals very little about the purely economic aspects of productive development; it does, however, highlight the importance of social factors and informal, extrainstitutional relations for economic development. Once again, the striking feature of the serf order was not rigidity but plasticity and amorphousness. The dynamic small-scale entrepreneurship of preindustrial Russia reflected not the "missing bourgeoisie" but the fluid and uncertain socioeconomic conditions—conditions that prevented effective concentration of capital and resources and the cohering of middle-class elements.[103] The slow pace of productive development was not due to any absence of social initiative, energy, or dynamism—all of which traditional wisdom holds to have been stifled by the institutions of autocracy; it resulted from the dissipation of that energy through weak organization. Energy and ideas were abundant; infrastructure and a reasonable measure of predictability were sorely lacking.[104]

CONCLUSION

Among Russian historians there is a marked tendency to associate dramatic change and development with periods of reform from above. This results partly from a dearth of research on the periods preceding the Petrine reforms, the Catherinean reforms, and the Great Reforms of Alexander II. Because knowledge of the late imperial era is much more extensive, there is greater awareness of spontaneous societal development, particularly in relation to the revolutionary upheavals of the early twentieth century. Inattention to the popular sphere surfaces again—because of limited research and limits on research—when historians portray the Stalinist revolution and the subsequent history of the Soviet Union, including its demise, as yet another transformation wrought from above. These analyses of reform from above are valid as far as they go. The creation of *raznochintsy* in service and other aspects of state building repeatedly testified to the close relationship between administrative policy and social development. However ubiquitous the role of the state, it cannot fully explain the autonomous socioeconomic development that occurred outside the framework of official policy. How, for example, does one explain the proliferation of cultural and professional associations in the 1860s? The Great Reforms did not create the people who formed these organizations, though it was the relative freedom of the era that enhanced their visibility and gave them a public voice. Moreover, even if the state emerges as the initiator of significant change, it is important to remember that policymakers formulated projects for reform based on their understanding and knowledge of the realities of Russian life. To paraphrase Catherine the Great, they did not write on blank paper, they wrote on human skin, and their proposals derived at least in part from what seemed feasible. As a by-product both of governmental policy and spontaneous socioeconomic activity, the phenomenon of the *raznochintsy* sheds light on the dynamic interplay between these larger dimensions of development.

Societal Representations

The *Raznochintsy* as Outsiders

SOCIETAL CONCEPTIONS of the *raznochintsy* referred to a variety of groups in a variety of contexts, precisely because it was not necessarily clear who belonged to that or any other social category. When the former seminarian and successful teacher-turned-writer N. G. Pomialovskii declared: "How terrible it is not to know what I am—a clever person or an inveterate fool, a deacon or a *chinovnik*, or simply a proletarian,"[1] he was expressing a social condition and a state of mind that were not confined to those radical *raznochintsy* who struggled to achieve prominence in the literary circles of the 1860s. While alcoholism and emotional instability must have exacerbated Pomialovskii's feelings of uncertainty and self-doubt, there is considerable evidence that social insecurity and the patterns of self-definition it both permitted and demanded were present throughout Russian society, at all levels and in all classes of the population.

The forms of public expression examined here contain virtually no instances of persons actually calling themselves *raznochintsy;* the isolated references that do occur are found in nineteenth-century fiction. Even in instructions to the Legislative Commission that emanated specifically from *raznochintsy,* individual signatories referred to themselves by occupation or service function; for example, as retired soldiers or chancery clerks *(kantseliaristy).* Nor in the eighteenth and early nineteenth centuries did individual petitioners who legally belonged to a *raznochinnyi* subcategory identify themselves in this manner; in the vast majority of usages the category *raznochintsy* was applied from the outside in reference to others. The societal definitions presented in this chapter fall into four main categories: (1) the *raznochintsy* as an amorphous, ambiguously defined social element among petty officialdom or the lower urban classes; (2) the *raznochintsy* as a segment of rural society that was neither peasant nor noble; (3) the *raznochintsy* simply as non-nobles, including the notion of *raznochintsy* as educated commoners; and (4) the *raznochintsy* as outsiders, a notion that also could incorporate the three preceding usages.[2]

In the study of social language it is impossible to equate the first written usage of a term with its origins. Further confusing the picture, the example of the *raznochintsy* reveals a striking similarity between legal-administrative and societal definitions. Before the visible emergence of a liberal, educated, and critically thinking public *(obshchestvo)* in the 1830s and 1840s, and more precisely, before N. K. Mikhailovskii's notion of *raznochintsy* as the radical democratic intelligentsia of the 1860s, there was no clear distinction between official and unofficial formulations. This is no surprise, given the absence of any clear pattern of chronological development or even of a specific definition that consistently appeared in one or another category of legal-administrative texts. The proliferation of literary images of *raznochintsy* in the mid-nineteenth century was analogous contextually to the production of many eighteenth-century depictions. Leaving aside the unprecedented role of a self-sufficient educated elite, the mid-nineteenth century was a time of fundamental change in social categorization; the elimination of serfdom altered the basis for all formal definitions operating in Russian society. In addition, the reformed legal framework for the first time assigned an explicit civic identity to a large segment of the population (the former serfs) previously excluded from much of statute law.

The literary and journalistic significance of the category *raznochintsy* thus resulted from the involvement of a rapidly expanding and increasingly independent educated elite in the process of redefining and restructuring social definitions. Initiated by bureaucratic means, this process echoed earlier official efforts to recategorize Russian society—efforts that in the early eighteenth century had led to the creation of *raznochintsy* as a legal-administrative concept. Although neither official nor societal efforts ever produced a consistent definition of the *raznochintsy*, both originated in the consistent need to categorize persons occupying the interstices of a fragmented and indeterminate social structure. In the mid-nineteenth century this need manifested itself most explicitly in relation to the educated, semi-educated, professional, and semi- or protoprofessional elites. The stabilization of legal-administrative terminology that had occurred since the late eighteenth century, and the simplification and conflation of formal categories that had begun in the second quarter of the nineteenth century and that continued in the reform era, had made the category *raznochintsy* less important for official purposes. By contrast, the ever more vocal middle elements of Russian society, whose delimitation first became evident in patterns of sociocultural self-definition, applied the category in ways similar to those of their bureaucratic predecessors.

THE LEGISLATIVE COMMISSION (1767)

When representatives of public opinion identified the *raznochintsy* as a social group, whether urban or rural, their definitions were no more precise than those of officialdom. Like legislators and administrators, the authors of the instructions to the Legislative Commission (1767) tended to define the *raznochintsy* in relation to other groups. The residents of Khar'-kov, for example, described their city as one populated by "a free Little Russian people" that was not divided into the categories found in Great Russian cities: "merchants, members of craft guilds and other *raznochintsy,* artists [masters], and artisans."[3] Similarly, the inhabitants of Nerchinsk (Ir-kutsk government) sought to augment the number of registered mer-chants in their town with recruits from the *raznochintsy,* who came under the office of the district governor *(voevoda)* rather than of the city magis-tracy. The Nerchinsk instruction mentioned, along with the *raznochintsy,* additional outsider groups involved in local trade, such as merchants from other cities, Cossacks, and soldiers.[4] These and similar instructions pre-sented the *raznochintsy* as an undefined, yet distinguishable subgrouping.

In debates concerning the rights of nonmerchants to conduct business in the towns, deputies also equated the *raznochintsy* with a more specific range of social categories involved in petty trade and handicraft produc-tion. The deputy from the city of Belgorod defined *raznochintsy* to include peasants, single householders, Ukrainians, and retired lower military ranks living in towns and villages.[5] Embedded in this listing were two separate definitions that recurred in other instructions. First, the *raznochintsy* ap-peared as an umbrella category for groups engaged in urban trades who were not legally registered as merchants and so did not come under the authority of the magistracy. The vast majority of urban instructions em-ployed the term in this vague manner without indicating specific sub-groups.[6] Second, in instructions that provided a more concrete accounting, the category could include all the groups mentioned by the deputy from Belgorod, as well as Cossacks or persons living under Cossack administra-tion, musketeers *(strel'tsy),* ecclesiastical servicemen and landless peasants *(bobyli),* religious minorities, Turkic nobles in service *(sluzhilye murzy),* Tatars who paid the *iasak* tax, Greeks, and artisans *(remeslenniki, promyshlenniki).*[7] Whether the *raznochintsy* appeared as an umbrella grouping or as a more precise listing of subcategories, the common point was that they always lived outside the domain of local town authorities. In this manner the in-structions to the Legislative Commission repeated the legal practice of de-fining the *raznochintsy* negatively by exclusion, in some cases making clear only that they were not nobles or peasants or Cossacks or single household-ers or merchants or ecclesiastical or state officials *(prikaznye).*[8] Some noble instructions went even further and referred to any landowners who were not nobles or to any peasants who were not privately owned serfs as *razno-chintsy,* just as merchants applied the term to persons who were not formal members of the urban community.[9]

The Belgorod deputy also associated the category *raznochintsy* with the lower service classes that eighteenth-century policy sought increasingly to delimit from the hereditary nobility.[10] These groups, which could be urban or rural, originated both in the traditional Muscovite categories of military servicemen (often collectively referred to as *prezhnikh sluzhb sluzhilye liudi*) and in the newer Petrine categories of soldiers and civil servants. Depending on the context and the vantage point of the observer, these groups appeared as both upwardly and downwardly mobile; in their own view, as expressed in the instructions of 1767, the movement clearly was downward. The single householders *(odnodvortsy)* and "ploughing soldiers" *(pakhatnye soldaty)* of the eighteenth and nineteenth centuries contained some remnants of the Muscovite service categories; others had disappeared into the peasantry or achieved recognition as nobles. The conflating of categories did not, however, signify a clearer delimitation of social boundaries.

Recognized in the legislation of Peter the Great, the single householders were free landowners who retained the right to seek official recognition of their noble ancestry. While permitted to own serfs, they nonetheless paid the capitation and remained subject to conscription on the same basis as state peasants. Still, their term of service was considerably shorter than that of most soldiers: fifteen years, as opposed to the normal term of life (or twenty-five years after 1793); they also enjoyed easier access to promotion in the army, though their opportunities were by no means comparable to those of nobles.[11] The instructions to the Legislative Commission generally depicted single householders as rural landowning *raznochintsy* who were neither noble nor peasant, and less often as a landless urban category.[12] In either case the references to land disputes, taxation and service obligations, the right to distill liquor, and access to education revealed that the groups within the category single householders sought recognition of a distinct status that they traced back to seventeenth-century social arrangements. Thus "ploughing soldiers" from the city of Odoev (Moscow government) claimed rights to graze livestock on lands granted "to our ancestors."[13] More explicit was the instruction from the landless single householders of Sviiazhsk (Kazan province), who served in the Ukrainian frontier force *(landmilitsiia)*, paid the capitation on the same basis as state peasants, and supported themselves as hired laborers. Desperate to preserve their separateness, these single householders requested grants of land and begged not to be equated with state peasants, but rather "to possess some sort of advantage *(preimushchestvo)* over them."[14] Their petition seems both a search for social definition and a wish for its attendant economic benefits.

A second body of instructions came from urban residents who were more consistent than the single householders in identifying themselves as *raznochintsy*. This group sometimes included individual single householders or Ukrainians, but its main constituents were non-noble or unranked state officials and retired lower military ranks—representatives of the newer service categories that proliferated as a result of the Petrine reforms. Whether or not they called themselves *raznochintsy* and whether or not they

submitted their instructions along with other groups of *raznochintsy* or separately, the non-noble administrative personnel (collectively called *prikaznye
sluzhiteli*) repeatedly objected to the recent prohibitions depriving them of
the right to acquire individual serfs or to possess populated estates (including those obtained by seventeenth-century ancestors as payment for service).[15] The officials argued that the demands of state service, which kept
them in their offices day and night, prevented them from tending to household affairs, so that their wives, "lacking out of necessity any shame, [were]
forced to lead the livestock, horses as well as cows, to water and also to
perform other onerous labor."[16]

In addition to neglect of the household economy and even danger to
their wives and children when they were away on official trips (lasting as
long as five years in Kazan province), low-level officials complained about
inadequate pay, lack of pensions, and the additional service obligations
that urban residents were required to perform. Work schedules made it
impossible to fulfill these duties without hiring substitutes at significant
expense; thus there was an economic need to possess at least a few serfs.
Adding insult to injury, some unranked administrative employees and retired lower military ranks also complained that they could not even take
wives from among the economic peasants, because they could not afford
to pay the fees charged for the release of these women.[17] Finally, the urban
raznochintsy drew a direct connection between their economic plight and
the uncertainty of their social status, noting that they lacked the resources
to educate their children in preparation for state service.[18] Clearly, they
regarded the unpaid labor of serfs as an important economic resource, to
which until very recently they had enjoyed unrestricted access.

Non-noble officials in Tobol'sk identified the social implications of the
serf issue even more directly when they justified the need to purchase individual serfs as a way to distinguish themselves from the lowborn *(podlyi
narod)*. They then tried to bolster their argument by noting the absence of
a Russian nobility in Siberia and the potential for agricultural development
that would result if they were permitted to own estates and serfs.[19] While
one can muster good economic reasons for the desire to own serfs, issues
of social status were equally important; certainly, loss of the legal right to
possess estates and serfs constituted downward mobility. The *raznochintsy*
expressed awareness of the social issue when they protested that their wives
shamelessly performed unseemly labor and when they stressed the need to
separate themselves from the ignoble masses. Low-ranking civil servants
and unranked administrative personnel in Tambov and Voronezh even requested permission to wear official dress and carry swords, in order to distinguish themselves from what they called "other *raznochintsy*."[20] One may
question the extent to which non-noble, and particularly unranked, officials were distinguishable from the general urban population even before

the legal prohibitions of serf ownership. (Merchants and lesser towns-people also possessed serfs.) But the important point here is that the *raz-nochintsy* expressed a yearning for recognized distinctions—a yearning that suggests a lack of firm boundaries and, if not a slippage in status, at least an underlying uncertainty. It is ironic that, even though the Petrine re-forms had institutionalized "automatic" ennoblement through service, both the traditional service categories represented by the single household-ers and the newer ones represented by the urban *raznochintsy* sought to differentiate themselves from other groups in society by preserving tradi-tional distinctions that appeared to be evaporating.

THE *RAZNOCHINTSY* AS NON-NOBLES

The earliest legal definition of the *raznochintsy* as non-nobles dates back to a law of 1746 that addressed the problem of illegal enrollment in the ranks of the nobility. A second legal usage appeared in 1755 with the establishment of Moscow University, where the term immediately acquired the meaning of educated commoner.[21] Noble instructions to the Legislative Commission employed the generic notion of *raznochintsy* as non-nobles and a more specific derogatory notion of *raznochintsy* as new service nobles, hence social upstarts who had risen through illegitimate means. While ac-knowledging that persons from the *raznochintsy* reached senior or staff of-ficer rank in state and military service and that they became landowners either by marrying noblewomen or by purchasing populated estates, the instructions still did not recognize them as legitimate nobility but instead vehemently objected to the lack of proper procedures for ennoblement, especially to the acquisition of noble rights and privileges without a direct grant of nobility from the autocrat.[22] Like other groups permitted to ad-dress the Legislative Commission, nobles expressed an awareness of the fluid social conditions and a desire for more explicit social delimitation. In the words of the noble landowners of Kashin district (Moscow govern-ment): "Grant general privileges to every category [*rod*] of persons—to the nobility, to the merchants, and equally to the *raznochintsy*—so that each category [*rod*] has its own privileges and one [category] does not enter into the privileges of another, and each enjoys that to which it is privileged."[23]

In nineteenth-century literature and memoirs the notion of the *raznochintsy* as non-nobles continued, but the definition was broader and the emphasis changed. The *raznochintsy* still appeared as social upstarts and unworthy service nobles, but because ennoblement through the Table of Ranks was well established and because growing numbers of nobles were in fact landless, there was no discussion of the mechanisms for attaining nobility and its concomitant privileges. The conditions of ennoblement remained a central problem for policymakers, but literature and memoirs did not directly address these concerns. Rather, societal usages tended to depict *raznochintsy* in cultural terms—a development that corresponded to the increasing importance of *raznochintsy* as educated commoners and to a broader articulation of cultural identities in educated society.

One of the earliest literary references to upwardly mobile *raznochintsy* appears in Nikolai Gogol's *Diary of a Madman* (1835). The narrator, Poprishchin, is a frustrated, indignant, and bitter official of low rank (a titular councillor at rank nine). After his superior berates him for showing an interest in the daughter of their department director, Poprishchin declares:

> I understand, I understand why he is angry with me. He is envious; he noticed perhaps the marks of favor that are directed primarily toward me. Why, I spit on him! As if a court councillor [rank seven] is of such great importance. He hangs a gold chain on his watch, orders boots at thirty rubles—well, the devil take him! Am I someone from the *raznochintsy*, the son of a tailor or a non-commissioned officer? I am a noble. I, too, can serve to [a high rank]. I am only forty-two—an age at which service is only beginning. Wait a little, [my] friend! I will be a colonel [rank eight] and perhaps, God willing, something even higher.[24]

Although, as a hereditary noble, Poprishchin obviously considers himself superior to civil servants from the *raznochintsy* and is careful to distinguish himself from these non-noble pretenders, his real frustration—aside from the more important emotional factors of unrequited love and mental instability—lies in the lack of the social recognition, both formal and informal, that he considers his due.[25] Again, the lack of clear social delimitation in Russian society is evident precisely because the legal definitions were of such fundamental importance.

In I. S. Turgenev's *On the Eve* (1859) Nikolai Stakhov—the father of the heroine, Elena—expresses similar feelings of exasperation, though from the secure position of a hereditary nobleman who is married to a wealthy heiress. He applies the term *raznochinets* in an openly derogatory manner to describe Dmitrii Insarov, a Bulgarian patriot and revolutionary, the orphaned son of a prosperous merchant. As a student at Moscow University, Insarov becomes a regular visitor at the Stakhov home. On one level, the depiction of Insarov as a *raznochinets* corresponds to the definitions of non-noble, educated commoner, and foreigner, but the derogatory manner in which Nikolai employs the term refers to more than social origins. Indeed, with the exception of Nikolai, Insarov is immediately and fully accepted into the social circle of the Stakhov family, and Nikolai disparagingly calls Insarov a *raznochinets* only at a moment of intense anger and utter shock.

When Elena informs her father that she and Insarov were secretly married, he explodes: "[You are] married! To that ragamuffin, that Montenegrin! The daughter of the lineal nobleman, Nikolai Stakhov, has married a vagrant, a *raznochinets!* Without the parental blessing!"[26] While the socio-economic position of Nikolai and his wife may be secure, their position as parents clearly is not. Their daughter has rejected their authority, their sensibilities, and their way of life by marrying a man who lacks ties to Russian society and who is obsessed with liberating his people from the Turks—"a vagrant, a *raznochinets.*" Like Poprishchin, Nikolai expresses disdain for *raznochintsy,* but his frustration does not stem from a lack of social recognition. It is rather the lack of filial recognition that he finds most distressing.

Another of Turgenev's characters, the tyrannical grandmother-landowner in "Punin and Baburin" (1874, action in the 1830s), expresses a corresponding disdain for *raznochintsy.* When her clerk, Baburin, objects to an unjust order to exile a serf boy, she proclaims: "I am not accustomed to debate or interference in my affairs. I have no use for learned philanthropists from the *raznochintsy;* I need meek servants [who do not have answers]."[27] Baburin's social origins are not precisely identified in the story. His companion, Punin, who becomes a "vagrant" after being expelled from the ecclesiastical domain, describes him as a republican and relates that "some say he is the son of a sovereign Georgian prince." Baburin's wife later calls him a townsman *(meshchanin),* which may have been his registered status. In any event his background is obscure, and despite his education, the grandmother views him as little more than a servant who owes her unquestioning obedience. When the narrator-grandson, Petr, again encounters him, Baburin mocks the earlier comments of the grandmother, saying "through [his] teeth that conversation with common people, with *raznochintsy,* cannot be very satisfying for me and that probably [it] will displease my grandmother *(babka).*"[28] In Baburin's sarcastic usage, the term *raznochintsy* again refers to commoners, who, regardless of learning or participation in socially mixed company, still represent cultural inferiors.

Expressions of contempt for *raznochinsty* also appear in the memoirs of radical and liberal nobles of the nineteenth century. Alexander Herzen used the term when discussing the unhappy marriage of N. Kh. Ketcher, a member of his Moscow circle in the 1830s and 1840s. The son of a Swedish craftsman who made surgical instruments and a fanatical admirer of the French revolution, Ketcher married an uneducated, lower-class woman who had been orphaned as a child and who had grown up in an Old Believer community. According to Herzen, Ketcher quarreled frequently with his friends and was unable to find intellectual or spiritual satisfaction in his wife, who was "submissive [and] meek to the point of slavery." Herzen likened Ketcher to Rousseau, whose unsuitable marriage to Thérèse alienated him from his friends: "Thérèse, poor, stupid Thérèse Rousseau, did she not make the prophet of equality into a finicky *raznochinets* who was constantly occupied with preserving his dignity?"[29] Because Rousseau and

Ketcher both were sons of skilled craftsmen, Herzen's usage corresponded to the notion of *raznochintsy* as educated commoners, yet he did not employ the category in a general or neutral way to indicate social position. Rather, Herzen was describing the moral and psychological downfall of a close friend and condescendingly likened him to a *raznochinets* in order to highlight his friend's emotional failings—failings that were exacerbated by marriage to an "undeveloped woman."

P. D. Boborykin, a minor writer from the middle provincial nobility, and Elena Stackenschneider, the daughter of a wealthy Court architect, both applied the label *raznochintsy* to persons who participated in the cultural life of St. Petersburg, but whose appreciation of literature, theater, and music they considered inadequate. Although neither framed the issue in terms of noble and non-noble, both associated the lack of culture with a lower, socially inferior stratum—not the best public, as Boborykin would have it.[30] In the case of Stackenschneider one of the *raznochintsy* was a professor and the other "claimed" to be the son of a general, but because she regarded them as cultural inferiors, she found it difficult to accept them as persons of high social standing.[31] Stackenschneider's usage of the term *raznochintsy* certainly was derogatory, though that did not prevent her from expressing enormous admiration for individual writers and artists of lower-class origin. On the contrary, the distinction was obvious: those whom she admired, she simply did not refer to as *raznochintsy*. Written in 1883, Stackenschneider's remarks reflected a confusion of social and cultural terminology, a translation of social definitions into cultural categories that carried an implied statement of values. Thus she also described Dostoevskii as a *meshchanin* (petit bourgeois) in appearance and behavior.[32] The disappearance of many juridically defined status groups in the Great Reforms of the mid-1850s to mid-1870s permitted cultural applications of social terminology to proliferate. The mingling of social and cultural attributes was nothing new; eighteenth-century notions of the *raznochintsy* as non-nobles or educated commoners often implied a statement of identity or values. Still, the growing importance of the value-laden usages revealed a new emphasis in patterns of sociocultural definition. Specifically, it was the emphasis on created definition or self-definition as a positive judgment and statement of values that helps explain the emergence of the concept of the intelligentsia.

THE *RAZNOCHINTSY* AS SOCIAL MILIEU

The representations of *raznochintsy* as non-nobles also suggested a category of educated commoners; their primary purpose was not to identify a specific group in society but to disparage social and cultural inferiors or, in the case of Herzen, to condemn a mode of behavior. Unlike authors who only referred to *raznochintsy* disparagingly, Boborykin and others extended the meaning of the category to describe a socially mixed milieu of educated and semieducated urbanites—a milieu that was first envisioned in the legislation of 1755 establishing Moscow University and that was subsequently described so nonchalantly in the dramatic works of A. N. Ostrovskii. In 1846 V. G. Belinskii, who praised education and literature as the means to eliminate social barriers and create a society of spiritually likeminded individuals, described the phenomenon: "The possession of education equalizes people. Already in our time it is not a rarity to meet a circle of friends in which one finds an exalted *barin* [aristocrat], and a *raznochinets,* and a merchant, and a townsman—a circle whose members have forgotten completely the external differences that divide them and who respect each other simply as people."[33] Although Belinskii depicted the event correctly, he had the chronology wrong. The cultural elites of the eighteenth century—writers, poets, translators, scientists, inventors, and artists—had always been a socially diverse group; the educated commoner was nothing new. What was new by the mid-nineteenth century was the extent of the phenomenon: the size of the educated or semieducated classes, the public recognition accorded the cultural elites, and the level of interaction, organization, and articulation outside of state institutions.[34]

Boborykin's exaggerated perception of this mixed society of educated individuals was that of a liberal landowner who easily shed his noble identity in order to join the urban literary elite; he proudly described the gymnasium in Nizhnii Novgorod, where Boborykin studied in the reign of Nicholas I, as a fully democratic institution attended by students from all social classes except for serfs. In particular, he boasted about the "*raznochinskii* milieu" in which he was educated and lived. By this he meant a socially diverse company, similar to that described by Belinskii, in which an educated individual was judged and accepted on the basis of talent and merit. In other passages he used the term *raznochintsy* to depict a range of urban groups, not all of them educated. These included prominent non-noble writers of the 1860s, merchants and townspeople, and an undefined lower-class urban stratum that was distinct from nobles, peasants, and the middle circle *(srednii krug).*[35] When Boborykin spoke of literature, theater, and music or of fellow students, the category *raznochintsy* was a neutral one that referred to educated commoners or to a socially diverse, cultured milieu, but when he used the term to describe a lower-class segment of urban society, the *raznochintsy* clearly were social and cultural inferiors. The confusion was indicative of the cultural meaning and the implied statement of values that became increasingly characteristic of social categories in the nineteenth century.

In a description of Khar'kov in the 1840s, V. N. Karpov included the children of poor *raznochintsy* in the student population of the university, as

well as the sons of rich landowners and merchants and another impoverished contingent from the ecclesiastical domain. According to Karpov,
himself a graduate of the local gymnasium and a state-certified artist *(khu-
dozhnik)*, the city's population was divided into two halves: the rich and the
poor, the privileged and the unprivileged. In the first category he placed
the minority—"persons endowed with elevated birth, with the privileges of
juridical status groups *(sosloviia)*, with wealth"—who lorded over the majority. The privileged categories included nobles, civil servants with rank, and
merchants. The exploited majority included townspeople, artisans, state
peasants, and serfs who worked in the city.[36] Although Karpov's memoirs
cover the period from the 1840s to the 1860s, they were first published
only in 1900 and presumably were written at the end of the nineteenth
century. Karpov limited his conception of the *raznochintsy* to a particular,
though ill-defined, group of commoner-students; unlike other legal, administrative, and societal usages, his typology of Khar'kov society in the
1840s did not include them as a distinct category.

As an independent non-noble artist, Karpov would fall under one definition of the *raznochintsy*, but in his memoirs he never referred to himself
as such. Three other writers, N. A. Polevoi, A. N. Ostrovskii, and N. G.
Pomialovskii—themselves frequently identified as *raznochintsy*—used the
term to define a stratum or subgroup with a variety of attributes. In *The
Painter* (1834), N. A. Polevoi depicts a struggling young artist named Arkadii, who abandons a modest career in the provincial bureaucracy to pursue more elevated endeavors in St. Petersburg. In a painful and emotional
encounter with a visitor from his father, Arkadii calls himself a *raznochinets*
to explain his aspirations and to highlight his unworthiness: "Who am I?
The son of a poor official with rank [*chinovnik*], an insignificant *raznochinets*, my brothers are clerks [*pod'iachie*] and I also would have become a
clerk."[37] Arkadii's definition of the *raznochintsy* is not legally correct, for he
is from the lesser nobility, and his usage is far from neutral. Imbued with
the ideas of early nineteenth-century romanticism, his notion of the *raznochinets* as commoner does not mean simply non-noble or déclassé noble.
Thus Arkadii seeks to avoid an ordinary life, in an ordinary civil service
position, in ordinary provincial surroundings.

A. N. Ostrovskii, who was legally a *raznochinets* only until age sixteen,
offered a relatively prosaic picture of that group.[38] Although Ostrovskii's
forty-eight plays include many characters who could be classified as *raznochintsy*, only two of them actually use the term to describe themselves. The
first, Anton Antonych Pogulaev in *The Abyss* (1866, action in the 1830s), is
a university graduate who works as a private tutor, all the while hoping to
pursue a journalistic career in St. Petersburg. His childhood friend Kisel'nikov is a university dropout of some means, engaged to the daughter of
a "well-known merchant" and planning to enter the civil service. When
Kisel'nikov introduces Pogulaev to his future father-in-law, the latter's

friend, Pereiarkov—a civil servant with a seminary education who has reached rank nine after twenty-five years of service—asks whether he is a university graduate from the *raznochintsy*. Pogulaev's affirmative response prompts a second inquiry: Is he a *raznochinets* "from the townspeople or from the children of government officials [*prikaznye deti*]?" Pogulaev answers that his father was a teacher, which Pereiarkov immediately classifies as a status belonging to the civil service. Pereiarkov and a retired colonel, Turuntaev, then go on to describe the wonderful career prospects that await a *raznochinets* with a university degree, including ennoblement and the acquisition of serfs.[39] The participants in this conversation identified the *raznochintsy* in a manner that corresponded to Ostrovskii's own family history: that is, as upwardly mobile, university-educated commoners whose origins lay in the lesser townspeople or non-noble bureaucracy.[40] The dialogue expressed no special praise or disdain but rather a simple statement of fact about the chances for a successful career and just the sort of questions one would expect older, established people to ask of a recent graduate.

Ostrovskii's second use of the term *raznochintsy* occurs in *Not of This World* (1884) during a discussion between Barbarisov, a conniving rogue, and his fiancée, Kapitolina, the daughter of a deceased general. Kapitolina's wealthy mother has just promised to give a significant sum of money to her other daughter, so that she and her estranged husband can buy an estate in the Crimea. Barbarisov, who is more interested in acquiring a fortune than a wife, reacts to the news with hostility and refers to the merchant origins of the general's widow. When Kapitolina takes offense, Barbarisov replies: "I am not boasting. [I am] not a titled personage, pardon me, [I am] of the *raznochintsy*. Yes, I have wits and ability. You could find yourself someone better, if I am not a [suitable] match."[41] Although there is no mention here of formal education, Barbarisov is, like Polugaev, an upwardly mobile commoner of some intellect and talent. But in contrast to Polugaev, he is a dishonorable social climber. A close look not only at the two individuals directly identified by Ostrovskii as *raznochintsy* but also at his *raznochinnye* characters in general reveals that there is no commonly shared ethos or lifestyle. Rather, they appear in a range of shapes and sizes, struggle with a variety of emotional and financial problems, experience different levels of success and failure in their careers and personal relationships, and finally take on an assortment of moral hues.[42]

Yet a third unadorned conception of the *raznochintsy* appears in the writings of N. G. Pomialovskii. The son of a deacon at a cemetery church outside of St. Petersburg, a graduate of the St. Petersburg seminary, a recognized teacher appointed to the elite Smolny Institute, and subsequently a struggling but permanent contributor to the radical journal *Sovremennik*, Pomialovskii epitomized the radical non-noble intellectual of the 1850s and 1860s, the *raznochinets* identified by literary critics, scholars, and revolutionaries beginning with N. K. Mikhailovskii in the early 1870s.[43] But as Christopher Becker notes, and as a cursory review of police reports from the Third Section (the tsar's personal gendarmerie) confirms, there is no "evidence that the men of the 1860s referred to themselves, or were commonly referred to by their immediate contemporaries, as *raznochintsy*."[44] Indeed, in all of his writings, Pomialovskii used the term *raznochintsy* only once, in the introduction to an unfinished novel, *Brother and Sister*, begun in 1862:[45]

> I consider it necessary to warn the reader that if he has weak nerves and seeks entertainment and elegant phrases from literature, then he should not read my book. . . . Let me explain. There is a huge stratum of society, an entire mass of people, who live a distinct life that is virtually unknown to our so-called educated society—this is the poor category of *raznochintsy*. Are they people or not? You will learn what sort of creatures they are, and you will be exposed to this purulent ulcer of our—yes, our—society.[46]

In Pomialovskii's view, the writer should "draw to the attention of society that mass of depravity, hopeless poverty, and ignorance that has accumulated in its bowels." Thus he writes for the "people who want to see the naked, unfeigned truth" about the conditions of life among the *raznochintsy*:

> extreme debauchery, striking ignorance, [people] who know nothing about the earth, sun, moon, and wind . . . and [who] view the events of life and nature like beasts; . . . poverty so ubiquitous that the feeling of suffering from it is lost and deadened; . . . inescapable oppression; . . . deep-rooted baseness and meanness of spirit; . . . the heathenism of this stratum, the ignorance of the basic principles of civilization. . . .[47]

For Pomialovskii, as for Polevoi and Ostrovskii, the *raznochintsy* represented a discernible, though not precisely defined, segment of society. Polevoi's *raznochintsy* were nondescript petty officials; Ostrovskii's were educated, upwardly mobile commoners; and Pomialovskii's succumbed to a larger social reality of endless poverty, suffering, and depravity. All three writers applied definitions that appeared in legislation and administrative practice. For them, the *raznochintsy* came from the diverse and diffuse lower urban classes, out of which individuals frequently moved and into which they easily fell.[48]

Ironically, the commonly understood notion of the *raznochintsy* as a select group of radical, non-noble intellectuals distinguished by their democratic spirit, social conscience, and unassuming way of life in no way originated among writers who themselves could be called *raznochintsy* or who had lived in the milieu of the *raznochintsy*. Belinskii and others associated the category with a new democratic ethos that united persons of diverse origins, but the *raznochintsy* simply constituted one subgroup of partici- pants in this greater social endeavor and were by no stretch of the imagina- tion depicted as its harbingers. That representation had to await the pen of the noble literary critic N. K. Mikhailovskii, though it was foreshadowed in the earlier writings of Alexander Herzen and Nicholas Ogarev.

In the early 1860s Herzen wrote of a "new Russia" rooted in the unprivi- leged strata of society and embodied in progressive figures such as Belin- skii, the circle of M. V. Butashevich-Petrashevskii, and most recently, Cher- nyshevskii. Herzen identified the *raznochintsy* as a new element in Russian intellectual life, impervious to tsarist repression and morally prepared by their poverty to continue the democratic struggle—an element that, unlike the nobility, was capable of rising above the interests of *soslovie*. In contrast to Mikhailovskii's more purely sociological *raznochintsy*, Herzen's moral *raz- nochintsy* comprised a socially mixed milieu that included poor nobles and ranked officials, ecclesiastical progeny, cadets, students, teachers, artists, military officers, copyists, merchants, shop assistants, and *raznochintsy*.[49] Herzen here depicted *raznochintsy* in traditional terms as a social category and also more broadly as a morally delimited cultural category.

Ogarev developed a similar usage in an article published in the radical émigré newspaper, *The Bell*, in 1864–1865.[50] He also identified the *razno- chinstvo* as a socially mixed group that would lead the struggle for represen- tative government in Russia. While not a bourgeoisie or third estate, the *raznochintsy* would replace the nobility-bureaucracy as the vital intellectual force of the country and play the historical role of the French third estate. Socially positioned between the nobility and the peasantry *(narod)*, the cate- gory included merchants and lesser townspeople and "that minority of the nobility that rejected their *soslovie*, or that *raznochinstvo* that did not join the bureaucracy at all or served with repugnance."[51] Ogarev's usage of the term *raznochintsy* was twofold. In a traditional application, he referred to the non-noble bureaucracy as *raznochinstvo*. At the same time, he formu- lated a politicocultural usage to describe the forward-looking segment of society that would converge with the peasantry to transform Russia. In as- cribing to the *raznochintsy* a particular political position, he anticipated the later definitions of Mikhailovskii, Plekhanov, and Lenin.

In his well-known and influential article, "Literary and Journalistic Notes for 1874," N. K. Mikhailovskii presented a more concrete sociopoliti- cal definition of the *raznochintsy*. He explained the ideological conflict be- tween the radical intellectual "fathers" of the 1840s and the "sons" of the 1860s as essentially a social phenomenon resulting from the arrival on the literary scene of the *raznochintsy*, a distinct group of radical non-noble writ- ers. Careful to distinguish them from the repentant nobles epitomized by D. I. Pisarev, Mikhailovskii equated the *raznochintsy*—who had nothing for

which to repent—with "a well-known social position." Thus, their characteristic traits included humble social origins, poverty, a burning desire for
knowledge, especially knowledge of the truth, and direct experience and
understanding of the life of the common people. In addition to these attributes, the *raznochintsy* held "a special view of things": they believed that
art and literature should serve social needs and that they, as enlightened
individuals, were obliged to pursue activities that would be useful for the
common people. They understood that civilization, both material and spiritual, progressed at the expense of the people, and above all they advocated
"the subordination of the general categories of civilization to the idea of
the people."[52] One can argue about the degree to which Mikhailovskii's
raznochintsy actually lived by or identified with the attributes he described;
as Mikhailovskii himself noted, there were "many transitional types between the pure *raznochinets* and the pure repentant noble" portrayed in
the article.[53]

Mikhailovskii's definition of the *raznochintsy* fell within the category of
the educated commoner, but he presented his conception in terms of a
created sociocultural ideal—an ideal that required both a particular sociological experience and "a special view of things." The intellectual attributes of the *raznochintsy* depended upon their specific social experience,
hence the crucial distinction between their behavior and the formalistic
code of the repentant noble. Mikhailovskii was not the only writer to depict
the *raznochintsy* in sociological terms, but he was the first to associate specific social traits with a particular world view. It was precisely this association
that came to dominate contemporary and historiographical treatments of
the *raznochintsy* and that has resulted in so narrow an understanding of the
category.

Beginning in the reign of Nicholas I, societal representations of the *raznochintsy* added a new cultural component to the multiplicity of legal, administrative, and social usages. Moving beyond earlier definitions of *raznochintsy* as non-nobles, educated commoners, and social inferiors, elite
writers of a liberal and radical persuasion began to associate the category
with a pluralistic sociocultural milieu and to imply in their usages a specific
statement of values. Some of these writers meant to condemn, others to
praise, and still others simply to describe. Increasingly, the use of social
terminology indicated subjective aspirations and moral judgments, a development that reflected the assimilation of German idealism and French utopian thought by the Russian educated elite.

Ideological usages of social terminology are particularly noticeable in
the history of the revolutionary movement. Beginning with Mikhailovskii's
definition of *raznochintsy,* the political meaning of the category acquired
increasing importance—a pattern that paralleled the development of the
concept of the intelligentsia. On the eve of the First World War, the Marxist

theoreticians G. V. Plekhanov and V̇. I. Lenin adapted Mikhailovskii's definition of the *raznochintsy* to the history of the revolutionary movement; it is
their conception that has had the greatest impact on subsequent historiography. In his *History of Russian Social Thought,* Plekhanov treats the *raznochintsy* both as a socioeconomic entity and as an ideological point of view.
According to Plekhanov's analysis, the nobility represented the only Euro-
peanized element in Russian society before the mid-nineteenth century,
when "noble hegemony" in art and literature had been superseded by
the "hegemony of the *raznochintsy,*" defined as the "democratic wing" of
Russia's "third estate" *(tret'e soslovie).* European culture had at last penetrated to the "bourgeoisie," represented by the "progressive *raznochintsy*"
who sought to avoid the fate of the "superfluous people"—"progressive
nobles" like Herzen and Ogarev—of the 1830s and 1840s.

Even so, Plekhanov argues, the *raznochintsy* remained insignificant as a
social force until the proletariat appeared on the political scene. With the
development of capitalism, the progressive *raznochinskaia* intelligentsia had
embraced the viewpoint of the proletariat and become Marxist. Others
from the same "stratum of *raznochintsy*" that had stood at "the head of the
intellectual movement" for decades were responsible for the "ideological
Europeanization" of Russia's "progressive" (i.e., politically oppositionist)
bourgeoisie. In the present period, Plekhanov concludes, there is no ideological hegemony of a single class or stratum; rather, there are two poles:
the proletarian and the bourgeois. Unable to conceive of the *raznochintsy*
in terms that did not correspond to the Marxist stages of history, Plekhanov
attempted to establish a socioeconomic basis for a specific intellectual position, but the historical reality of the *raznochintsy* was far too complex to fit
his formulation. Thus Plekhanov associated the *raznochintsy* with both the
proletariat and the bourgeoisie; in a very un-Marxist manner, he defined
these groups not as socioeconomic classes but as ideological positions. Just
as the "progressive nobles" of the 1830s and 1840s "went over to the point
of view of the laboring masses," the *raznochintsy* became either proletarian
or bourgeois.[54]

Lenin's conception of the *raznochintsy* is close to Plekhanov's, though it
is more simplistic and hence also less contradictory. Lenin identifies three
stages in the development of the revolutionary movement, each of which
he associates with the dominance of a particular group in society: the noble
stage of the Decembrists and Herzen (1825–1861), the *raznochinskii* or
bourgeois-democratic stage (1861–1895), and the proletarian stage (since
1895). Lenin also identifies the *raznochintsy* with a concrete social element,
defining them as the "educated representatives of the liberal and democratic bourgeoisie who did not belong to the nobility but rather to the
bureaucracy, townspeople, merchants, peasants." He equates the *raznochinskii* stage with liberal and anarchist populism and with individuals like

Chernyshevskii—Belinskii was a precursor—who combined utopian social-ism, the "spirit of the class struggle," and opposition to capitalism.[55] Once again, the categories of analysis corresponded more closely to ideological than to socioeconomic positions.

"THE OUTSIDER AS INSIDER"

What is one to make of the varied and nuanced conceptions of the *raznochintsy* that appeared in elite society?[56] Was there a common image or shared experience that one can discern in the repeated references to *raznochintsy* as non-nobles, nonmerchants, educated commoners, right-thinking intellectuals, social and cultural inferiors, or the diverse and vul-nerable urban masses? The one inclusive definition that could encompass a range of seemingly differentiated meanings was that of the *raznochintsy* as outsiders. Implicit in the earliest legal definitions of *raznochintsy*, the out-sider designation was the unavoidable outcome of policies that aimed to confine dynamic socioeconomic processes within relatively fixed adminis-trative hierarchies and delimitations. These policies and the outsider usage that accompanied them continued into the 1880s, when the conservative Kakhanov Commission decried the exploitation of peasants and noble landowners by a morally dissolute social element identified as *meshchane* and *raznochintsy*. Much to the distaste of tradition-minded officials, the "outsiders" were settling in rural areas and as owners of allotment land were participating in the village assembly.[57] A similar usage occurred in Saratov province among *zemstvo* statisticians who in 1912 applied the cate-gory *raznochintsy* to indicate persons who bought or rented allotment land.[58] The "arrival of the raznochintsy" in the countryside of postemancipa-tion Russia suggests the broad significance of the outsider in imperial soci-ety. Long after the disappearance of the formal urban categories that origi-nally framed the concept of the *raznochintsy* as outsiders, it continued to play a role in administrative discourse.[59]

In societal sources the *raznochintsy* as outsiders also appeared in the early eighteenth century. Already in 1724 I. T. Pososhkov referred to "*raznochin-nye* entrepreneurs" *(promyshlenniki)* who encroached on merchant trades as "persons of other ranks/occupations" *(inochintsy)*, that is, as nonmerchants whose occupational activities should be restricted.[60] The instructions to the Legislative Commission explicitly and consistently identified *raznochintsy* as outsiders. In these usages the category was devoid of any precise social composition; its meaning was defined by the group or groups applying the label. To nobles, these *raznochintsy* were new nobles, non-nobles, or categories of peasants other than serfs; to merchants and townspeople, they were urban residents who did not belong to the formal taxpaying com-munity *(posad);* and to the officials of administrative domains *(vedomstva)*, they were individuals subordinate to other commands.

The majority of literary, journalistic, and memoir sources employed the label *raznochintsy* either to express disapproval or to describe social outcasts. This may explain why so few people who legally belonged to the group ever applied the term to themselves;[61] indeed, the very existence of a category to define "others"—be they non-nobles, nonmerchants, or educated commoners—was negative and exclusive. As occurred in legislative and more formal societal usages, the informal representations of *raznochintsy* were most consistent in defining them as outsiders. Thus nineteenth-century noble memoirists and fictional characters implied a notion of outsiders when they treated the *raznochintsy* as social and cultural inferiors. Socioeconomic issues also could be at stake, specifically the rewards of service and the norms determining an appropriate marriage. In addition, among noble and non-noble writers and characters, the *raznochintsy* as outsiders acquired a sociocultural meaning that defined educated and semieducated commoners, many of whom were upwardly mobile. In some of these usages *raznochintsy* represented a less cultured or less worthy element of elite society; in others they emerged as equals or even as models to emulate, though still newly arrived.

The representatives of society and government whose views were expressed in the instructions to the Legislative Commission and in nineteenth-century literature and memoirs attempted to distinguish themselves from others by excluding outsiders. Equally important, however, were the individuals and communities that sought to be excluded. The outsider in Russian society wore the face of Janus. Runaways, for example, pursued two possible courses. They attempted either to change their formal status or to evade registration altogether and so remain permanently outside the legal framework of society. Persons in a legitimate transitional status behaved similarly. Thus in 1833 the former serf of a merchant in Arzamas claimed to be unaware that he had only nine months after his emancipation to choose a formal station in life; although his ignorance was probably intentional, he presumed that he need not decide before the next census.[62] Among ethnic and religious minorities, entire communities attempted to remain outside the formal institutions of society either by living under their own officially recognized laws and customs (Poles, Baltic peoples, Cossacks, Siberian natives, Jews, and so on) or by refusing to acknowledge the authority of the tsarist government (pretenders, some Old Believers, Caucasian tribes, rebellious Poles, and so on). Official policy always aimed toward legal-administrative integration, assimilation, and standardization; given the particularistic nature of status definitions and the structure of discrete administrative domains, this goal remained elusive.

The army's experience with minorities and Old Believers was indicative. In the prereform era some minorities were fully or partially integrated into the regular military structure. Ukrainians and Baltic peoples, for example, did not appear in the sources as separate groups; thus official lists of conscripts permit identification only by religion or place of origin. Jews after 1828 and Poles after 1831 also served on the same basis as Russians, though Jewish conscripts often were taken in boyhood to facilitate conversion and assimilation. By contrast, other minorities fulfilled military obligations in separate units or hosts. Finns, Cossacks, and some Siberian nationalities succeeded in preserving distinct terms and institutions of service, and hence also their desired particularistic status in society.[63]

From the state's viewpoint, schismatics and Old Believers of various types constituted an especially problematic group. By refusing to shave their beards or take the oath of allegiance, Old Believers—even when they did not do so explicitly—in effect renounced tsar, church, and country. Early in the reign of Alexander I the authorities reacted by administering the oath after the schismatics joined their units and by assigning them to distant regiments, with as few as possible in each. By the mid-1850s conscripts who refused to shave or pronounce the Orthodox oath faced court-martial. Those who repented, in effect converting, received assignments to service without punishment. Those who refused were sent to convicts' companies of the Engineering Department, where after work they were subjected to daily measures designed to encourage or force conversion; if they eventually accepted the official church, they also were appointed to regular service.[64]

The relationship of Old Believers and other minorities to the subcategories of *raznochintsy* remains unclear. Sometimes minorities were specifically identified as *raznochintsy;* at other times, minorities themselves applied the term *raznochintsy* to outsiders, including Russians, who lived within their communities or close by.[65] Like the *raznochintsy,* Old Believers and minorities in general could occupy a multiplicity of formal statuses. The concept of the *raznochintsy* encompassed a notion of outsiders as unwanted or inferior groups, but there also were significant groups of people who remained outsiders by choice. Along with ethnic and religious minorities, the list included any number of fictional and literary personages who abandoned successful or potentially successful careers and so elected outsider status in order to pursue a higher, culturally or religiously defined social ideal. The preference for outsider status that some groups exhibited was a traditional feature of Russian society and one, moreover, that was not limited to peoples who had suffered conquest and persecution in the course of imperial expansion. Even the intellectuals and rebels who became victims of authoritarian repression chose the role of outsiders when they courageously decided to speak their truth.

As so often happens in concrete historical situations, abstract categorizations, even when societal in origin, do not necessarily correspond to social facts, though they may play a role in specific dimensions of actual life. In contrast to repeated representations of *raznochintsy* as outsiders in a variety of contexts and sources, church and local administrative-judicial records reveal that they also were parishioners, neighbors, commercial associates, and partners in crime.[66] Siberian sources from the late 1750s depicted *raznochintsy* not only as urban and rural property owners but also as criminals involved in the theft and illegal sale of state liquor.[67] In Briansk in 1770, *raznochintsy* joined with their neighbors, identified as merchants, to petition for the removal of an enterprise producing kvass and bread; according to the petitioners, the establishment disturbed the neighborhood and posed a serious fire hazard.[68]

Following the provincial reforms of Catherine the Great, local officials continued to describe *raznochintsy* as urban homeowners who, regardless of their tax obligations, performed the same labor services as other citizens.[69] In Moscow province, efforts to delineate social categories more clearly led to the creation of "*raznochinskie* [*sic*] streets" and wards *(kvartaly)*, which could be adjacent to either upper- or lower-class areas.[70] The following maps illustrate that as parishioners and neighbors, *raznochintsy* were integrated into local communities in a variety of ways. At the same time, from the perspective of specific administrative domains and groups in society, they were also outsiders. Clearly, the category *raznochintsy,* and particularly the notion of *raznochintsy* as outsiders, must be viewed first and foremost as a subjective cultural construction. Only then is it possible to explain the diversity and malleability of definitions.

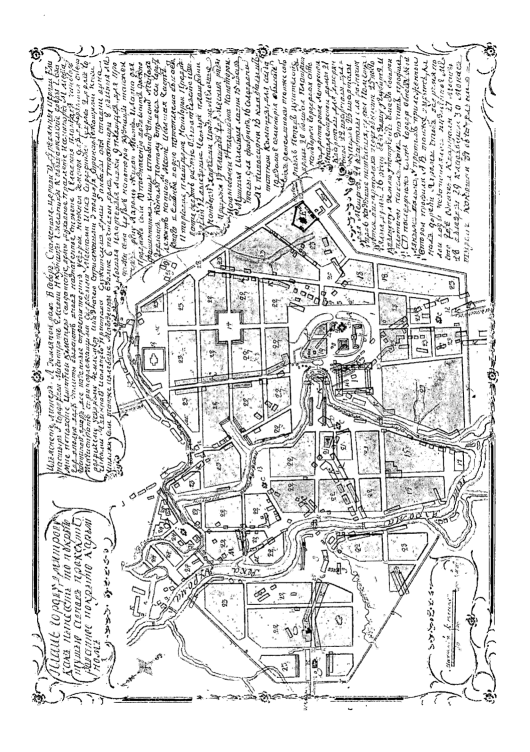

City of Dmitrov, Moscow province, 1787.

Plan showing a ward for *raznochintsy* (grid 24).

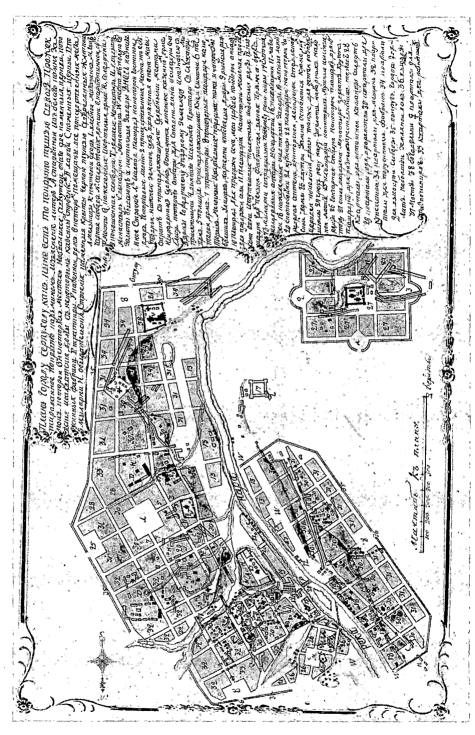

City of Serpukhov, Moscow province, 1787.

Plan showing a ward for *raznochintsy* (grid 39).

City of Klin, Moscow province, 1787.
Plan showing mixed wards for *raznochintsy*, administrative office employees, and church employees (grids 18, 19, and 22).

City of Volokolamsk, Moscow province, 1787.
Plan showing a ward for *raznochintsy* (grid 29).

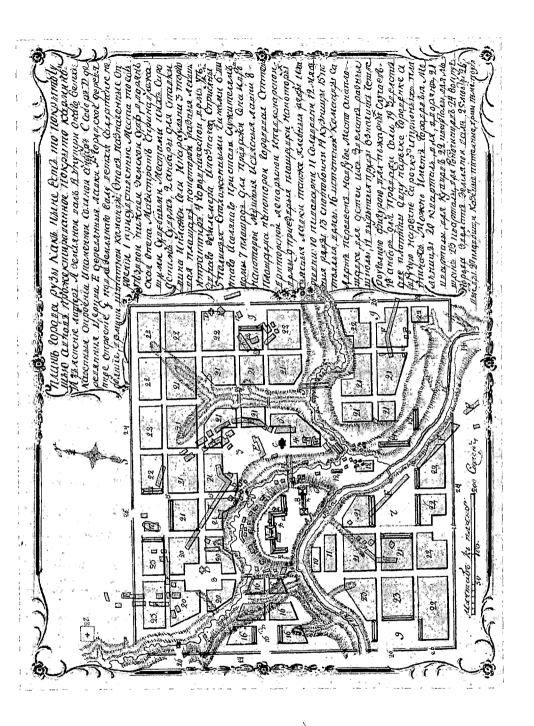

City of Ruza, Moscow province, 1787.

Plan showing a ward for *raznochintsy* (grid 23).

Self-Definition and Identity

AS INDIVIDUALS AND COMMUNITIES defined themselves in relation to the state or each other, they applied and interpreted legal formulas in response to diverse circumstances, needs, and aspirations. Indeed, it was precisely the flexibility and inconsistency of these formulas that permitted their voluntaristic interpretation by both officialdom and society. The plasticity of formal definitions, revealed in administrative and societal applications of the law, resonated in the formation of sociocultural identities. Legal self-definition occurred when individuals sought to change their formal identity or to obtain official recognition of an unrecognized status, when administrative domains competed for taxpayers, specialists, and functionaries, and when communities, landlords, and administrative agencies clashed over individual petitions for a change of status. The legal uncertainties directly contributed to the articulation of informal definitions— definitions that violated official categories and that in the nineteenth century increasingly implied a statement of values. Thus writers, memoirists, and fictional characters blended social concepts such as *raznochintsy* into cultural categories and at the same time, created new cultural concepts such as *obshchestvo* (liberal educated society) and the intelligentsia, which in turn acquired a social meaning. The cultural definitions and self-definitions could encompass intellectual and more organized political, social, or community affiliations, including some forms of passive resistance and rebellion. Once perceived as politically significant, the cultural definitions entered official language and hence began to color the government's representation of society.

LEGAL SELF-DEFINITION

As officials applied the legal category *raznochintsy* (and social definitions generally) in concrete administrative and judicial practice, they interpreted and hence re-created its meaning. These interpretations then resounded back to the lawmakers themselves, who continued to issue new legislative formulations in response to perceived misunderstandings or abuses. Beyond these official processes of creation, interpretation, and re-creation, there was a second and no less crucial dynamic underlying the concept of the *raznochintsy,* namely, how society received, translated, and remade the legally defined category. To explain this process, one must consider the nature and content of ideal social types and identities as expressed by officials, intellectuals, and groups in society; divergences between ideal types/identities and the concrete realities of individual and group life chances; and the possibility of competing ideals and identities. Close study of the *raznochintsy* reveals that self-definition could be legal, social, or cultural; one central fact emerges from all of the legislative, administrative, and societal usages: social definitions were changeable, often inconsistent, and always ambiguous.

Although society had no institutionalized voice in the production of legal definitions, individuals and communities sought changes in formal status with some minimal success. In striving to change their registered status, they engaged in a process of legal self-definition—a process encouraged by widespread social insecurity and the uncertainties of formal prescriptions. Whether successful or not, they expressed their own particular interpretation of the law. Not surprisingly, legal self-definition often clashed with administrative practice, as officials assigned formal status and individuals or communities sought to alter it. Self-definition also provided cover for illegal actions. As already indicated, socioeconomic development extended far beyond the framework of officially recognized institutions and relationships. Even the lowliest elements in society, perhaps more so than the elite, could passively resist the authorities by evading state regulations or by falsifying individual identities; such actions then generated official responses in the form of new legal formulations.

The most suggestive examples of legal self-definition involved serfs who petitioned district courts for their freedom on the basis of legislation permitting illegally enserfed persons to seek their freedom.[1] The authorities considered petitions from individuals who had fallen into bondage through unlawful means or whose masters were not entitled to own serfs. A study of thirty suits submitted in Perm province during the reigns of Alexander I and Nicholas I found that only four were decided in favor of the serfs.[2] The successful petitions all involved the illegitimate children of women who belonged to the state peasantry. Whereas some suits were based on erroneous or unproven claims, the authorities also rejected legitimate petitions that should have resulted in emancipation, either because officials misinterpreted the law or because landlords effectively delayed the proceedings until the statute of limitations or the period for appeals had expired. Lack of documentation provided additional grounds for denial, usually to the benefit of the serfowner; thus, if peasants had been registered to landlords before 1815, the Senate rejected the peasants' petitions even when the landlords could not produce bills of sale.[3]

To understand the formation of social identities, it is important to examine how petitioners defined themselves and justified their claims, how they interpreted and hence re-created the laws. There is some evidence that serfs were familiar with the legal texts that regulated emancipation from unlawful bondage; in formal petitions they revealed a selective understanding of the law, while articulating what they regarded as legitimate grounds for emancipation. One suit from Vladimir province, denied by the Senate in the 1820s, involved factory workers purchased by a serf of Count Sheremet'ev in his master's name. When Sheremet'ev sold the peasants, they refused to submit to their new owner. Instead, they demanded freedom on the basis of laws forbidding *raznochintsy* (here, the Sheremet'ev serf who had first acquired them) to possess serfs.[4] Many claims were also based on accusations of hardship and abuse by landlords, including excessive work burdens and unjust or life-threatening punishments.[5] Neither the courts nor the law treated these "moral" issues as sufficient grounds for liberation; judicial officials might instruct local administrators to take measures to prevent such abuses, but the landlords were not punished.[6] Clearly, a gap existed between the expectations of serfs who believed they had a right to freedom and the official criteria for emancipation.

The petitions submitted to the Perm courts revealed a striking desire for liberation, despite almost insurmountable obstacles. Some serfs claimed that their ancestors had been freed in the first half of the eighteenth century but had returned to their landlords when they could not secure a living. In the 1820s the descendants of these freedmen saw sufficient evidence of economic opportunity to seek emancipation; the authorities rejected their petitions, both because the ten-year statute of limitations had expired and because it was not always clear how the free ancestors had become serfs. In a similar case the relatives of a dragoon discharged from service in 1730 failed to establish their relationship to the emancipated individual. The descendants of this *raznochinets* became aware of his free status only in 1807, when they discovered a document showing that he and his relatives had paid the capitation directly. They immediately seized the opportunity to escape bondage, but because it was unclear how the dragoon's descendants had lapsed into serfdom, the court concluded they had not adequately proven a relationship to the freedman. In addition to problems of documentation, serfs who sought freedom faced overt intimidation by their masters, including imprisonment (until the prescribed period for appeals expired), physical abuse, fines, and loss of property. Landlords also maintained close ties to local officials, who likewise feared them. The richest and most powerful landowners, families like the Golitsyns and Demidovs, further benefited from ministerial connections. The yearning for freedom thus seems even more remarkable when one considers the frightful barriers that petitioners had to overcome. Clearly, and more important, there was a perception that legal emancipation was indeed possible.

When examining legal self-definition by groups, it is necessary to distinguish community identities from the claims of competing administrative domains. Whereas the boundaries of administrative domains and their subordinate communities usually were synonymous, their interests often clashed. Individual aspirations, the needs of the community, and the functions of administrative domains interacted to produce a morass of competing claims and conflicting definitions. In a case presented to officials in Perm province in 1800, a serfowner claimed authority over an unranked administrative clerk named Vedernikov.[7] Vedernikov was the illegitimate son of a sacristan's wife who had left her husband in 1760, when the husband voluntarily became enserfed to a factory owner. Vedernikov had petitioned the local court for formal recognition of his free status and had then obtained an appointment to state service. Subsequently, the factory owner managed to persuade him to withdraw his petition, an action that the lower court approved. A higher court objected, however, arguing that Vedernikov already was a state man *(kazennyi chelovek)*, that is, a government official, and so could not be registered to a factory owner. The final outcome of this case is unknown, but the competing claims it manifested are significant. At one point Vedernikov sought recognition as a freeman and a career in the civil service. The bureaucracy, always short of qualified personnel, assigned him to service. The factory owner needed serf laborers, while the treasury and army stood to lose a potential taxpayer and recruit. A multiplicity of interests thus produced divergent interpretations of the law. The judicial arbitrariness and inconsistency so evident in this case can be traced, once more, to the plasticity and ambiguity of the legal definitions that permitted so many varied and contradictory applications.

Similar dynamics were visible in conflicts between individuals and their communities. In 1781 a coachman from Nizhnii Novgorod registered as a merchant and in 1782 was selected to serve as an official *(burgmistr)* of the magistracy. In January 1783 the provincial authorities released him from this post because of poor health, but then in September the community again chose him to supervise the collection and distribution of salt. The former coachman considered this assignment illegal and petitioned for release, citing a community ruling *(vygovor)* of 1761 that exempted *raznochintsy* who enrolled in merchant status from administrative obligations for five years. The provincial authorities agreed that if such a decision existed, the petitioner should be freed from these duties. Again, conflicting needs resulted in divergent interpretations of the law. More than twenty years after a ruling that aimed to give newer merchants a chance to establish themselves, the community reversed itself and assigned the newcomer-outsider to carry out the burdensome functions older members sought to escape.[8] Still, the former coachman was able to apply the law, in order to define for himself an advantageous position within the merchant society.

A final type of legal self-definition revealed the strength of traditional community ties—ties that defied both formal law and socioeconomic realities. At the end of the eighteenth century, some groups still employed Muscovite categories to define themselves and pressed claims on the basis of seventeenth-century social and economic arrangements. Thus in 1782 thirty-one petitioners from the city of Vasil' (Nizhnii Novgorod province) identified themselves as the descendants of petty Muscovite servicemen *(prezhnikh sluzheb sluzhilye liudi)*. Previously from the city of Kozmodem'-iansk, they had served there as "police" troops *(razsyl'shchiki)* attached to the provincial administration *(voevodskaia kantseliariia)*. In the second revision they had been registered to the "ploughing soldiers" of Vasil', where they now paid the capitation and provided manpower for the Ukrainian frontier force. Although they were supposed to resettle in Vasil', they continued to live in Kozmodem'iansk and there fulfilled the service obligations of town residents. The local governor supported their desire to remain in their homes and ordered that in the next revision the petitioners be registered in Kozmodem'iansk.[9] Here one witnesses the strength of traditional identities even after more than half a century of poll tax reform and governmental efforts to conflate Muscovite social categories.

The persistence of community ties was especially striking among former peasants *(bobyli)* of the Dukhov monastery near Nizhnii Novgorod. In 1799, even though some of them lived in Nizhnii Novgorod and others in nearby Kunavinskaia suburb *(sloboda)*, they petitioned local authorities through a single representative. According to the petitioners, local townspeople had long coveted the land and population of the monastery—a situation that in 1632 forced Patriarch Filaret to intervene to protect the integrity of the Dukhov community. Despite such efforts, the community still "had lost its existence." The former peasants claimed not to know precisely how or when this occurred, but they were certain it resulted from coercion by the neighboring townspeople. They also reported that since the secularization of church property, they came under the College of Economy and had in 1769 received new lands to farm. Finally, they argued, in addition to paying the capitation and providing conscripts, some of them lived in the city, and although they lacked the right to engage in urban trades, they still performed the service duties of townspeople.

Continuing to call themselves *bobyli*, the twenty-nine petitioners requested that the former lands of the Dukhov monastery be returned to them; they failed, however, to produce documents establishing the boundaries of their lost community. Eventually a deed *(gramota)* of 1686 revealed that the monastery community had been absorbed into the Kunavinskaia suburb *(sloboda)*. Local authorities thus rejected the petition as unfounded.[10] One can only marvel at the tenacity of these people who managed to preserve their sense of community, despite the dislocations caused by a century of administrative restructuring and the confiscation of church property. One must question their professed ignorance of the circumstances surrounding the demise of their community, yet the selective memory they exhibited, whether conscious or unconscious, enabled them to perpetuate traditional bonds and to continue to define themselves as a group.

Systematic study of the *raznochintsy* provides much evidence that Russian society lacked firm boundaries and secure structures; still, the unbreakable ties of communities that had even ceased to exist in law might also suggest just the opposite conclusion. Could not the strength of these traditional bonds indicate a rigid adherence to social distinctions? The desire to preserve distinctions was indeed significant, but then one must consider why these people clung so tenaciously to time-honored definitions. The uncertainty of social status and the plasticity of social boundaries offer an explanation, for these realities of Russian life both permitted and necessitated a dynamic process of legal self-definition that was central to the formation of social identities. When serfs and other individuals attempted to change their status, they relied upon their own understanding of formal laws. Similarly, communities in danger of losing their formal or historic specificity selectively interpreted laws in an effort to preserve traditional distinctions—distinctions that no longer corresponded to legislative norms or socioeconomic realities.

Although the dynamics of self-definition revealed the importance of formal law in the formation of social identities, this did not mean that identities or socioeconomic realities necessarily corresponded to legal norms. Historical memory, which repeatedly proved stronger than actual life, also could be selective and deliberately manipulative. Both the state and society readily manipulated the formal *soslovie* definitions that were so important in determining the life chances of an individual or class. Societal self-definition could become "self-fashioning"—that is, personal adaptation to existing power structures—or it could become popular resistance to superordinate authority in the form of conscious evasion. Successful escapes from serfdom represent just one example of how even the lowliest elements of society could use existing structures of authority to good advantage. Equally important and closely related were the phenomena of impostors and false identities, which concealed a variety of social conditions. One court case from 1797 involved a copyist's wife who had deserted her husband and then tried to enter a monastery by claiming to be the homeless daughter of a deceased colonel. According to the colonel's son, the wife was the child of a servant girl who had lived in the house of his late father, and although the son denied it, she may very well have been his illegitimate half-sister.[11]

In a particularly complex instance of disputed identity, an impostor attempted to register in Arkhangel'sk by identifying himself as Filipp Grigor'ev Simonov, the adopted son of a Moscow townsman. In 1846 the impostor had journeyed to Arkhangel'sk with a merchant employer, carrying a passport issued by the Moscow city council *(duma)* and receipts confirming the payment of all taxes. When he requested registration in Arkhangel'sk, authorities there sent inquiries to their Moscow counterparts. Moscow declared the man an impostor, as did his "adoptive" mother, who claimed she had lived with her son, the real Filipp Grigor'ev (now married and himself a father). The ensuing investigation exposed numerous anomalies and contradictions. Several intermediaries actually had helped to formalize the identification papers of the impostor—the Arkhangel'sk Filipp—but key witnesses had died or been drafted. The facts of the case never were established definitively; it is likely that the merchant who originally employed the Arkhangel'sk Filipp had taken advantage of an error in the Moscow city records, which listed two Filipp Simonovs. Because of this double entry, the merchant was able to obtain a passport for a fourteen-year-old boy of unknown origins, the present Arkhangel'sk Filipp. Finally, in 1860, officials in Arkhangel'sk abandoned their efforts to determine the identity of the Arkhangel'sk Filipp. They decided that so young a boy could not have falsified his origins deliberately, nor, because of his documented association with the Moscow city government, could he be a vagrant or runaway. No doubt with some monetary encouragement from his merchant patron, the officials allowed the impostor to register, noting that "the Arkhangel'sk society of townspeople has declared its agreement to accept him in the townspeople of the city of Astrakhan [*sic*]."[12]

The possibility of impostors, combined with repeated errors in record keeping, often makes it difficult to evaluate the authenticity of the popular aspirations and representations expressed in cases of legal self-definition. This is a general problem with any petition or judicial source and cannot be resolved here.[13] For the purposes of this study, the significance of self-definition and the relationships that petitioners attempted to rectify, formalize, or conceal lies not in the veracity of their representations but in what these reveal about the larger uncertainties of social categorization. The very persistence of such cases, which repeatedly occupied local courts and regularly required intervention by the Senate, shows that they were taken seriously at all levels of government. Most importantly, they indicate that formal social affiliations were not always easy to identify or maintain.

This malleability of social definitions, so strikingly revealed in the concept of the *raznochintsy*, suggests the importance of "self-fashioning" in the larger structure of society.[14] Social structure did not exist on a purely legal or economic basis; it was, at least in part, a subjective construction, formulated and understood by individuals or groups who defined themselves in relation to others and who were in turn redefined by those others. As a subjective construct, social structure constantly interacted with external ("objective") legal and economic pressures that lay beyond the control of the self-defining population. The *raznochintsy* represented an exaggerated example of the subjective and often arbitrary nature of social definitions;

given Russia's weak legal tradition and the lack of autonomous institutional bases, it is fair to say that even the external elements of law and productive development could be arbitrary and discretionary, and thus subject to significant fluctuations. The result was a society in which subjective factors, be they self-definitions or arbitrary administrative interpretations of laws, played a greater role in the development of social structure than might otherwise have been the case.

Historians traditionally identify the *raznochintsy* as a category of persons who occupied a transitional or indeterminate status, yet they do not discuss the relationship of the varied and changeable contours of the *raznochintsy* to the larger structure of society. Along with unrecognized claims to noble status, the related problem of delimiting the nobility, and the stubborn persistence of unlawful serfdom and trade, the phenomena of legal self-definition and conscious evasion suggest that the ambiguity of status most readily implied in the category *raznochintsy* was a more generalized feature of Russian society. It is possible, then, to think of imperial Russia as a society of *raznochintsy*. Together with the noble-serf paradigm and the "*soslovie* paradigm"—neither of which has exhausted its potential for significant research—Russian historians also must consider the notion of a *raznochin-nyi* culture, where formal social boundaries often were inoperative. Akin to the mestizo civilization of New Spain, this was a society where legal and illegal economic relationships combined with voluntaristic processes of sociocultural self-definition to produce an overlapping and intermingling of statuses, ethnicities, and cultural identities. The result was a fluid, porous social fabric with a distinct lack of structure, predictability, and security.

THE INTELLIGENTSIA AS CULTURAL SELF-DEFINITION

The concept of the intelligentsia represents the most striking example of cultural self-definition in imperial Russia. Most historians employ the term as if it had a straightforward, commonly accepted definition, but detailed studies reveal a variety of confusing interpretations. The discussion that follows makes no attempt to treat the complex social language of the intelligentsia, either concretely or historiographically. The subjective, normative, and polemical essence of the category intelligentsia already has received scholarly treatment.[15] The purpose here is to suggest that if one views the intelligentsia as a self-proclaimed, self-defined subculture—and more specifically, as a means by which educated Russians sought to delimit themselves—it is possible to reconcile the term's contradictory meanings. Given the porousness of social boundaries and the plasticity of formal categories, self-definition played a prominent role in the formation of social and cultural identities. Thus the history of the intelligentsia is best understood as part of a broader, long-term pattern of social development and not as the radical departure that the intellectual creators of the concept would have us believe.

According to the traditional mythology of the Russian intelligentsia, the *raznochintsy* figure prominently in discussions of the chronology and essential nature of the phenomenon, as well as the origins of the revolutionary movement. Divergent chronologies constitute a major source of inconsistency in definitions of the intelligentsia, for historians have yet to explain adequately the origins of the group. Although *intelligentsia* as a collective term appeared only in 1861, few scholars take as their starting point the terminology and its applications. This inattention to language is just one reason for the failure to formulate an adequate definition. Historians who date the birth of the intelligentsia to sometime in the eighteenth century integrate social and cultural explanations by associating an identifiable frame of mind with a specific social context.[16] Those who focus on the philosophical circles of the 1830s and 1840s stress its intellectual origins, whereas those who examine the 1850s and 1860s depict a sociological process.[17] All seek to establish a relationship between the concept of the intelligentsia and the social reality it is supposed to represent; most also regard the intelligentsia as a distinct group in society. Even those scholars who emphasize social and intellectual differentiation within the intelligentsia or who define it as a concept rather than a social entity still insist that by 1870 the abstraction had evolved into a stratum or subculture.

The insistence on treating the intelligentsia in sociological terms creates serious problems in interpretation. Unable to overcome the contradiction between the intelligentsia as "self-image" and the presence of the intelligentsia as an identifiable group in society, historians attempt to incorporate both definitions.[18] The notion of "self-image" implies a multiplicity of conceptions that undermines attempts to formulate a sociological or "objective" scholarly definition. Both Western and Soviet historians seek to overcome this difficulty by eliminating the subjective element. Noting that the diverse conceptions of the intelligentsia "accurately reflected the self-image of various groups of writers and politically active men in Russian society," Daniel R. Brower concludes that "the very subjectiveness of the definitions should have precluded their use in historical research."[19] Soviet scholars go the farthest in seeking to formulate an "objective" scientific definition. Even so, one historian counts over sixty definitions of "intelligentsia" in Soviet scholarship, the most common being a social group composed of "persons professionally employed in mental labor [*umstvennyi trud*]."[20] This definition, essentially that which was used to delineate Soviet social categories, equates the intelligentsia with the professions of modern industrial society.

Locked into viewing the intelligentsia as a social group, scholars are unable to devise a definition that can delineate its boundaries satisfactorily. The prerevolutionary scholar Mikhail Gershenzon unwittingly suggested a solution when he castigated intellectual historians for their failure to apply "the laws of scientific inquiry," describing their studies as nothing more than a pile of "poetry and politics, creative minds and masses, thought and feeling, words and deeds."[21] The dissertation of Otto Müller—to date the only work that offers a solution to the dilemma posed by defining the intelligentsia as a social stratum—reveals that this pile of contradictory meanings and usages can produce an alternative and ultimately more successful conception.[22]

Noting that political polemics and philosophical reflection undermined the collective notion of the intelligentsia, Müller examines numerous distinctions within the category—distinctions based on ethnicity, geography, chronology, social status, politics, and philosophical-ethical values. Repeatedly, the subjective conceptions of individual authors posed ideological or ideal types that doomed any effort to delineate a sociological entity or develop a value-free definition. Müller's close scrutiny of nineteenth-century texts and his willingness to embrace a multiplicity of meanings and conceptions make it impossible to uphold sociological interpretations of the classic Russian intelligentsia.[23] Yet, however frequently he relates Russian usages of the term *intelligentsia* to developments in French and German philosophy, Müller does not explain the Russian social context in which these European ideas were applied,[24] nor does he examine the relationship between the concept of the intelligentsia and the larger structure of Russian society. It is precisely this relationship that the phenomenon of the *raznochintsy* helps to illuminate.

Historians generally introduce the *raznochintsy* in order to examine the composition of the intelligentsia and its formation as a distinct group in society, revealing just how easily the choice of language can alter interpretation. Many historians associate the formation of the intelligentsia as a self-defined, self-proclaimed subculture with the rise to prominence of a radical "democratic intelligentsia" (*raznochinnaia* or *raznochinskaia* intelligentsia) in the 1860s. Thus they link sociological conceptions of the intelligentsia to the phenomenon of the *raznochintsy* either by treating the two groups as synonymous or by attributing the radicalization and alienation of the intelligentsia to the influence of the *raznochintsy*. Deeper understanding of the *raznochintsy* reveals problems in relying upon the category to establish a sociological interpretation of the intelligentsia.

Michael Confino provides a partial answer to the problems created by historians who attribute changes in the nature of the intelligentsia to the arrival of the *raznochintsy*. He is careful to point out that, even in the 1840s and 1850s, most intellectuals, including those from the *raznochintsy*, were loyal to the government and that already in the eighteenth century a significant number of intellectuals were of humble birth.[25] Confino challenges the assumption, first articulated by Mikhailovskii, that the more radical ideological trends of the 1860s stemmed from "a democratization of the social basis of the intelligentsia." Rather, nihilism represented a "revolt of gentry sons and daughters" against their biological fathers, "by means of which the *raznochintsy* obtained a role and became a part of the phenomenon." The more prominent role of *raznochinskie* intellectuals was not the "result of quantitative growth" but of changes in their occupational distribution, "with more of them in autonomous intellectual activities."

Seeking to explain the role of the *raznochintsy* in the nihilist movement of the 1860s, Confino identifies them as former seminarians whose poverty, rough manners, "neophyte atheism," and intellectual dogmatism ("inherited from theological studies") gained legitimacy and even were idealized in the ethos of the intelligentsia. He avoids the major pitfalls associated with sociological interpretations of the "democratic intelligentsia" by confining his analysis to a specific historical context: the development of nihilism in the era of the Great Reforms. As a result, Confino can establish a correspondence between the nihilist ideal and the beliefs and life experiences of the radical ex-seminarians—without, however, directly attributing ideological radicalization to their influence. Confino's definition of an intelligentsia ethos, limited by time and place, thus anticipates Müller's political interpretation. Nevertheless, there are problems in equating the ex-seminarians with the *raznochintsy*. The phenomenon of the *raznochintsy* cannot be confined to any specific sociological entity, and even if one treats the *raznochintsy* in social terms, the former seminarians represented just one of the numerous subgroups comprising this diverse category. Confino's failure to distinguish the *raznochintsy* from the seminarians does not impinge on his analysis, which is limited to nihilism, where his definition is appropriate. But other historians who apply the definition more broadly do so at great risk.

Careful analysis of the category *raznochintsy* reveals its basic irrelevance to the chronological development of the intelligentsia. However one defines the intelligentsia, the *raznochintsy* cannot explain its origins, nature, or social composition, nor can the *raznochintsy* account for the emergence of the intelligentsia as a self-conscious social element. The role of *raznochintsy* in the development of a revolutionary intelligentsia—and particularly the relationship between radicalism and social origins during the 1860s and 1870s—remains problematic. As Daniel R. Brower notes, the rise of the *raznochintsy* as a source of radicalism was a myth—a myth that "reflected wishful thinking by those who saw no hope for the revolutionary cause as long as nobles dominated the movement."[26]

Because the *raznochintsy* were visible participants in social unrest already in the mid-eighteenth century, it is impossible to attribute the radicalization of the intelligentsia a century later to their "arrival." They had "arrived" and acted long before.[27] Any definition of the intelligentsia must include the *raznochintsy* already from the beginning—whether as "revolutionaries," latent revolutionaries, or politically quiescent members of the

educated and cultural elites. The role of the *raznochintsy* in peasant disturbances indicated not alienation from society but integration and involvement; even retired officers and provincial secretaries sometimes participated. Indeed, their role in these disturbances raises questions about the
supposed isolation of the lower bureaucracy from "the people" well before
the revolutionary crisis of the twentieth century.[28] The implications of their
involvement are similar to those already suggested by historians who challenge traditional assumptions about a profound sociocultural alienation
separating priests and serfs in the prereform era and peasants and propagandists in the movement to the people in 1874.[29]

There is precious little evidence to suggest that the phenomenon of the
raznochintsy had a decisive impact on the formation of the intelligentsia
and revolutionary movement. As a socially democratic but not self-conscious group with a large contingent of educated commoners, the "intelligentsia" existed at least a century before there was any articulation of the
concept.[30] Most frequently, the *raznochintsy* enter historiographical discussions in order to address the issue of radicalization in the 1860s; thus scholars focus on the supposedly new cultural prominence of the *raznochintsy* to
explain the radicalization of the intelligentsia and its crystallization as a
self-conscious group. More narrowly, they examine the relationship between radicalism and the composition of the student youth. This approach
clearly is misguided. In social terms, the *raznochintsy* did not represent either a new or a newly dominant element within the cultural and educated
elites. In ideological, intellectual, or political terms, there was no "special
view of things" or identifiable ethos that differentiated the *raznochintsy*
from other groups in society. It is grossly distorting to describe Chernyshevskii, Dobroliubov, N. V. Uspenskii, Pomialovskii, and F. M. Reshetnikov as
"the *raznochintsy*." Nor, as Otto Müller conclusively shows, was there a single conception of the intelligentsia. In a word, it is possible to understand
the category *raznochintsy*, its role in the formation of the intelligentsia, and
the intelligentsia itself only by paying close attention to concrete articula-
tions of these concepts and their relationships in a larger cultural or political context.

The failure to formulate neutral scientific terms of analysis plagues
scholarly treatments of the *raznochintsy* and intelligentsia, precisely because
both groups represented subjective categories. One must, therefore, aban-
don the notion of the intelligentsia as a social entity that can be delineated
either sociologically or philosophically. For only by defining membership
as a form of conscious identification or positive identity is it possible to
incorporate legal, socioeconomic, and intellectual differences. Once this is
done, it also becomes impossible to equate the intelligentsia with the educated elites or professions. The democratic social composition of the intelligentsia and its formation as a self-defined, self-proclaimed subculture
were not simply the result of radical views, though such views promoted

voluntarism and an egalitarian disregard for social distinctions. Rather, the intelligentsia originated in the lack of rigid social boundaries and in the social intermingling that had been characteristic of Russian society since earliest times.

The formation of the intelligentsia reveals with particular clarity the extent to which educated society remade the formal social definitions of imperial Russia. The concept of the intelligentsia emanated directly from the cultural elite, whereas the concept of the *raznochintsy* was remade in the context of an emerging intelligentsia subculture. When one considers the extent to which lawmakers, administrators, and representatives of society defined the *raznochintsy* subjectively, it becomes possible to explain their role in the "birth of the intelligentsia." Thus Mikhailovskii's remaking of the concept of the *raznochintsy,* an important element in the articulation of an intelligentsia subculture, fails to delineate the boundaries of a social group; rather, it makes sense only if one views the intelligentsia as identity, self-definition, and consciousness. As such, the meaning and the role of the intelligentsia in the development of modern Russia are as varied and sometimes elusive as the individuals and groups who incorporated the category into their speech, writings, perceptions, and actions.

In a diary entry for the year 1866, F. M. Reshetnikov underscored the problematics of self-definition in the development of the intelligentsia. Regarded by publicists and historians as a quintessential representative of the *raznochinskaia* intelligentsia, Reshetnikov described the nihilists of his day in the most unflattering terms:

> These are stupid people. A boy who gets it into his head that he is a nihilist, i.e., he does not believe in God, does not recognize the government, wears long hair, glasses, talks nonsense and acts like a scoundrel; in church he is terribly vile; he is terribly repulsive on Nevskii, in the passage, where he plays dirty tricks on girls, women. If you ask him: what is a nihilist?—he cannot explain it to you. People who consider themselves nihilists and obtain a position or have money explain nihilism to girls; [they] pose as intelligent [people], but in essence they are so base that there is no reason to talk with them. They not only do not want to stand up for a *muzhik* [peasant], they do not want consciously or sincerely to call him a citizen. . . . Nihilism—this is a fashionable phrase that does not explain anything.[31]

According to Reshetnikov, there was no "objective" reality to nihilism; it was an invention, something that people got into their heads to call themselves—without, however, any corresponding commitment to a set of ideas or values. For Reshetnikov, the nihilists were not real because they lacked sincerity and moral purity, a judgment that is strongly reminiscent of the idealist premises of Herzen and his circle. There is here no hint of a sociological entity, only the unfulfilled promise of a political one.

Reshetnikov's critique of the nihilists centered on their relationship to the people—a relationship that is central to any discussion of the intelligentsia. A key problem that plagued this relationship was the difficulty experienced by self-proclaimed members of the intelligentsia *(intelligenty)* and revolutionaries who sought to forge direct social and organizational ties to the general population. Before the 1890s this was an issue that was more talked about than sought after, though there were noteworthy exceptions such as the Sunday School movement, the movement to the people, and the educational activities of the followers of N. V. Chaikovskii. Publicists, theoreticians, and historians after them frequently attribute the lack of stable ties to an insuperable sociocultural gulf that divided the educated elites from the common people. This explanation seems insufficient, however, when one considers that the number of educated and semieducated persons in Russian society grew continually throughout the imperial period. As a steady stream of newcomers entered the educated elites directly from "the people," as the base and middle levels of the educational pyramid solidified following the reforms of Alexander I, and as primary education exploded after 1870—the demarcation between the educated and uneducated became progressively less severe.[32] Thus, by the later nineteenth century, the village schoolteacher blended imperceptibly into the literate peasantry, the worker *intelligent* into the skilled factory labor force. Daniel Field makes a similar point when he argues that historians, attempting to explain the failed movement to the people in 1874, exaggerate the sociocultural divide separating peasants from propagandists.[33] The phenomenon of the *raznochintsy* suggests an even broader explanation: the lack of formal structures in Russian society, the fragmented nature of social groups and identities, and the impossibility of establishing stable ties within the context of secure, historically enduring social institutions. Even without repression— and repression was crucial in preventing the solidification of newly conceived organizational ties—Russia lacked uniform social structures through which potential leaders could communicate their ideas.

The second problem that affected the relationship of the intelligentsia to the larger population lies in the very idea of "the people." Slavophiles, populists, conservatives, liberals, and radicals—all treated the people as an undifferentiated mass of toilers, future citizens, or latent revolutionaries. Only the Marxists offered a more complex view of social relations, but the ideological construct they imposed on Russian society was even more distorting than the notion of a single stratum of nonantagonistic toilers. It is incredible that critically thinking intellectuals who knew their country so well and who were keenly aware of its social and ethnic diversity could entertain such simplistic views of the people. Still, the existence of a sociocultural gulf that prevented genuine understanding does not adequately explain this problem. A more plausible rationale is the enormous complexity, fluidity, and fragmentation of society.

If one recognizes the indeterminate social delimitations in imperial Russia, then the Slavophile vision of Muscovite social concord and the populist thesis of a "single people" become more readily understandable.[34] I. S. Aksakov's belief in the organic, harmonious unity of society remains idiosyncratic. Although it is clearly wrong to equate a lack of firm social boundaries with an absence of social conflict,[35] one can see that the Slavophile historical vision had some basis beyond mere nostalgia for an idealized past. The populist conception of a single stratum of toilers was probably closer to the mark; certainly, it is necessary to consider what their success in the 1917 elections to the Constituent Assembly suggests about their understanding of Russian society. While both the Slavophile and populist conceptions of the people are far too simplistic to provide a satisfactory framework for analyzing Russian social development, they do seem less utopian and more rooted in the realities of Russian life when one considers the flexibility and porousness of the imperial social structure.

It was not, then, the archaic simplicity of the serf system that intellectuals depicted in their notion of "the people" but rather the absence of any stable, clearly delimited social structure. Society was far too diverse for polemicists and theoreticians in pursuit of political goals to take full account of the ambiguous social realities. Thus the idea of insurmountable social and cultural barriers separating the educated elites from the common people reinforced the notion of the intelligentsia as a distinct stratum in society. The inability to forge effective ties was in reality a failure to overcome social fragmentation—fragmentation that was a traditional feature of Russian society and by no means limited to the relationship between the Westernized cultural elites and the common people. As the educated elites became more activist and professionalized and as their sphere of activity moved increasingly beyond the framework of state service, they became acutely conscious of their relationship to the larger society, and painfully aware of their isolation from the people and from each other. Social fragmentation, not cultural Westernization, was at the root of this isolation and the feelings of alienation that it bred.

Students of the intelligentsia invariably identify alienation as one of the group's salient characteristics. It is interesting, however, that not only were the men of the 1840s integrated into elite society in terms of informal status and formal privileges, but the so-called *raznochintsy* of the 1860s—while in most cases not as privileged as Chernyshevskii—at least had very promising career prospects in military or civil service. They were not, then, alienated in the sense that society rejected them but rather in their choosing to reject the conventional norms of society. The intelligentsia's self-declared alienation and its fixation on forging a relationship with the people thus suggest that in addition to Müller's political definition, one might also regard the concept of the intelligentsia as a search for effective social bonds. It was precisely the failure to create stable bonds that helps to account for the growing radicalism and voluntarism of the educated public in the late imperial period.[36]

RUSSIA'S "ABSENT" MIDDLE?

Historians of Russia address the issue of the middle classes in a variety of ways, usually in terms of Western European experience[37]. Thus the middle layers of society appear as the "missing bourgeoisie"—missing both economically and politically, as the stillborn creation of the state, or as a newly conscious civil society encompassing the intelligentsia, the professions, and a politicized entrepreneurial class. Following Max Weber's Oriental-Occidental typology, Vatro Murvar attributes the "missing bourgeoisie" to the basic classlessness of Russian society and to the "monist-patrimonial authority of the tsar."[38] Murvar correctly stresses the absence of social structures and institutions that could challenge the authority of the ruler, but then he assumes that the weakness of society automatically translated into effective monarchical power. In Russia this clearly was not the case;[39] the limits of state power were very real, so that one has to look beyond patrimonialism for explanations of societal weakness.

Alfred J. Rieber indicates a very different reason for Russia's failure to develop a national bourgeoisie.[40] He also emphasizes the role of the state in defining social arrangements. But where Murvar sees classlessness, Rieber points to rigid social hierarchies and the traditional castelike features of society to explain the inability of the merchant elite—described as "a well-defined social group"—to overcome regional, ethnic, and socioeconomic particularism and to consolidate as a class. Noting the failure of merchants to forge stable ties among themselves and with other middle groups in society, Rieber aptly identifies social fragmentation as the foundation for the absence of class. He then attributes that fragmentation to the resilience of the *soslovie* principle rather than to the traditional porousness and plasticity of social boundaries.

A second approach to the problem of the middle classes focuses on governmental efforts to create a "middle estate" modeled after its Central and Western European counterparts. Beginning with the administrative and social reforms of Catherine the Great, legislators related status definitions to economic development, believing that if the government fashioned an effective administrative-social structure, economic development would ensue. The lack of firm structures in society certainly played a role in dissipating the beneficial results of economic initiative and entrepreneurship, both of which were abundant in imperial Russia. Moreover, the constraints of serfdom and the subordination of socioeconomic institutions to the fiscal needs of the state undermined the security and hence the development that the officially created structures were supposed to guarantee. Thus the distinction between productive development and the fiscal demands of the state—a distinction that was evident in legal defini-tions of *raznochintsy*—also found expression in the reforms of Catherine the Great, in the guild reform of 1824, and again in the urban reforms of 1846–1870. The paradoxical result of this effort to create corporative structures while maintaining the primacy of fiscal considerations was to produce social categories defined by occupation, tax obligations, and legal privileges that had more in common with "tax classes" than juridical es-tates. In other words, rather than delineating a "middle estate" in a social sense, tsarist policy established a legally defined "economy-society" *(Wirt-schaftsgesellschaft)*.[41]

Russia's "missing bourgeoisie" is obviously a vast subject that extends well beyond the scope of this study. Still, it is important to examine a few concrete conceptions of the "middle estate" in order to consider what the phenomenon of the *raznochintsy* reveals about the middle layers of society. Although Russian legislators clearly had the European experience in mind when they designed policies toward the "middle estate," the application of European patterns of development to the study of the Russian middle has produced only minimal understanding. The failure of Russia's middle to play the expected historical role, as the backbone of economic moderniza-tion and political democracy, does not justify treating it as the artificial creature of the state or as an immature, inert "missing bourgeoisie." Rather, it reveals the very different parameters and characteristic features of Russia's middle groups.

It was not until the reign of Catherine the Great that lawmakers con-sciously began to articulate a larger class structure. Responding to French political theorists such as Montesquieu, who attributed despotism and pov-erty in Russia to the absence of a "third estate," highly placed officials and intellectuals, including the empress herself, formulated projects to create the missing social element.[42] Most observers, drawing upon the French model, also attributed Russia's perceived economic backwardness to a lack of urban development manifested in the absence of a "third estate." Con-ceiving of this estate as "a static juridical middle stratum" wedged between the nobility and peasantry, they associated it with urban crafts, the arts, sciences, and trade; they also believed that its ranks could be augmented by foundlings and selectively freed peasants.[43] Official interest in fashioning a "third estate" was evident in Catherine the Great's Charter to the Towns (1785)[44] and later in the Digest of Laws (1832). Still, in conception and law, the middle estate—like virtually every other social category in imperial Russia—remained fragmented, fluid, and internally differentiated.

Catherine the Great's instruction to the Legislative Commission (1767) identified the "middle sort of people" *(srednii rod liudei)* as free persons occupied in the arts, sciences, navigation, trade, and crafts, who were nei-ther nobles nor tillers of the soil. According to the empress, the noble calling *(zvanie)* was founded on the principles of virtue, honor, service, loyalty to and love of the fatherland and sovereign; whereas membership in the "middle estate" depended upon sound behavior, industry, and hard work. Combining functional, cultural, and moral attributes, Catherine also included in the "middle sort" non-noble graduates of all church and state schools regardless of their formal status and non-noble children of low-ranking state officials and chancery clerks *(prikaznye liudi)*. The failure to formulate a precise legal or socioeconomic definition—already implied in the negative notion of the "middle sort" as free persons who were neither nobles nor peasants—became fully apparent, when she remarked that among the children of these officials and clerks, "there are different degrees of privileges."[45]

More specific conceptions of the various categories included in the middle estate appeared in the "Project of Laws on the Rights of the Middle Sort of State Inhabitants" (1769).[46] The project repeated Catherine's listing of the constituent groups and then added freedmen and foreigners who registered as townspeople *(meshchane)*, as well as foundlings and illegitimate children who were raised by townspeople. The members of the middle estate were then divided into three subgroups according to occupation. The first included persons in the sciences and services: white clergy, scholars, non-noble civil servants with rank, unranked administrative office employees, artists, and technical specialists. The second contained persons involved in trade: merchants, factory owners, shipowners, and navigators. Finally, the third subgroup served as a broad classification for all other persons legally employed in work appropriate to townspeople: artisans, freedmen, and a vague category, "simple townspeople and townspeople-*raznochintsy*," encompassing persons who were not employed in the urban occupations already identified. Some specific possibilities included employees in shops and service establishments, purveyors of prepared foods, artisans who were not organized into guilds, and stewards who worked for merchants. The project attempted to incorporate in the "middle sort" a wide range of free urban categories, excluding only high clergy, nobles, military servicemen, and peasants. Here there was no single middle estate in a legal, social, or economic sense; instead, there was a gradation of diverse classes and status groups, highly differentiated as well as overlapping, formally wedged between the noble and clerical elites above and the unprivileged rural categories below.

The Charter to the Towns (1785) formalized the fragmentation already evident in the 1769 project.[47] The "middle sort," called townspeople *(meshchane)*, corresponded to all legally registered city residents *(gorodovye obyvateli)*. Within this broad classification, artists, scholars, some wealthy merchants, and some elected city officials constituted a separate subcategory of distinguished citizens—a subcategory that represented legislated status honor. Merchants registered in a first, second, or third guild; artisans, in special craft organizations. Most urban residents belonged to the ordinary townspeople (also called *meshchane*), but the law still retained the traditional designation *posadskie* for others.[48] Lacking coherence as a sociological entity, the "middle estate" included legally differentiated subcategories occupied in trade, manufacturing, the arts, sciences, and crafts; there was no concept of "citizenship" based on heredity and territory, such as existed in the German home towns, to provide the basis for a larger group identity.[49] Although heredity played a role, "citizenship" was realized only in legal registration and residency. Communities might seek to exclude new registrants, but the "middle estate" in Russia remained the most open of the formal categories in a society where social boundaries in general were permeable.[50]

Russia's "middle estate" contained all the cultural and socioeconomic ingredients of the European middle classes, but it lacked the institutionalized structures needed to overcome social diversity and fragmentation. In a manuscript entitled "Introduction to the Code of State Laws" (1809), M. M. Speranskii implicitly recognized this problem when he chose to disregard socioeconomic attributes and define Russian social structure in primarily political terms.[51] Attempting to combine equality of civil rights with a reform of serfdom that would define in law the obligations of peasants toward their lords, Speranskii divided Russian society into three classes distinguished by degrees of political and civil freedom. Private serfs (third class and lowest degree of freedom) lacked both political and civil freedom. Merchants, townspeople, and state peasants (second class) possessed civil, but not political, freedom. The nobility (first class) enjoyed the highest degree of freedom, possessing civil, but again not political, rights, although nobles shared authority over serfs with the autocracy. Thus, according to Speranskii, "there can be only two sources of all divisions [of juridically defined social categories]: civil [*grazhdanskie*] and political [*politicheskie*] rights."[52]

Although in his notion of "civil rights" Speranskii approached a conception of larger social aggregates, he then distinguished two types of civil freedom, personal and material, and left intact traditional differences in tax and service obligations, property rights, and access to state service. In addition, he delineated two categories of civil rights: general rights enjoyed by all subjects (who possessed a civic identity in the first place) and special rights enjoyed only by specific social categories. By "special civil rights," he meant exemption from obligatory service and the right to own populated estates. Within this framework Speranskii identified three juridically defined social categories *(sostoianiia)* with distinct rights: the nobility, the "middle estate" *(srednee sostoianie)*, and the laboring population *(rabochii narod)*.

According to Speranskii's conception, the "middle estate" possessed general, but not special, civil rights. Its members performed service based on their calling *(zvanie)* and trade *(promysel);* like the nobility, their political rights depended on ownership of property. They could attain personal nobility through service, although advancement to hereditary nobility required imperial recognition of special merits. Speranskii's more refined and nuanced distinctions were in essence very close to the cruder, relatively clumsy formulations of the Catherinean era—with, however, two fundamental differences. Returning to Petrine practice, Speranskii made hereditary nobility contingent upon service, so that the children of hereditary nobles were considered personal nobles until they completed a specified term of service. In addition, the children of personal nobles—traditionally referred to as *ober-offitserskie deti* and by legal definition counted among the *raznochintsy*—belonged to the "middle estate." Speranskii took a more original position in defining the composition of the "middle estate"; he was unique in not limiting that category to urban society, thus including merchants, townspeople, artisans *(remeslenniki),* single householders, and all peasants *(poseliane)* who owned property. (This automatically excluded serfs.) In the case of peasants, workmen *(masterovye),* laborers, and domestic servants, it was the lack of property—as opposed to the appropriate occupation or socioeconomic function—that relegated them to the laboring class.[53]

Although Speranskii's most novel proposals were not enacted into law, discussions in the Committee of 6 December 1826 revealed the influence of his thinking on the proper organization of society. In the first version of its "Project for a Supplementary Law on Social Categories [*sostoianiia*]," the committee defined four primary groups: nobility, clergy, urban "citizenry" *(grazhdanstvo),* and peasantry.[54] While the project did not incorporate Speranskii's notion of a "middle estate," it did define the urban citizenry independently of economic rights that required guild membership or official certification. Within the urban population it distinguished four *sosloviia* by legal rights, tax and service obligations, access to education, and the rewards of service: citizens with rank, distinguished citizens, honored citizens, and townspeople (the traditional *meshchane).* According to the project, the highest strata of the urban population were closer to the nobility in education and lifestyle, while the lowest levels of urban society, occupied in trades and manual labor, approached the peasantry. Between these two extremes were artists, scholars, and scientists, who promoted enlightenment, and merchants, who enriched the state through trade. The proposed reform thus sought to find secure degrees of formal status for the constituent elements of a diverse category positioned between the nobility and peasantry.

The Committee of 6 December 1826 did not use the expression "third estate" or even anything comparable; its primary aims were to delineate precisely and clearly the main categories comprising Russian society and to establish adequate regulations and procedures to govern changes in formal status, particularly ennoblement through service. Thus the committee expressed concern about the lack of correspondence between rank *(chin)* and office *(dolzhnost')*, the ease with which commoners attained nobility, and the socioeconomic diversity and insecurity of the urban classes. There was no attempt to eliminate mobility, just to control and hopefully limit it. Like officials of the Catherinean era, the committee sought to provide for each social category, within its circle, "all the [necessary] means for the correct and beneficial use of the strengths and abilities given to it by God."[55] Alarmed by the amalgamation of social groups at all levels of society, members of the committee and of the State Council, which reviewed the project, were particularly hostile toward the *raznochintsy*, defined as the children of personal nobles and no doubt understood to be upwardly mobile.[56] The government's position was hopelessly contradictory; by limiting access to the nobility, it only increased the number of personal nobles and *raznochintsy*.

The potential restructuring of the "middle estate" suggested by the projects of Speranskii and the Committee of 6 December 1826 did not lead to fundamental social reform before emancipation in 1861. Thus, despite significant and long-standing movement between urban and rural categories, their formal conflation in a "middle sort" did not occur even in the 1832 Digest of Laws. It is significant that the codifiers avoided Speranskii's designation of a "middle estate" *(srednee sostoianie)*, returning instead to Catherine's term "middle sort" *(srednii rod)*. Like the Charter to the Towns, the Digest of Laws equated the social category *(sostoianie)* of formal urban "citizens" with the "middle sort of people" and included in its ranks guild merchants (local, from other cities, and honored citizens), townspeople *(meshchane* and *posadskie)*, and artisans or members of craft guilds.[57] The broad legal framework of social categories remained unchanged, though codification did promise more effective implementation of juridical distinctions. At the same time, within and between the broad formal categories so carefully constructed during the eighteenth century, the proliferation of protoprofessional elements and the dynamism of illegal or semilegal socioeconomic relationships continued to transform juridical definitions and violate social barriers.

Explicit patterns of professionalization did not appear in Russia before the 1860s, but the formation of educated and semieducated elites and the articulation of protoprofessional attitudes were evident already at the end of the eighteenth century. Given the absence of autonomous guild structures, the emergence of professional classes resulted primarily from state-directed occupational training and specialization; the phenomenon of the *raznochintsy* was closely related to the development of manpower resources for the numerous specialties and occupational categories that were thus created. It is important, then, to consider what the category *raznochintsy* reveals about processes of "professionalization" and how these processes related to the larger structure of society. The history of the *raznochintsy* suggests that even before the establishment of *zemstvo* assemblies and well before the industrial takeoff of the 1880s and 1890s, Russia experienced protoprofessional training and work outside of state institutions. As occurred in so many areas of Russian life, societal development moved well beyond formal institutions and definitions—with significantly more specialized activity than was officially recognized.

Historians of the professions in imperial Russia generally take as their starting point the establishment of a state school to train specialists needed in a particular area of military or civil service; this allows them to explore the connection between the tradition of state service and the development of a professional ethos that emphasized service to society. Referring to the Academy of Sciences, the universities, and specialized military schools, historians also tend to characterize tsarist educational policy as top-heavy, elite-oriented, and indifferent to the general population. Thus, in their view, educational expansion affected only a small cultural elite that served the military and administrative needs of the state. The visible achievements of Russian education did indeed seem concentrated at the top of the cultural pyramid, at least until the later nineteenth century, but the focus of state policy clearly was not. Actually, only in the reign of Alexander I— when it attempted to create an integrated system of parish and district schools, gymnasia (secondary schools), and universities—did the government devote substantial resources to institutions of higher learning. Only then can one say that elite education developed more rapidly or received more attention than primary education. To be sure, during the eighteenth century, and even more so in the reigns of Alexander I and Nicholas I, the creation of state schools resulted primarily from specific administrative, military, or economic needs; more often than not, these schools were not higher educational institutions. Rather, there was considerable activity in the development of low-level specialized training that also provided a basic primary education.[58]

The close relationship between education and social development is well documented. It is generally assumed that in the second half of the nineteenth century, the spread of education—brought on by the requirements of administrative, military, and economic modernization— contributed to a loosening of social barriers and a restructuring of social identities. By contrast, the first half of the nineteenth century, and particularly the reign of Nicholas I, is seen as a time when the *soslovie* principle reigned supreme, and educational policies rigidly reinforced traditional social boundaries.[59] There is no question that, like their eighteenth-century predecessors, prereform lawmakers attempted to order educational institutions according to the specific needs and functions of clearly delineated social categories.[60] Their ability to do so was another matter. Thus, as late as 1837, in state and particularly in private schools, children of lower-class townspeople, peasants, and even serfs continued to study "higher philology" in violation of laws limiting their education to technical subjects.[61]

Already in the first half of the nineteenth century, one has to ask whether the spread of education, the socially diverse composition of student populations, and the proliferation of specialized schools actually undermined social boundaries, or whether the patterns of institutional development mirrored existing features of Russian society. In a word, did education transform society? Or did society, and particularly its fragmentation, shape educational institutions by modifying policy at the moment of implementation? The history of the category *raznochintsy*, when viewed in its broadest possible relationship to society, supports the latter interpretation—an interpretation that high-level officials also voiced. The 1828 regulation governing primary and secondary schools subordinate to St. Petersburg, Moscow, Khar'kov, and Kazan universities designated specific institutions and curricula on the basis of social categories, yet from the outset, lawmakers recognized the correlation between curriculum and social origin as " 'a primary, but not exclusive function' of educational institutions."

Minister of Education Prince K. A. Lieven vividly described the impossibility of realizing "*soslovie* barriers" in the Russian educational system:

> In states where social categories [*sostoianiia*] are strictly separated from one another; where movement from one to another, in particular from the middle into the noble, is extremely difficult and very rarely occurs; [in states] that grant nobility only [as a reward] for lengthy and superior services—in such . . . states it is very easy to introduce such an order [i.e., the organization of education according to social categories]. But in Russia, where there is no middle category or citizenry; where only the merchant *soslovie* in some fashion represents such [a category]; where artisans are in all respects equal to farmers and almost always corrupt; where a prosperous peasant can at any time become a merchant, and often is both together; where the extent of the noble *soslovie* is so boundless that at one end it touches the foot of the throne and at the other is almost lost in the peasantry; where every year many [persons] from the urban and peasant *sosloviia* enter the nobility after receiving officer rank in military or civil service—in Russia such an arrangement of schools is difficult.[62]

Granted that officials who sought to limit ennoblement might have exaggerated the real prospects for social mobility, the important point here is that the minister of education considered the socially diverse character of Russian schools to be the result, not the cause, of indeterminate social boundaries. More important, what distinguished Russia from other, presumably European states was not the rigidity, but the plasticity of social barriers.

Regardless of time and place, the development of education is closely related to the emergence of professional classes. In Russia, where education often brought changes in formal status, the exclusion of individuals from social categories subject to the capitation created a range of *raznochinnye* protoprofessionals.[63] Children of personal nobles, state servicemen without a rank and their children, graduates of state schools who had the potential to attain a rank or even nobility but chose not to enter service— all were among the subgroups of *raznochintsy* defined by service and formal education. Official protoprofessional callings *(zvaniia)* such as teacher, artist, and dentist gave individuals a new legal status whether or not they were employed by the state.[64] By the 1860s *raznochintsy* who abandoned civil service careers also could become professional writers and journalists; others found work as specialists outside the framework of officially recognized degrees and certifications.

In imperial Russia the traditional free professions or "great person professions" of law, medicine, the ministry, and university teaching never fully developed; they never achieved sufficient autonomy in their "essential work" or control over the regulation of their membership to be regarded as anything more than "aspirant occupations" or "semiprofessions."[65] With the partial exception of lawyers—who were organized into bar associations after 1864 but still excluded from participation in significant areas of the judiciary—none of the traditional or newer technical professions ever gained authority over training, licensing, employment, and ethics.[66] According to modern sociologists, specialized knowledge, group consciousness, and occupational aspirations are not sufficient to attain professional status, nor is employment in a bureaucracy—a condition that was widespread in Russia—of crucial importance to the presence or absence of professional status. Rather, recognition as a profession hinges on societal acceptance and "the relationship between administrative and professional authority."[67] The extent of societal recognition is a subject that Russian historians have yet to consider, but one can say with certainty that the political and institutional conditions of autocratic rule in the nineteenth century did not permit the mechanisms of professional self-administration to evolve.

Police repression obviously played a formidable role in thwarting societal impulses to organize, though its precise impact is difficult to assess when speaking of social and cultural definitions.[68] The social fragmentation of the revolutionary era, particularly in the aftermath of 1905 and again in 1917, strikingly revealed the weakness of professional associations and identities.[69] Just as the "woman question" in late imperial Russia tended to be subsumed in the larger issue of social justice (the peasant and worker questions), professional identities became absorbed into the concept and ethos of the intelligentsia. In the absence of autonomous organizations, "professionalization" centered on the ideal of service. Categories like the "third element," *obshchestvo* (liberal educated society), and *obshchestvennost'* (public service) reflected the difficulty of distinguishing aspirant professions from the broader notion of the intelligentsia. The conflation of the professions with the intelligentsia was justified to a degree; in the struggle to achieve professional status, particularly the authority to fulfill a self-defined service ideal based on expertise, many semiprofessionals became politicized and radicalized, and hence joined the ranks of the activist intelligentsia.[70] The absence of institutionalized professions by no means indicated a lack of vital, professionally oriented activity; it did, however, contribute to the fragility of "professional" unity.[71]

Owing to the traditional lack of social structures, the need for social recognition, and the uncertainty of social status, the first steps toward professionalization began in the 1860s as a process of self-definition manifested in the search for organizational ties and channels of self-expression. Indeed, it is the ambiguity of status definitions and the splintered development of society and economy that make it so difficult for scholars to distinguish the professions from the intelligentsia. The difficulty can be partly overcome if one treats both as self-defined sociocultural concepts and remembers that, precisely because of the amorphous social boundaries, voluntaristic processes of self-definition were characteristic of all Russian society. The voluntarism of self-definition, combined with the lack of firm structures, also underlay the inability of educated and economic elites to develop a common outlook. In addition, because of political repression, the identities and associations that did form rarely became institutionalized. Thus the intelligentsia and "missing bourgeoisie" remained fragmented, and the professional classes failed to coalesce into a newly conscious civil society.

Attention to the lack of structure in Russian society provides a fresh view of the problem of the middle classes. It allows the historian to recognize the presence of a dynamic, independent, and enterprising middle, while explaining the late and ineffective development of a political bourgeoisie on the Western European model. The "missing bourgeoisie" of Russia was not missing because of impenetrable social barriers, lack of economic development and education, or unyielding political repression. It was missing because Russian historians have been unable to avoid Western European definitions of the middle classes—definitions that are formulated in terms of socioeconomic status, political liberalism, general education, and professionalization. If one applies alternative criteria and delimits the Russian middle in terms of self-definition—specifically, as the "autonomous" or spontaneous carving out of an identity or status, of a public or social role— then one can see that Russia's middle classes maintained a stubborn historical presence and constituted a much more significant social element than is traditionally assumed. The concept of the *raznochintsy*—a concept that acquired a broad spectrum of meanings and applications—faithfully reflected the nature of the Russian middle. As a sociocultural category, it both represented and explained the ambiguous, changeable forms of the "middle" in a variety of contexts.

Like Russian society as a whole, the middle classes were fragmented and porous; the intelligentsia, sometimes depicted as a substitute middle class, could be included in their ranks—along with a range of entrepreneurial, semieducated and educated social types (protoprofessionals, semiprofessionals, professionals, civil servants, independent tradesmen, and farmers). The indeterminate structure of Russian society accounts for the failure of the eighteenth-century nobility to impose formal limits on autocracy, the inability of the late imperial educated elites to coalesce into a civil society, and the prevailing historiographical view of Russian society as a malleable tool in the hands of an activist government—a view shared by contemporary intellectuals and high officials. So, too, the lack of structure accounts for the slow emergence of a modern society, defined in terms of economic development, occupational specialization, and professionalization. The dissipation of human resources in the form of professional skills and expertise paralleled the dissipation of economic resources among potential investors and entrepreneurs. Beyond squandered resources, the continued absence of firm structures reinforced the traditional uncertainties of social status and so further politicized and fragmented modern patterns of association resulting from industrialization and professionalization. It was this politicization and fragmentation, exacerbated by police repression, that made Russia's socioeconomic transformation so violent and revolutionary.[72]

CONCLUSION

The search for social bonds was central to the notions of a supraclass or supra*soslovie* intelligentsia and a liberal educated public— embodied in the concepts *obshchestvo* (liberal educated society) and *obshchestvennost'* (public service), standing above the interests of any particular social group and opposed to the autocracy.[73] In 1846 Belinskii spoke of "a strong need for society [*potrebnost' obshchestva*] and a striving toward society [*stremlenie k obshchestvu*]."[74] His call to overcome the distinct *soslovie* subcultures and "the spirit of separation" serves as evidence not of rigid social barriers but of a search for social and spiritual ties in an extremely fragmented society. Similarly, when historians of the professions in late imperial Russia speak of "a quest for public identity," they implicitly raise the issue of social fragmentation and its central role in the revolutionary crisis of the early twentieth century.[75] But they treat the fragmentation as a recent phenomenon, and they see in the "quest" for new identities the origins of a civil society. The fragmentation was actually a very traditional feature of Russian society; the "modern" concept of civil society, no less than the "traditional" concept of the intelligentsia, resulted from the same lack of stable structures that produced the need to invent social bonds. The notions of the intelligentsia and civil society thus represented efforts by the educated elites to establish ties beyond the family, neighborhood, and parish.[76] Regardless of how this search for public identity, and the process of self-definition that it entailed, were articulated—whether as intelligentsia, professional autonomy, or civil society—the traditional social fragmentation easily reasserted itself in the revolutionary situations of the early twentieth century.

The social splintering of the revolutionary era was more than a manifestation of crisis; it was its root cause. Thus the fragmentation of society explains the multiple images of the intelligentsia and the failure of the professions to constitute themselves as a civil society. The classless or supraclass society—whether of the intelligentsia, autocratic, or Soviet socialist variety—seemed attainable precisely because social boundaries were so porous and changeable. Like the concepts of the intelligentsia and civil society, both the notion of an autocracy above class interests and the appeal of a revolutionary socialist transformation reflected a search for sources of unity, stability, and structure—all of which were excruciatingly difficult to find in both traditional and newly industrializing Russia. Throughout the imperial period the indeterminate structures in society encouraged dynamic patterns of social and cultural self-definition. It is in this context of self-definition, then, that the utopianism and voluntarism of state and society are best understood.[77]

In his analysis of the revolutionary situation of the early twentieth century, Leopold Haimson defines the intelligentsia as a "collective representation" assumed by some members of the educated elite, who in turn formulated additional representations of identities for groups in society. These representations then played a significant role in shaping patterns of political behavior, as social groups chose to embrace identities that were meaningful for them.[78] Professor Haimson attributes these fluid and shifting social identities—which contributed significantly to the disintegration of society and the acute social conflict—to a growing discrepancy between legal status and socioeconomic realities brought on by modernization in postemancipation Russia. The history of the *raznochintsy* suggests that the fluid social identities belonged to a traditional pattern of self-definition that was not limited to the acceptance or rejection of intelligentsia-inspired representations. Moreover, the ambiguity of shifting social identities—while clearly accentuated by urban-industrial-capitalist development—was not so much the result of this development as the reason Russia failed to modernize without disintegrating into revolutionary upheaval.

Conclusion

OVER MORE THAN A CENTURY and a half, new definitions of the category *raznochintsy* appeared and existing ones evolved. If the written sources are correct—and one cannot be absolutely certain of this when speaking of language—legal definitions tended to precede societal; at the very least, there was a close correspondence between legal and societal usages. To be sure, in the postemancipation period, radical publicists and revolutionaries transformed the *raznochinets* into a sociopolitical type—a pattern that paralleled the development of the political concept of the intelligentsia and the assignment of politicocultural meanings to traditional social terminology (such as *meshchanstvo* and *obshchestvo*). Yet even these ideological usages can be identified as offshoots of earlier official definitions. In 1911 the Marxist theoretician G. V. Plekhanov still could use the category *raznochinets* in a nonideological manner to describe an educated commoner, the patriotic publicist M. P. Pogodin, who clearly was not at the forefront of the liberation movement. According to Plekhanov, only with the arrival of Chernyshevskii and Dobroliubov did the *raznochintsy* as educated commoners necessarily become progressive.[1] Indeed, there was no societal definition of the *raznochintsy* that did not also have a corresponding legal-administrative usage or antecedent. Even if it is impossible to determine the exact chronology of a particular application, there is no question that a dynamic, interactive relationship existed.

The earliest recorded definitions of the *raznochintsy* were legal, with societal usages following close behind. Beginning in the reign of Peter the Great, legislation applied the label either as an umbrella term or to indicate outsider status; these usages overlapped, varied, and evolved throughout the imperial period, appearing repeatedly in official and societal sources. The first certain legal usage (1718) defined the *raznochintsy* negatively as a lower-class element that did not belong to the peasantry or urban taxpaying community. At about the same time, Ivan Pososhkov used the category to identify nonmerchants who engaged in urban trades and who, in his view, should be excluded from these occupations. In both instances the *raznochintsy* were defined negatively as outsiders who came from a range of taxed and untaxed social categories. The exact chronological development of this usage is unclear; because the legal and societal applications were so close in time and meaning, they must be regarded as coterminous.

As a legal umbrella term, the category *raznochintsy* dated back to the reign of Peter the Great, where it referred to the lower service categories of Muscovy and imperial Russia. Following legal precedent, the authors of the urban instructions to the Legislative Commission (1767) also employed the category as an umbrella label for lesser service categories; in nineteenth-century legislation and the Digest of Laws, *raznochintsy* continued to indicate petty servicemen below the Table of Ranks.[2] The lower-class meaning of *raznochintsy* that had already appeared in legal sources of the early eighteenth century took on new significance by the mid-nineteenth century, when official and literary sources applied the term as a general designation for lower-class urban categories. It is therefore possible to identify the legal origins for societal concepts of the *raznochintsy* as lesser servicemen and later as the amorphous and diverse urban masses.

The negative category of *raznochintsy* as outsiders and its use as an umbrella designation had by 1746 acquired a new legal dimension: *raznochintsy* as non-nobles. This broad usage underwent further modification in 1755, when the legislation establishing Moscow University referred to non-noble students as *raznochintsy*. This marked the beginning of the notion of *raznochintsy* as upwardly mobile educated commoners—a notion that survived in population, and especially education, statistics of the nineteenth century. Even when applied in a purely descriptive or administrative manner, the definitions of *raznochintsy* as non-nobles remained negative. Beginning with the Legislative Commission (1767), where the various definitions of *raznochintsy* as outsiders predominated, the label most frequently indicated nonmerchants or nonmembers of the formal urban community but was also applied on occasion to non-nobles or even to new service nobles. In fact and in fiction nineteenth-century nobles used the term in a derogatory manner to describe upwardly mobile educated commoners whom they viewed as social upstarts and cultural inferiors. Officials also depicted *raznochintsy* as interlopers who legally and illegally crossed social and community boundaries. The widespread derogatory usages were consistent with legal definitions of the *raznochintsy* as nonmembers of a given community or category.

Whereas nineteenth-century literature and journalism provided prosaic depictions of *raznochintsy* as upwardly mobile educated commoners with a range of individual attributes and moral qualities, in the second quarter of the century the development of a self-conscious opposition in educated society produced positive images that implied a deliberate statement of values. At first, the *raznochintsy* appeared as participants in a liberal, socially mixed cultural milieu of progressive educated individuals; this image anticipated subsequent, more direct portrayals of the *raznochinets* as a symbol of correct thinking. Created by radical publicists and revolutionaries, the *raznochinets* as a model hero also tended to be an educated commoner, although Alexander Herzen and Nicholas Ogarev could include radical noble youths of the 1860s in the category, and the Marxist theoretician

G. V. Plekhanov could describe the aristocratic socialist Herzen as a *razno-chinets* in his thinking. The emphasis was clearly not on social origins but on political values, attitudes, and behaviors.

The sociological meaning of the category *raznochintsy* as the democratic intelligentsia of the 1860s—a meaning that has caused much confusion in subsequent histories of the revolutionary movement—was a late usage (1874) that evolved from legal and societal sources. It was no accident that liberals and radicals took the term *raznochintsy*, which in its broadest application referred to outsiders in a variety of contexts, and applied it to specific persons who sought to delimit themselves from officialdom by creating an oppositionist public role.[3] Given the weakness of autonomous structures and organization in imperial Russia, it also was no accident that educated and semieducated elites used language to construct public identities by transforming traditional social terminology into politicocultural categories. In re-creating these categories, the elites defined themselves as sociocultural entities in a society where social definitions always were indeterminate.

The chronological development of the category *raznochintsy* clearly reveals the absence of discrete stages of meaning; although it is possible to identify the introduction of new definitions at specific points in time, the added dimensions did not supersede or displace existing ones. With the exception of hereditary *raznochintsy*, petty servicemen, and the urban lower classes, definitions of the category generally implied outsider status; formally, this meant nonmembers of a given category or community. Informally, in the eighteenth century the outsider usage usually referred to nonmerchants; in the nineteenth century, to non-nobles and educated commoners. In this latter instance the *raznochinets* as outsider appeared as a social upstart, cultural inferior, or positive political hero. Neither in law nor in administrative practice nor in public opinion was the notion of *raznochintsy* as outsiders an objective category. In most cases it was a label imposed on specific subcategories of people from the outside, not an appellation that the *raznochintsy* applied to themselves. Only among radical writers in the postemancipation period did the re-created designation of *raznochinets* acquire stature in oppositionist circles and become clearly associated with progressive thinking. The outsider by exclusion had become the outsider by choice, and the language of tsarist law had become the language of sociocultural identity.

This study assumes that the category *raznochintsy*—having been formulated in a variety of legal, social, and cultural contexts—also reflected more general features of imperial Russian society. Specific interpretations of the *raznochintsy* invariably bring to the fore compatible explanations of larger historical issues. Consequently, a particular conception of the *raznochintsy* can skew the analysis of more general problems even as it exposes the limitations of alternative definitions, and especially the ways in which those definitions distort existing historiography. In urging historians to recognize and embrace the "fictive element" and "literary basis" of historical writing, Hayden White notes that "historical narrative does not *image* the things it indicates; it *calls to mind* images of the things it indicates, in the same way that a metaphor does." For this reason, "histories ought never to be read as unambiguous signs of the events they report, but rather as symbolic structures, extended metaphors that 'liken' the events reported in them to some form with which we have already become familiar in our literary culture."[4] This study thus represents an image of Russian society derived from an image of the category *raznochintsy* that in turn is based upon a variety of documentary images contained in legal, administrative, literary, journalistic, and memoir sources. Clearly, the multifaceted conceptions of the *raznochintsy* provide striking evidence of the "figurative level of historical discourse."

A central theme of this book has been the lack of structure in Russian society—a lack of structure that encouraged voluntaristic self-definition in society and arbitrariness in government, that permitted the re-creation of social categories as politicocultural concepts, and that transformed sociocultural constructs into sociological facts. The chronological evolution of the category *raznochintsy* reflected this pattern, beginning with the legal definitions of the early eighteenth century, continuing with societal representations of the *raznochintsy* as outsiders and educated commoners, and ending with the application of the label to the radical democratic intelligentsia of the 1860s. More broadly, the lack of structure was manifested in the fluidity and uncertainty of social status, in vague and inconsistent terminology, in the multiplicity of juridically defined social categories, in discrepancies between legal definitions and socioeconomic realities, and in disputes over formal registration in a particular community or category. If one accepts plasticity as a fundamental feature of Russian society, it becomes possible either to reinterpret or to explain more fully important patterns of historical development.

Social structure represents the first dimension of Russian history that needs modification in light of the phenomenon of the *raznochintsy*. Ambiguous social definitions and the absence of constituted bodies engendered an underlying uncertainty of status that was not confined to the poor and persecuted elements of society. Claimants to nobility faced repeated disappointments, and formally recognized nobles discovered that exclusive legal privileges such as the right to possess serfs were not in fact exclusive. Serfdom may have been the foundation of Russia's social and institutional order, but the boundaries of serfdom were far too indeterminate and dynamic to define in any predictable manner the structure of relations throughout society. As John Stuart Mill wrote in a famous essay on Samuel Taylor Coleridge: "All students of man and society who possess that first requisite for so difficult a study, a due sense of its difficulties, are aware that the besetting danger is not so much of embracing falsehood for truth, as of mistaking part of the truth for the whole."[5]

Ambiguity also resulted from the multidimensional nature of social categories. Imperial Russia lacked a consistent method for defining social groups. Nobility constituted a calling *(zvanie),* a rank *(chin),* a formal social category *(sostoianie),* and a status group *(soslovie).* Similarly, an individual could occupy multiple formal statuses: a serf could be a certified artist, a peasant could register as a merchant, and a *raznochinets* as outsider could belong to almost any social category. To be sure, the government aspired to delineate a systematic social order, yet its own taxation policies, service needs, and educational goals constantly created new definitions and categories, while simultaneously re-creating the old. Adding to the ambiguities of official delimitation were societal self-definition (legal and cultural) and spontaneous productive development. As the concept of the *raznochintsy* so strikingly revealed, the transformation of Muscovite ranks into imperial social categories was never fully accomplished. Imperial Russia was not a society composed of discrete chronological sediments of social formations superimposed one upon the other. It was a society with very few permanent delimitations, a society where the absence of structure—not the rigidity of traditional structures—hampered development toward a modern industrial system by dissipating resources, both material and human. Mobile, mosaic-like, and voluntaristic, Russian "society" defied persistent efforts by enlightened rulers, officials, and intellectuals to impose system, symmetry, and structure.

Once historians recognize this indeterminate structure, specific problematics of nineteenth-century society and culture become more intelligible. The dynamism of Russia's cultural elites, who burst onto the political scene in the 1860s, the birth of the concept of the intelligentsia, the "missing bourgeoisie," the absence of fully evolved free professions, and the failure of the educated public to coalesce into a civil society—all of these phenomena seem less startling when viewed in the larger context of Russian society's traditional fragmentation. In addition, Slavophile notions of pre-Petrine social harmony, the populist thesis of a "single people," and the social, political, and cultural concepts of *obshchestvo* (liberal educated society), *raznochintsy* (people of various ranks), the intelligentsia, *obshchestvennost'* (public service), and *nadklassnost'* (classlessness in the sense of a supraclass or a government above class interests)—all represented efforts to construct identities, societal structures, and even social entities in a society of fluid, porous, and uncertain boundaries.[6]

The voluntarism and utopianism of Russia's reformist and revolutionary rulers from Peter the Great, to Catherine the Great and Alexander the Great, to Lenin and Stalin—rulers who were supported by important segments of the educated and semieducated elites—resulted not from the passivity but from the amorphousness of society. It was this amorphousness that permitted and made plausible legal self-definition, the construction of broader sociocultural identities, and eventually the extreme voluntaristic belief in an ideologically defined new society composed of new human beings. Because the more objective legal and economic attributes of social categories were so varied and changeable, culture—defined as lifestyle, religion, spiritual values, and ideas—became virtually indistinguishable from social identity, at least among the educated classes. Similarly, self-definition (or "self-fashioning") represented not only adaptation but also resistance to the prevailing structures of power.

There is significant evidence to suggest that societal fragmentation existed primarily within the framework of governmental policy and formal social categories. By contrast, at the parish level and from the perspective of the church, society was integrated and coherent. Coherence also manifested itself in the spontaneous productive development that so frequently engendered violations of legal boundaries. The absence of stable social structures beyond the parish, neighborhood, or local community suggests that society became fragmented as it intersected the administrative framework; for individuals and self-conscious communities, both social integration and the fragmentation of formal institutions were equally operative. No single work can account fully for the plasticity of Russian society. It is therefore important for historians to think in terms of multiple, overlapping, and competing social frameworks—frameworks that did not necessarily possess clear legal and socioeconomic definition. From such a perspective, delimitation can be discerned in the shifting interstices where numerous legal, socioeconomic, and cultural categories and subcategories met and diverged. Contiguity obviously is crucial in delineating these categories, as is the need to distinguish between legal-administrative, socioeconomic, and cultural definitions.[7]

Usages and Meanings of the Category *Raznochintsy*

A Typology and Chronology*

I. LEGAL-ADMINISTRATIVE

    A. Outsiders or nonmembers of a given category or community

        1701: Persons who were not subordinate to the ecclesiastical domain

        1718: Lower-class nonpeasants; lower-class residents of towns who were not members of the taxed urban community *(posad)*†

        1720s to 1730s: Offspring of ecclesiastical ranks, who did not continue in the occupation of their fathers†

        1746: Non-nobles†

        1880s: Non-nobles and nonpeasants who settled in the countryside, bought allotment land, and participated in the village assembly

    B. Umbrella category or cluster of specific categories

        1724: Low-ranking civil servants, unranked administrative employees in government offices, employees of the Court and stables, and retired soldiers†

        1732: Senior officers' children (later, children of personal nobles), children of the almshouse poor, single householders, and lesser Muscovite servicemen

        1743: Tatars and tributary natives

---

*This is not a complete record of all the applications discussed in this book; it contains either the earliest or most representative examples of the most important usages and meanings.

†Eighteenth-century usage that continues in the nineteenth century.

> 1755: Non-noble students in state schools (educated commoners)†
> 1767: Foreign merchants
> 1811: Free commoners exempt from the capitation
> 1826: Non-noble civil servants and children of personal nobles
> 1846: Scholars, artists, performers, and others who were neither personal nobles nor honored citizens but who enjoyed comparable rights
> 1858: Persons of transitional status, required to register in a taxed category within a prescribed period

C. Hereditary social category (1736)†

> 1755: Taxed Siberian farmers
> 1764: Taxed residents of Siberian towns occupied in trade, crafts, or manufacturing
> 1775: Taxpayers of diverse origins (including runaways) under the authority of the Astrakhan city magistracy
> 1869: Subcategory of *raznochintsy* called "simply *raznochintsy*"

D. Church (until 1841)‡

> Nobles, petty servicemen and gentry, single householders, coachmen, "police" troops *(razsyl'shchiki),* and monastery employees

II. SOCIETAL

A. Outsiders or nonmembers of a given category or community

> 1724 (I. T. Pososhkov, *The Book of Poverty and Wealth*): Non-merchants who encroached on merchant trades
> 1767 (Instructions to the Legislative Commission): Non-merchants, nonmembers of the taxed urban community *(posad),* non-nobles, and service nobles
> 1912 (*zemstvo* statistics): Persons who bought or rented allotment land

B. Non-nobles

> 1. Derogatory (social and cultural inferiors)
>> 1767: Instructions to the Legislative Commission
>> 1830s to 1880s: Educated commoners, cultural inferiors, and unscrupulous social climbers
>> 1834 (Polevoi): Painter son of poor provincial official and déclassé noble

---

‡See chapter 3 for the subcategories applied in individual parish records.

> 1835 (Gogol): Ranked official of non-noble origins
>
> 1859 (Turgenev): Educated commoner and foreigner

2. "Neutral" descriptive usages

> 1866 (Ostrovskii): Upwardly mobile educated commoners

C. Social milieu and right-thinking intellectuals

> 1846 (Belinskii): One element in a socially mixed company of progressive and enlightened individuals
>
> 1860s (Herzen and Ogarev): Socially mixed, forward-looking segment of society that would lead the democratic struggle
>
> 1874 (Mikhailovskii): Non-noble, radical democratic intelligentsia of the 1860s
>
> 1914 (Plekhanov and Lenin): Bourgeois-democratic element that dominated the revolutionary movement prior to the proletarian stage

D. Umbrella category or cluster of specific categories

> 1767 (Instructions to the Legislative Commission):
> Muscovite categories of lesser servicemen
> Single householders (urban and rural)
> Non-noble or unranked state officials and retired soldiers
> 1862 (Pomialovskii): Lower urban classes

List of Abbreviations

AHR	*American Historical Review*
CASS	*Canadian-American Slavic Studies*
ch.	*chast'*
CMRS	*Cahiers du Monde russe et soviétique*
d.	*delo*
DNGUAK	*Deistviia Nizhegorodskoi gubernskoi uchenoi arkhivnoi komissii*
ES	*Entsiklopedicheskii slovar' F. A. Brokgauz–I. A. Efron*
FOG	*Forschungen zur osteuropäischen Geschichte*
f.	*fond*
GARF	Gosudarstvennyi arkhiv Rossiiskoi Federatsii
IZ	*Istoricheskie zapiski*
JGO	*Jahrbücher für Geschichte Osteuropas*
JMH	*Journal of Modern History*
KLE	*Kratkaia literaturnaia entsiklopediia*
kn.	*kniga*
l. (ll.)	*list (listy)*
op.	*opis'*
PSZ	*Polnoe sobranie zakonov Rossiiskoi imperii*

PVM	*Prikazy voennogo ministra*
RGADA	Rossiiskii gosudarstvennyi arkhiv drevnikh aktov
RGIA	Rossiiskii gosudarstvennyi istoricheskii arkhiv
RGVIA	Rossiiskii gosudarstvennyi voenno-istoricheskii arkhiv
RI	*Russkii invalid*
RR	*Russian Review*
RS	*Russkaia starina*
SEER	*Slavonic and East European Review*
SIRIO	*Sbornik Imperatorskogo Rossiiskogo istoricheskogo obshchestva*
SR	*Slavic Review*
st.	*stat'ia*
SZ	*Svod zakonov Rossiiskoi imperii*
t.	*tom*
TPlUAK	*Trudy Poltavskoi uchenoi arkhivnoi kommissii*
TPUAK	*Trudy Permskoi uchenoi arkhivnoi kommissii*
TsGIAgM	Tsentral'nyi gosudarstvennyi istoricheskii arkhiv goroda Moskvy
TVUAK	*Trudy Vladimirskoi uchenoi arkhivnoi kommissii*
ZMVD	*Zhurnal ministerstva vnutrennikh del*
ZRGUAK	*Zhurnal Riazanskoi gubernskoi uchenoi arkhivnoi kommissii*

CHAPTER 1: HISTORIOGRAPHY AND PROBLEMATICS

1. V. O. Kliuchevskii, *Istoriia soslovii v Rossii,* reprinted in *Sochineniia v deviati tomakh,* vol. 6 (Moscow, 1989).

2. Gregory L. Freeze, "The *Soslovie* (Estate) Paradigm in Russian Social History," *AHR* 91 (1986): 11–36.

3. V. V. Vinogradov has traced the origins of the word *soslovie* back to the church literary style of the fourteenth to sixteenth centuries. V. V. Vinogradov "Vozniknovenie i razvitie slova soslovie," *Etimologiia 1966* (Moscow, 1968): 133–37.

4. Marc Raeff, *The Well-Ordered Police State: Social and Institutional Change through Law in the Germanies and Russia, 1600–1800* (New Haven, 1983); Christoph Schmidt, "Über die Bezeichnung der Stände *(sostojanie-soslovie)* in Russland seit dem 18. Jahrhundert," *JGO* 38 (1990): 199–211.

5. Richard Pipes, *Russia under the Old Regime* (New York, 1974).

6. Leopold H. Haimson, "Civil War and the Problem of Social Identities in Early Twentieth-Century Russia," in Diane P. Koenker, William G. Rosenberg, and Ronald Grigor Suny, eds., *Party, State, and Society in the Russian Civil War: Explorations in Social History* (Bloomington, Ind., 1989), 24–47.

7. Alfred J. Rieber, *Merchants and Entrepreneurs in Imperial Russia* (Chapel Hill, N.C., 1982).

8. Edith W. Clowes, Samuel D. Kassow, and James L. West, eds., *Between Tsar and People: Educated Society and the Quest for Public Identity in Late Imperial Russia* (Princeton, 1991).

9. For a recent treatment, see Michael Confino, "Servage russe, esclavage américain (note critique)," *Annales Économies, Sociétés, Civilisation* 45 (1990): 1119–41. See chapter 4.

10. Raeff, *The Well-Ordered Police State;* Hans-Joachim Torke, *Die Staatsbedingte Gesellschaft im Moskauer Reich: Zar und Zemlja in der altrussischen Herrschaftsverfassung 1613–1789* (Leiden, 1974).

11. Marc Raeff touches on this in *Origins of the Russian Intelligentsia: The Eighteenth-Century Nobility* (New York, 1966). See also Michael Confino, *Domaines et seigneurs en Russie vers la fin du XVIIIe siècle* (Paris, 1963); idem, *Société et mentalités collectives en Russie sous l'ancien régime* (Paris, 1991).

12. On utopia building in the early Soviet period, see Richard Stites, *Revolutionary Dreams: Utopian Vision and Experimental Life in the Russian Revolution* (New York, 1989).

13. Christopher Becker, "*Raznochintsy:* The Development of the Word and of the Concept," *SR* 18 (1959): 63–74.

14. G. N. Vul'fson, "Poniatie 'raznochinets' v XVIII–pervoi polovine XIX veka," in *Ocherki istorii narodov Povolzh'ia i Priural'ia,* vypusk 1 (Kazan, 1967), 107–24.

15. This is precisely the approach of M. M. Shtrange, who extends the definition of democratic intelligentsia to include not only revolutionaries, but also that segment of the educated elite which was non-noble in origin. M. M. Shtrange, *Demokraticheskaia intelligentsiia Rossii v XVIII veke* (Moscow, 1965).

16. I. B. Sidorova, "Polozhenie raznochintsev v russkom obshchestve (XVIII–pervaia polovina XIX v.)" (kand. diss., Kazan, 1982) and avtoreferat kand. diss.; idem, "Kto takie raznochintsy? (Polemika v literature)"; and idem, "Otrazhenie nuzhd raznochintsev v gorodskikh nakazakh 1767 goda," in *Voprosy otechestvennoi, zarubezhnoi istorii, literaturovedeniia i iazykoznaniia,* ch. 1 (Kazan, 1981), 24–33 and 33–40.

17. The reader is directed to the bibliography for a more complete listing of the large number of works that indirectly examine the *raznochintsy.*

18. For some of the literary treatments, see Albert Kaspin, "Ostrovsky and the Raznochinets in His Plays" (Ph.D. diss., University of California, Berkeley, 1957).

19. Elise Kimerling Wirtschafter, *From Serf to Russian Soldier* (Princeton, 1990), 32–40; idem, "Social Misfits: Veterans and Soldiers' Families in Servile Russia," *The Journal of Military History* (forthcoming, July 1995); *Materialy dlia geografii i statistiki Rossii: Smolenskaia guberniia* (St. Petersburg, 1862), 157–61. For a literary depiction, see Sviachenko, "Khronika zhizni soldatskogo syna Dmitriia Zhurby," *Sovremennik* 110, no. 9 (September 1865): 33–113; no. 10 (October 1865): 283–361.

20. S. M. Troitskii, *Russkii absoliutizm i dvorianstvo v XVIII v.: Formirovanie biurokratii* (Moscow, 1974); P. A. Zaionchkovskii, *Pravitel'stvennyi apparat samoderzhavnoi Rossii v XIX v.* (Moscow, 1978); Walter M. Pintner, "The Evolution of Civil Officialdom, 1755–1855," in Walter McKenzie Pintner and Don Karl Rowney, eds., *Russian Officialdom: The Bureaucratization of Russian Society from the Seventeenth to the Twentieth Century* (Chapel Hill, N.C., 1980), 190–226; idem, "Civil Officialdom and the Nobility in the 1850s," in ibid., 227–49; idem, "The Russian Higher Civil Service on the Eve of the 'Great Reforms,' " *Journal of Social History* (Spring 1975): 55–68; idem, "The Social Characteristics of the Early Nineteenth-Century Russian Bureaucracy," *SR* 29 (1970): 429–43; Helju Aulik Bennett, "*Chiny, Ordeny,* and Officialdom," in Pintner and Rowney, eds., *Russian Officialdom,* 162–89; idem, "Evolution of the Meanings of *Chin:* An Introduction to the Russian Institution of Rank Ordering and Niche Assignment from the Time of Peter the Great's Table of Ranks to the Russian Revolution," *California Slavic Studies* 10 (1977): 1–43; idem, "The *Chin* System and the *Raznochintsy* in the Government of Alexander III, 1881–1894," (Ph.D.

diss., University of California, Berkeley, 1971); Hans-Joachim Torke, "Das russische Beamtentum in der ersten Hälfte des 19. Jahrhunderts," *FOG* 13 (1967): 7–345, esp. 101–32.

21. L. E. Shepelev, *Otmenennye istoriei—chiny, zvaniia i tituly v Rossiiskoi imperii* (Leningrad, 1977), 25–33; Zaionchkovskii, *Pravitel'stvennyi apparat,* 26, 41–42, 137.

22. At the same time that the government raised formal educational requirements for promotion, it also expanded the educational opportunities available for sons of poor office workers. Harold A. McFarlin, "The Extension of the Imperial Russian Civil Service to the Lowest Office Workers: The Creation of the Chancery Clerkship, 1827–1833," *Russian History* 1 (1974): 1–17; idem, "Recruitment Norms for the Russian Civil Service in 1833: The Chancery Clerkship," *Societas—A Review of Social History* 3 (Winter 1973): 61–73; Pintner, "The Russian Higher Civil Service"; idem, "The Evolution of Civil Officialdom" and "Civil Officialdom and the Nobility" (see n. 20 above).

23. M. Vladimirskii-Budanov, *Gosudarstvo i narodnoe obrazovanie v Rossii XVIII v.,* vol. 1 (Iaroslavl, 1874; reprint, Cambridge, 1972); S. V. Rozhdestvenskii, *Istoricheskii obzor deiatel'nosti ministerstva narodnogo prosveshcheniia, 1802–1902* (St. Petersburg, 1902); Ben Eklof, *Russian Peasant Schools: Officialdom, Village Culture, and Popular Pedagogy, 1861–1914* (Berkeley, 1986).

24. Garrison schools for sons of soldiers first opened in 1732 and continued to operate in modified forms until 1856, when the legal category of "soldiers' children" *(soldatskie deti, kantonisty)* was abolished. Elise Kimerling [Wirtschafter], "Soldiers' Children, 1719–1856: A Study of Social Engineering in Imperial Russia," *FOG* 30 (1982): 61–136.

25. M. D. Kurmacheva, *Krepostnaia intelligentsiia Rossii: Vtoraia polovina XVIII–nachalo XIX veka* (Moscow, 1983).

26. V. R. Leikina-Svirskaia, "Formirovanie raznochinskoi intelligentsii v Rossii v 40-kh godakh XIX v.," *Istoriia SSSR* (1958): 83–104; idem, *Intelligentsiia v Rossii vo vtoroi polovine XIX veka* (Moscow, 1971); Vladimirskii-Budanov, *Gosudarstvo i narodnoe obrazovanie;* Rozhdestvenskii, *Istoricheskii obzor;* Gregory L. Freeze, *The Parish Clergy in Nineteenth-Century Russia: Crisis, Reform, Counter-Reform* (Princeton, 1983), 319–29; Nancy Mandelker Frieden, *Russian Physicians in an Era of Reform and Revolution, 1856–1905* (Princeton, 1981), 3–52; Alfred J. Rieber, "The Rise of Engineers in Russia," *CMRS* 31 (1990): 539–68; Etta L. Perkins, "Mobility in the Art Profession in Tsarist Russia," *JGO* 39 (1991): 225–33; idem, "Careers in Art: An Exploration in the Social History of Post-Petrine Russia" (Ph.D. dissertation, Indiana University, 1980).

27. With the establishment of the Military Orphanage in the reign of Paul, the government maintained separate sections for nobles' and officers' children. Even so, capable soldiers' sons could gain admittance. Kimerling [Wirtschafter], "Soldiers' Children."

28. See chapter 6 for a detailed discussion of the phenomenon of the *raznochintsy* in the development of the intelligentsia and professions.

29. For a superior start see Otto W. Müller, *Intelligencija: Untersuchungen zur Geschichte eines politischen Schlagwortes* (Frankfurt, 1971). Other noteworthy studies include Alan Pollard, "The Russian Intelligentsia: The Mind of Russia," *California Slavic Studies* 3 (1964): 1–32; S. I. Khasanova, "K voprosu ob izuchenii intelligentsii

dorevoliutsionnoi Rossii," in G. N. Vul'fson, ed., *Revoliutsionno-osvoboditel'noe dvizhenie v XIX–XX vv. v Povolzh'e i Priural'e* (Kazan, 1974), 37–54; and the essays contained in Richard Pipes, ed., *The Russian Intelligentsia* (New York, 1961).

30. Leikina-Svirskaia, "Formirovanie"; idem, *Intelligentsiia v Rossii;* N. M. Pirumova, *Zemskaia intelligentsiia i ee rol' v obshchestvennoi bor'be* (Moscow, 1986); V. S. Antonov, "K voprosu o sotsial'nom sostave i chislennosti revoliutsionerov '70-kh godov," *Obshchestvennoe dvizhenie v poreformennoi Rossii: Sbornik* (Moscow, 1965), 336–43; Clowes, Kassow, and West, eds., *Between Tsar and People;* Rieber, "The Rise of Engineers"; Perkins, "Mobility in the Art Profession"; idem, "Careers in Art"; Michael Pushkin, "The Professions and the Intelligentsia in Nineteenth-century Russia," *University of Birmingham Historical Journal* 12 (1969–1970): 72–79; Richard S. Wortman, *The Development of a Russian Legal Consciousness* (Chicago, 1976). Two recent studies that do not begin with the history of a state school are Louise McReynolds, *The News under Russia's Old Regime: The Development of a Mass-Circulation Press* (Princeton, 1991) and William E. Pomeranz, "Justice from Underground: The History of the Underground *Advokatura,*" *RR* 52 (1993): 321–40.

31. A fine recent example is Irina Paperno, *Chernyshevsky and the Age of Realism: A Study in the Semiotics of Behavior* (Stanford, Calif., 1988).

32. Shtrange, *Demokraticheskaia intelligentsiia v Rossii;* Leikina-Svirskaia, "Formirovanie"; idem, *Intelligentsiia v Rossii.* Following Shtrange is Michel Laran, "La Première Génération de l''intelligentsia' roturière en Russie (1750–1780)," *Revue d'histoire moderne et contemporaine* 13 (1966): 137–56.

33. M. A. Rakhmatullin, *Krest'ianskoe dvizhenie v velikorusskikh guberniiakh v 1826–1857 gg.* (Moscow, 1990), 83–89; idem, "K voprosu o vliianii raznochinnykh elementov goroda na krest'ianskoe dvizhenie v 20-e gody XIX v.," in *Goroda feodal'noi Rossii: Sbornik statei pamiati N. V. Ustiugova* (Moscow, 1966), 547–58; idem, "Soldaty v krest'ianskom dvizhenii 20-kh godov XIX v.," in *Voprosy voennoi istorii* (Moscow, 1965), 351–58; M. F. Prokhorov, "Vliianie gorodskikh nizov i raznochintsev na klassovuiu bor'bu krest'ian Rossii v seredine XVIII v.," in *Russkii gorod (issledovaniia i materialy)* vypusk 8 (Moscow, 1986), 132–54.

34. Daniel R. Brower, *Training the Nihilists: Education and Radicalism in Tsarist Russia* (Ithaca, N.Y., 1975); idem, "The Problem of the Russian Intelligentsia," *SR* 26 (1967): 638–47; Michael Confino, "On Intellectuals and Intellectual Traditions in Eighteenth- and Nineteenth-Century Russia," *Daedalus* 101 (1972): 117–49. Cf. Michael Pushkin, "*Raznochintsy* in the University: Government Policy and Social Change in Nineteenth-Century Russia," *International Review of Social History* 26 (1981): 25–65; Robert J. Brym, "A Note on the *Raznochintsy,*" *Journal of Social History* 10 (1976–1977): 354–59.

35. Martin Malia goes further than both Brower and Confino in questioning the relationship between lower-class origins and the radicalism of the 1860s, insisting that the radical intelligentsia had formed by the 1840s and that its origins were intellectual. Martin Malia, "What Is the Intelligentsia?" in Pipes, ed., *The Russian Intelligentsia,* 1–18.

36. Pollard, "The Russian Intelligentsia," 1–32; D. N. Ovsianiko-Kulikovskii, *Istoriia russkoi intelligentsii,* ch. 2 (St. Petersburg, 1909), 83–99.

37. B. N. Mironov, *Russkii gorod v 1740–1860-e gody* (Leningrad, 1990).

38. N. B. Golikova, *Ocherki po istorii gorodov Rossii kontsa XVII–nachala XVIII v.* (Moscow, 1982); E. V. Anisimov, *Podatnaia reforma Petra I* (Leningrad, 1982); A. A.

Kizevetter, *Posadskaia obshchina Rossii XVIII st.* (Moscow, 1903); M. M. Gromyko, "Razvitie Tiumeni kak remeslenno-torgovogo tsentra v XVIII v.," in *Goroda feodal'-noi Rossii*, 397–409; Mironov, *Russkii gorod;* P. G. Ryndziunskii, *Gorodskoe grazhdanstvo doreformennoi Rossii* (Moscow, 1958); Manfred Hildermeier, *Bürgertum und Stadt in Russland, 1760–1860: Rechtliche Lage und soziale Struktur* (Cologne, 1986); Gilbert Rozman, *Urban Networks in Russia, 1750–1800, and Premodern Periodization* (Princeton, 1976); Bernd Knabe, "Die Struktur des russischen Posadgemeindes und das Katalog der Beschwerden und Forderungen der Kaufmannschaft, 1762–1767," *FOG* 22 (1975).

39. Anisimov, *Podatnaia reforma;* Mironov, *Russkii gorod;* Rozman, *Urban Networks.*

40. See chapter 3.

41. Kizevetter, *Posadskaia obshchina;* Ryndziunskii, *Gorodskoe grazhdanstvo;* Hildermeier, *Bürgertum und Stadt.*

42. On the category "trading peasants," see chapter 4.

43. Anisimov states this very clearly. Anisimov, *Podatnaia reforma.*

44. It is worth noting that *raznyi*—in addition to meaning "various," "different," and "diverse"—also means "other" *(drugoi)*. Hence the meaning of *raznochintsy* or "persons of diverse ranks" is equivalent to "persons of other ranks," i.e., outsiders. Vladimir Dal', *Tolkovyi slovar' Velikorusskogo iazyka*, 4 vols. (St. Petersburg, 1912).

45. See chapters 2 and 5.

46. John P. LeDonne, *Ruling Russia: Politics and Administration in the Age of Absolutism, 1762–1796* (Princeton, 1984).

47. Andreas Kappeler, *Russland als Vielvölkerreich: Entstehung, Geschichte, Zerfall* (Munich, 1992). More specialized studies that address these issues include Andreas Kappeler, *Russlands Erste Nationalitäten: Das Zarenreich und die Völker der Mittleren Wolga vom 16. bis 19. Jahrhundert* (Cologne-Vienna, 1982); Robert H. McNeal, *Tsar and Cossack, 1855–1914* (London, 1987); Michael Khodarkovsky, *Where Two Worlds Met: The Russian State and the Kalmyk Nomads, 1600–1771* (Ithaca, N.Y., 1992); R. N. Pullat, ed., *Problemy istoricheskoi demografii SSSR: Sbornik statei* (Tallin, 1977); "Pravo sostoianiia raznykh klassov narodonaseleniia Bessarabskoi oblasti," *ZMVD*, ch. 3 (1843): 48–64.

48. Jews were forbidden to live in the capitals of St. Petersburg and Moscow, except in special circumstances. A. S. Myl'nikov, "Vykhodtsy iz slavianskikh zemel' v Peterburge (XVIII–nachalo XIX v.)," in *Peterburg i guberniia: Istoriko-etnograficheskie issledovaniia* (Leningrad, 1989), 69–80; N. V. Iukhneva, "Evrei Peterburga v period reform 1860-kh godov: Sotsial'no-demograficheskaia kharakteristika," in ibid., 81–112; idem, "Peterburg: Mnogonatsional'naia stolitsa," in idem, *Staryi Peterburg: Istoriko-etnograficheskie issledovaniia* (Leningrad, 1982), 7–51.

49. The memoirs of N. N. Shipov, a serf entrepreneur (and hence a kind of informal *raznochinets*) and V. N. Karpov, a *raznochinets*-entrepreneur with the degree of artist *(stepen' khudozhnika)*, suggest the full range of integrative economic possibilities, including multilingualism. *V. N. Karpov, Vospominaniia—N. N. Shipov, Istoriia moei zhizni*, reprint (Moscow-Leningrad, 1933).

50. Gromyko, "Razvitie Tiumeni," 397–409 (see n. 38 above). Ia. E. Vodarskii defines the Siberian *raznochintsy* differently, both as untaxed and separate from retired military personnel. Ia. E. Vodarskii, "Chislennost' russkogo naseleniia Sibiri

v XVII–XVIII vv.," in *Russkoe naselenie Pomor'ia i Sibiri (period feodalizma)* (Moscow, 1973), 194–213.

51. Mironov, *Russkii gorod,* 107–8.

52. Daniel R. Brower, *The Russian City between Tradition and Modernity, 1850–1900* (Berkeley, 1990); idem, "Estate, Class, and Community: Urbanization and Revolution in Late Tsarist Russia," *The Carl Beck Papers in Russian and East European Studies,* paper no. 302 (Pittsburgh, 1983).

53. Brower, "Estate, Class, and Community," 17–20.

54. Clowes, Kassow, and West, eds., *Between Tsar and People;* Alan Kimball, "Russian Civil Society and Political Crisis in the Era of Great Reforms, 1859–1863" (unpublished manuscript, Eugene, Ore., 1989).

55. On the connection between self-fashioning (i.e., the crafting of a public role) and power relationships, see Stephen Jay Greenblatt, *Renaissance Self-Fashioning: From More to Shakespeare* (Chicago, 1980). Greenblatt actually argues against the notion that human autonomy plays a role in constructing identities; rather, he sees the human subject as the ideological product of the relations of power in a particular society (p. 256). What Greenblatt fails to consider, however, is the possibility that self-fashioning might constitute successful resistance to or avoidance of imposed structures, if not in the case of renowned individuals, then perhaps in the case of the anonymous and—from the state's point of view—undergoverned general population (the so-called masses). On the conscious creating of behavior *(zhiznetvorchestvo)* in Russian romanticism of the prereform period, see the essays in Alexander D. Nakhimovsky and Alice Stone Nakhimovsky, eds., *The Semiotics of Russian Cultural History* (Ithaca, N.Y., 1985).

56. Roger Chartier, "Intellectual History or Sociocultural History? The French Trajectories," in Dominick LaCapra and Steven L. Kaplan, eds., *Modern European Intellectual History: Reappraisals and New Perspectives* (Ithaca, N.Y., 1982), 41–42.

57. Ibid.; also Dominick LaCapra, "Rethinking Intellectual History and Reading Texts," in ibid., 47–85.

58. Clifford Geertz, *Local Knowledge: Further Essays in Interpretive Anthropology* (New York, 1983), 34; idem, *The Interpretation of Cultures* (New York, 1973).

CHAPTER 2: THE LEGAL FRAMEWORK

1. Wirtschafter, *Russian Soldier,* 3–25.

2. Official sources usually referred to the occupational component of status as *zvanie* (calling), but here, too, the usages were not always consistent, so that the status of hereditary noble (generally thought of as *soslovie*) could be called the *dvorianskoe zvanie* regardless of occupation. This illustrates the importance of *zvanie* (occupation, profession, service function) to the concept *soslovie.* For illustration, see "Gorodskie vybory v S.-Peterburge," *ZMVD* (May 1850): 227–68; "Gorodskie vybory v S.-Peterburge i otchet S.-Peterburgskoi obshchei dumy," *ZMVD* (April 1856): 131–61; "Ob ustroistve remeslennogo sosloviia i remeslennoi promyshlennosti," *ZMVD* (November 1853): otdelenie 2, 1–40.

3. See chapter 3. See also Hildermeier, *Bürgertum und Stadt;* Freeze, "The *Soslovie* (Estate) Paradigm."

4. Daniel Morrison, " 'Trading Peasants' and Urbanization in Eighteenth

Century Russia: The Central Industrial Region" (Ph.D. diss., Columbia University, 1981); Hildermeier, *Bürgertum und Stadt*, 137–51; Mironov, *Russkii gorod*, 101–4, 170–77; Anisimov, *Podatnaia reforma*, 197–204; Ryndziunskii, *Gorodskoe grazhdanstvo*, 61–96; Kizevetter, *Posadskaia obshchina*, 17–24. Registered members of craft guilds also could be serfs. A. I. Kopanev, *Naselenie Peterburga v pervoi polovine XIX veka* (Moscow-Leningrad, 1957), 30–39.

5. *Polnoe sobranie zakonov Rossiiskoi imperii* (hereafter *PSZ*): 1st ser. (I) 1649–1825, 45 vols. (St. Petersburg, 1830); 2d ser. (II) 1825–1881, 55 vols. (St. Petersburg, 1830–1884); 3d ser. (III) 1881–1913, 33 vols. (St. Petersburg, 1885–1916). Here *PSZ* (II), vol. 3, no. 2153. The rules on promotion in service illustrate this point very clearly. Wirtschafter, *Russian Soldier*, 40–53; Zaionchkovskii, *Pravitel'stvennyi apparat*, 24–56.

6. Alfred J. Rieber, "The Sedimentary Society," in Clowes, Kassow, and West, eds., *Between Tsar and People*, 343–66.

7. The serf millionaires represent the most dramatic example. For a recent discussion of the issue as it pertains to towns, see Hildermeier, *Bürgertum und Stadt*. Similarly, discussions in the secret Committee of 6 December 1826 addressed the lack of correspondence between rank *(chin)* and office *(dolzhnost')*. See *Sbornik imperatorskogo Rossiiskogo istoricheskogo obshchestva*, hereafter *SIRIO*, 148 vols. (St. Petersburg 1867–1916), 74:248–487; 90:359–607.

8. *PSZ* (I), vol. 5, no. 3169. For a similar usage, see *PSZ*, vol. 8, no. 5319. Kizevetter defines the *posad* as the registered commercial and manufacturing community of taxpayers dating back to the seventeenth century. Membership was tied to residence and participation in payment of the *tiaglo* (later the capitation), so that only taxpaying members of the community could trade within its boundaries. Kizevetter, *Posadskaia obshchina*, iii–v, 1–4, 27–30. Legislation from 1699 and 1711, which some historians cite to define the *raznochintsy*, did not employ the term in the actual text of the decrees. One must assume that these usages, which appeared in the title of the laws, originated with the nineteenth-century editors; they included in the category bell ringers *(zvonari)*, coachmen, gunners/cannon founders *(pushkari)*, gatekeepers *(vorotniki)*, and artisans who were not yet registered members of the urban community. L. O. Ploshinskii, *Gorodskoe ili srednee sostoianie russkogo naroda v ego istoricheskom razvitii, ot nachala Rusi do noveishikh vremen* (St. Petersburg, 1852), 168. Becker makes this point in "Raznochintsy," 64 n. 3. On Speranskii's role in generating titles for the *Polnoe sobranie zakonov*, see Marc Raeff, *Michael Speransky: Statesman of Imperial Russia, 1772–1839* (The Hague, 1957), 320–44.

9. Citing an earlier decree of 1718, the 1720 law suggested that the *raznochintsy* category included all manner of military servicemen *(s polkovoi i gorodovoi sluzheb)*, dragoons and soldiers, musketeers *(strel'tsy)*, Cossacks, inhabitants of Cossack villages *(stanichnikovye)*, Turkic nobles *(murzy)*, and Tatars. *PSZ* (I), 6:3501. The *odnodvortsy* occupied a distinct middle position in Russian society. Like peasants, they paid the capitation and were subject to conscription, though their term of service was only fifteen years; like nobles, they were permitted to own serfs. Thomas Esper characterizes the *odnodvortsy* as downwardly mobile nobles who persistently sought to regain their former status. Thomas Esper, "The Odnodvortsy and the Russian Nobility," *SEER* 45, no. 104 (1967): 124–34. On the *iasak* tax, see LeDonne, *Ruling Russia*, 281, 289; Marc Raeff, *Siberia and the Reforms of 1822* (Seattle, 1956), 91–96;

Kappeler, *Russlands Erste Nationalitäten*. On the numerous Muscovite categories of servitors, see Kliuchevskii, *Istoriia soslovii;* Richard Hellie, *Enserfment and Military Change in Muscovy* (Chicago, 1971); and John L. H. Keep, *Soldiers of the Tsar: Army and Society in Russia, 1462–1874* (New York, 1985).

10. Later laws also referred to *bobyli* and runaway peasants as *raznochintsy. PSZ* (I), vol. 8, no. 6858; vol. 10, no. 7438; vol. 12, no. 9061; vol. 17, no. 12605. On the *bobyli* and *iamshchiki,* see Jerome Blum, *Lord and Peasant in Russia from the Ninth to the Nineteenth Century* (Princeton, 1961), 168, 240–42, 500–501; Keep, *Soldiers of the Tsar,* 105. For the *kuplennye,* see Richard Hellie, *Slavery in Russia, 1450–1725* (Chicago, 1982), 46–48, 67–71, 238, 343–53.

11. Another decree of 1746 named merchants; single householders and state peasants; and "other *raznochintsy*" as categories liable for the capitation. RGADA, f. 291, op. 1, ch. 1, d. 2618; *PSZ* (I), vol. 12, no. 9256. On the *pod'iachie,* see Borivoj Plavsic, "Seventeenth-Century Chanceries and their Staffs," in Pintner and Rowney, eds., *Russian Officialdom,* 19–45.

12. *PSZ* (I), vol. 14, no. 10521.

13. *PSZ* (I), vol. 12, no. 9267; vol. 33, no. 26469.

14. *PSZ* (I), vol. 20, nos. 14348, 14412. Kizevetter, *Posadskaia obshchina,* 38–45, 74–75.

15. See also *PSZ* (I), vol. 14, no. 10242; *PSZ* (II), vol. 3, no. 2463; vol. 7, no. 5791; vol. 9, no. 6788.

16. *PSZ* (I), vol. 7, no. 4474. The specific positions mentioned either fell below the Table of Ranks (e.g., *podkantseliarist*) or did not confer noble status *(sekretar').* According to Pintner, the designations for unranked clerical employees included in descending order *kantseliarist, podkantseliarist, kopeist,* and *pisar'.* (See Pintner, "The Social Characteristics," 432 n. 6.) It is therefore unclear whether the law treated the *kopeisty* and *pisari* as *raznochintsy.* The wording of the law suggests not, but logic would indicate that they also must have been included. The use of the term *pod'iachie* is difficult to explain except as a holdover from the seventeenth century. Muscovite terminology often appeared in laws of the earlier eighteenth century. On unranked employees of the civil service, see McFarlin, "The Extension of the Imperial Russian Civil Service"; idem, "Recruitment Norms."

17. PSZ (I), vol. 7, no. 4565.

18. *PSZ* (I), vol. 26, no. 19692. *Chinovniki* were officials who possessed a rank *(chin)* in the Table of Ranks.

19. The categories of urban inhabitants considered "citizens" *(grazhdane)* included merchants registered in a guild, townspeople *(meshchane)* or members of the taxpaying urban community *(posadskie)*, artisans *(remeslenniki)* or members of craft guilds *(tsekhovye)*, free persons *(vol'nye liudi)* ascribed to towns in some provinces, and laborers *(rabochie liudi)*. The notion of "citizen" in no way implied political rights. *Svod zakonov Rossiiskoi imperii,* 15 vols. (St. Petersburg, 1857), hereafter *SZ* (1857), t. 9, kn. 1, razdel 3, glava 1, otdelenie 1, st. 423–25; glava 3, st. 554.

20. Mikhail Chulkov, *Slovar' iuridicheskii ili svod rossiiskikh uzakonenii vremiannykh uchrezhdenii, suda i rasprava,* 5 vols. (Moscow, 1792–1796) 2:223.

21. *PSZ* (I), vol. 8, no. 5319; Kizevetter, *Posadskaia obshchina,* 27–30. This usage is particularly pronounced in the instructions to Catherine's Legislative Commission. Kievan law and society also included a category of free, déclassé persons in need of assistance, the *izgoi,* who existed outside the recognized status groups or

ranks, but who could achieve *reclassement* through service or commerce. Marc Szeftel, "La Condition juridique des déclassés dans la Russie ancienne," *Archives d'histoire du droit oriental* 2 (Brussels, 1938): 431–42.

22. See chapter 4.

23. *PSZ* (I), vol. 14, no. 10346. Again suggesting the non-noble meaning, a manifesto of 1763 established classes at Moscow University, the Academy of Sciences, and the Kazan gymnasium to train underaged *raznochintsy* and children of state officials for service. Noble youths were to receive training for the civil service in the cadets corps. *PSZ* (I), vol. 16, no. 11988.

24. In Becker's view, this legislation marks the beginning of a particular educational usage of the term *raznochintsy* as "commoner student," but subsequent laws establishing the St. Petersburg Practical Technological Institute (1828) and the Kherson School of Commercial Navigation (1834) instructed town councils to select students from merchants of the third guild, townspeople, members of craft guilds, and *raznochintsy*. Becker, "*Raznochintsy*," 66–67; *PSZ* (II), vol. 3, no. 2463; vol. 9, no. 6788.

25. *PSZ* (I), vol. 9, no. 6858; vol. 17, no. 12605. This usage also was common in the urban instructions to the Legislative Commission.

26. *SZ* (1857) t. 2, ch. 1, kn. 2, razdel 1, st. 415.

27. Müller, *Intelligencija*.

28. On the *Polizeistaat*, see Raeff, *The Well-Ordered Police State*.

29. Kliuchevskii, *Istoriia soslovii*; Vinogradov, "Vozniknovenie i razvitie slova soslovie"; Schmidt, "Über die Bezeichnung"; Freeze, "The *Soslovie* (Estate) Paradigm."

30. On implementation of the capitation, see Anisimov, *Podatnaia reforma*; V. M. Kabuzan, *Narodonaselenie Rossii v XVIII–pervoi polovine XIX v. (Po materialam revizii)* (Moscow, 1963).

31. According to Vul'fson, all types of *raznochintsy* had become exempt from the capitation by the 1860s; this conclusion does not, however, take into account all usages and definitions. Although the descendants of the taxed *raznochintsy* who were ascribed to urban, craft guild, or peasant communities would have merged with those groups, new *raznochinnye* elements, not always untaxed, were continually being added. Vul'fson, "Poniatie," 111–13; Sidorova, "Otrazhenie," 36–37. *PSZ* (I), vol. 6, nos. 3624, 3747, 3817; vol. 7, nos. 4533, 4565, 4566, 5002; vol. 9, nos. 6858, 7006; vol. 12, nos. 9061, 9267, 9332, 9383. Census data also treated the *raznochintsy* as untaxed. "Vedomost' o narodonaselenii Rossii za 1851 god, po 9 narodnoi perepisi," *ZMVD* (November 1853): otdelenie 3, 61–76.

32. See the 1729 *Instruktsiia komisara ot zemli*, which was based on decrees from 1724 and 1725. The instructions are available on microfilm from General Microfilm Company in *Eighteenth-Century Russian Publications* (Watertown, Mass., n.d.).

33. The coachmen *(iamshchiki)* drove state horses maintained at official postal stations. Free from taxation and conscription, the *iamshchiki* should not be confused with urban or domestic serf coachmen. *PSZ* (I), vol. 14, no. 10449.

34. The 1727 decree exempted them from palace and armory work. *PSZ* (I), vol. 7, no. 5002.

35. *PSZ* (II), vol. 9, no. 6746.

36. On the *raznochintsy* as a lower-class category, see Kopanev, *Naselenie Peter-burga*, 52.

37. *PSZ* (I), vol. 6, no. 3817 (1721); vol. 7, no. 4145 (1723). Similarly, the term also referred to individuals who had left the urban community in order to avoid taxes and had managed, allegedly because of debt, to register as peasants or mortgagers *(zakladchiki)*. The *raznochintsy* who had escaped a registered taxpaying status were to return to their community of origin. *PSZ* (I), vol. 7, no. 4624 (1724).

38. *PSZ* (I), vol. 8, no. 6215; vol. 10, nos. 7389, 7438; vol. 11, no. 8811; vol. 12, no. 9061.

39. On the lancers and cavalrymen, see Keep, *Soldiers of the Tsar*, 80–87; Hellie, *Enserfment and Military Change*, 24–26, 210–25.

40. Other legislation also identified *raznochintsy* as both taxed and untaxed. *PSZ* (I), vol. 9, no. 6858; vol. 17, no. 12605.

41. *PSZ* (I), vol. 11, no. 8836.

42. By contrast, the 1729 *Instruktsiia komisara ot zemli* had referred to single householders and natives paying the *iasak* as state peasants, which suggests that peasant categories also were pliable.

43. A law of 1752 called factory workers of illegitimate or unknown birth *raznochintsy*. *PSZ* (I), vol. 13, no. 9954.

44. *PSZ* (I), vol. 12, no. 9383.

45. See chapter 3 for discussion of this issue. Until the local reforms of Catherine the Great, central Russia (excluding the Baltics, Ukraine, and Siberia) was divided into governments *(gubernii)*, headed by a governor, and provinces *(provintsii)* and districts *(uezdy)*, both headed by a *voevoda*. LeDonne, *Ruling Russia*, 39–49.

46. It is known, for example, that communities conscripted such persons out of turn, in order to relieve themselves of any unnecessary economic burden and to protect wealthier members who had to shoulder the additional taxes regardless. Wirtschafter, *Russian Soldier*, 21–22.

47. *PSZ* (I), vol. 18, no. 12987.

48. Kimerling [Wirtschafter], "Soldiers' Children"; Wirtschafter, *Russian Soldier*, 35–40.

49. *PSZ* (I), vol. 18, no. 12987.

50. For the example of Astrakhan, see chapter 1.

51. *PSZ* (I), vol. 15, no. 10992 (1759).

52. Some examples of failed claimants to the privileges of nobility can be found in RGVIA, f. 395, op. 325, d. 10, ll. 10–11; f. 801, op. 61, d. 202, ll. 390–93; op. 61/2, d. 250, ll. 947–55ob.; and f. 14414, op. 10/291, sv. 60, d. 326, ch. 21. See also Troitskii, *Russkii absoliutizm*, 182–87, 236–39. For a full discussion, see chapter 4.

53. *PSZ* (I), vol. 12, no. 9256. Here the term *raznochintsy* was used in two ways. First, it corresponded to a specific poll tax category. Second, it referred to a variety of poll tax categories, including Cossacks, junior clerks in the civil service *(pod'iachie)*, soldiers' children, formal members of the taxpaying urban community *(posadskie liudi)*, and *raznochintsy*.

54. Immovable property included land held as *votchina* or *pomest'e*. *PSZ* (I), vol. 8, no. 5633. Blum, *Lord and Peasant*, 358–62; "Krest'iane," *Entsiklopedicheskii slovar'* (hereafter *ES*), Izdateli: F. A. Brokgauz, I. A. Efron (St. Petersburg, 1895),

16:683. On the monastery employees *(monastyrskie slugi)*, see Hellie, *Enserfment and Military Change*, 53 and 361 n. 149; Blum, *Lord and Peasant*, 194.

55. *PSZ* (I), vol. 12, nos. 9267, 9332; *ES*, 16:683.

56. *PSZ* (I), vol. 12, nos. 9267, 9332.

57. *PSZ* (I), vol. 15, nos. 10796, 10855; *PSZ* (II), vol. 3, no. 2378; *ES* 16:683.

58. The urban *nakazy* are found in *SIRIO*, vols. 93, 107, 123, 134, 144, 147 (St. Petersburg, 1894–1915). François-Xavier Coquin, *La Grande Commission Législative, 1767–1768: Les cahiers de doléances urbains (Province de Moscou)* (Paris, 1972), 110, 161–63.

59. *PSZ* (I), vol. 15, no. 11490; vol. 16, no. 11638.

60. *PSZ* (II), vol. 3, no. 2378. Similarly, a decree of 1827 forbade the sale of serfs to citizens *(grazhdane)* of Finland. *PSZ* (II), vol. 2, no. 1009. On the 1812 prohibitions, see RGIA, f. 1149. op. 2, d. 44.

61. Kopanev, *Naselenie Peterburga*, 24.

62. Zaionchkovskii, *Pravitel'stvennyi apparat*, 39–42; John P. LeDonne, *Absolutism and Ruling Class: The Formation of the Russian Political Order, 1700–1825* (New York, 1991).

63. *PSZ* (II), vol. 3, no. 2378; vol. 8, no. 6129; vol. 9, no. 6941; vol. 10, no. 8539; vol. 11, no. 9203; vol. 15, no. 13051; vol. 17, no. 15693; vol. 20, no. 19283; vol. 22, no. 20825.

64. *PSZ* (II), vol. 20, no. 19283. Nobles who unwittingly acquired serfs from ineligible masters or illegally hired out their serfs also did not receive compensation for the loss of human resources.

65. The law exempted these serfs from all court expenses, permitting them to use simple paper and excusing them from payments levied for appeals *(apelliatsionnye poshliny)*. *PSZ* (II), vol. 22, no. 20825.

66. *PSZ* (II), vol. 11, no. 9203.

67. Deliberations in the secret Committee of 6 December 1826 reflected this thinking.

68. Zaionchkovskii, *Pravitel'stvennyi apparat*, 39–42; LeDonne, *Absolutism and Ruling Class*.

69. *PSZ* (I), vol. 32, no. 25604; vol. 35, no. 27356.

70. Illegal serfdom took two forms: either the serfowners did not enjoy the right to possess serfs, or free persons fell into serfdom through illegal means. See chapter 4.

71. Nobles who lost their serfs were entitled to compensation from the state, but only if they could document that they had no knowledge of the serfs' illegal subjugation to *raznochinnye* masters. *PSZ* (II), vol. 3, no. 2378; vol. 12, no. 10149.

72. The subject of marriages between nobles and non-nobles deserves serious, comprehensive study. The question immediately arises as to whether such unions represented upward or downward mobility, and for whom. For a brief discussion of marriages between nobles and newly ennobled merchants, see Hildermeier, *Bürgertum und Stadt*, 113–17.

73. *PSZ* (I), vol. 7, nos. 4827, 4828; vol. 11, no. 8738; vol. 15, no. 11204; vol. 16, no. 11708; vol. 17, no. 12498; vol. 19, no. 13635.

74. *Raznochintsy* here referred both to all categories lacking the noble right to own serfs and to a specific category within this larger group. *Arkhiv Gosudarstvennogo Soveta*, t. 4, vypusk 1, ch. 2, 253–58.

75. Ibid.

76. The law set a five-year limit on these temporary labor agreements, but then allowed renewal. *PSZ* (I), vol. 33, no. 26469.

77. *PSZ* (I), vol. 38, no. 29416.

78. *PSZ* (I), vol. 39, nos. 29936, 30040.

79. *PSZ* (I), vol. 40, no. 30407; *PSZ* (II) vol. 3, no. 1696; vol. 15, no. 13051.

80. *Raznochintsy* were employed in factories under contract as apprentices *(ucheniki)*, journeymen *(podmaster'ia)*, and craftsmen *(mastera)*. Those who already had been ascribed in other categories could remain at the factories for only five years. *PSZ* (I), vol. 9, no. 6858; vol. 12, no. 9383; vol 13, no. 9954; vol. 17, no. 12605. See also A. M. Safronova, "Dokumenty ob organizatsii V. N. Tatishchevym shkol v slobodakh pri gornykh zavodakh Urala v 20-kh gg. XVIII v.," in *Istochniki po istorii russkogo obshchestvennogo soznaniia perioda feodalizma* (Novosibirsk, 1986), 73; Arcadius Kahan, *Russian Economic History: The Nineteenth Century*, ed. Roger Weiss (Chicago, 1989), 179–85.

81. *PSZ* (I), vol. 3, no. 1723; *PSZ* (II), vol. 5, nos. 3485, 3564; vol. 9, no. 6745; vol. 28, no. 27742.

82. *PSZ* (I), vol. 3, no. 1723; vol. 12, no. 9383.

83. *PSZ* (I), vol. 3, no. 1723.

84. A decree of 1728 required *raznochintsy* residing in the towns of Viatka province *(provintsiia)* to perform a range of service obligations alongside registered members of the community *(posadskie)*. These included quartering, repair of bridges, guard duty, and fire fighting. *PSZ* (I), vol. 8, no. 5319; vol. 14, no. 10242.

85. The affected categories included secretaries (low-ranking civil servants), administrative employees in government offices *(sluzhiteli i pod'iachie do podkantseliaristov)*, and Court and stable employees. *PSZ* (I), vol. 7, no. 4474.

86. *Raznochintsy* were to be registered with the St. Petersburg municipal council *(ratusha)*. *PSZ* (I), vol. 9, no. 6727, punkt 3. See also *PSZ* (I), vol. 14, no. 10242.

87. *PSZ* (I), vol. 14, no. 10242.

88. The term *raznochintsy* did not appear in the charter. *PSZ* (I), vol. 22, no. 16188.

89. Hildermeier, *Bürgertum und Stadt*, 42–45; Wallace Daniel, "Grigorii Teplov and the Conception of Order: The Commission on Commerce and the Role of the Merchants in Russia," *CASS* 16 (1982): 410–31; idem, "The Merchantry and the Problem of Social Order in the Russian State: Catherine II's Commission on Commerce," *SEER* 55 (1977): 185–203.

90. *PSZ* (I), vol. 22, no. 16188. The following groups received the title *(zvanie)* distinguished citizen: elected urban officials who served a second term with distinction, scholars *(uchenye)* with an academy or university degree or comparable certification, artists (i.e., architects, painters, sculptors, and composers) certified by the Academy of Arts, capitalists of any occupation *(zvanie)* possessing at least fifty thousand rubles, bankers declaring at least one hundred thousand rubles in capital, wholesale traders who did not own shops, and owners of seafaring ships.

91. *PSZ* (I), vol. 26, no. 19692.

92. Two male children counted as one laborer. This 1824 law divided the townspeople *(meshchane)* into traders *(torguiushchie meshchane)*, who paid additional

taxes for the privileges of that title, and ordinary townspeople *(posadskie)*. *PSZ* (I), vol. 39, no. 30115.

93. The 1832 law identified the following groups as free: persons released from their previous statuses, including peasants and sacristans; children of personal nobles and civil servants below senior officer rank *(ober ofitserskii chin);* and retired lower military ranks (privates and noncommissioned officers), their widows, and their unmarried daughters. Military personnel and their families in this last group were also exempt from taxation, if ascribed in the townspeople category. *PSZ* (II), vol. 7, no. 5842.

94. *PSZ* (II), vol. 7, no. 5791.

95. Mironov, *Russkii gorod;* Hildermeier, *Bürgertum und Stadt;* Daniel R. Brower, "Urbanization and Autocracy: Russian Urban Development in the First Half of the Nineteenth Century," *RR* 42 (1983): 377–402; Kopanev, *Naselenie Peterburga,* 41–48.

96. Nobles even registered in all three merchant guilds. "Vedomost' o narodonaselenii Rossii za 1851 god po 9 narodnoi perepisi," *ZMVD* (November 1853): otdelenie 3, 61–76. On the absence of derogation, see Troitskii, *Russkii absoliutizm,* 361–63. On lower-class entrepreneurs, see Shipov, *Istoriia moei zhizni;* Karpov, *Vospominaniia* (see chap. 1, n. 49, for both). S. I. Smetanin posits the existence of a transitional category of persons (including peasants, *raznochintsy,* and retired soldiers) who belonged to urban society by virtue of their socioeconomic position. Citing data from the cities of Perm province, Smetanin argues that between 1803 and 1860 the size of this group increased from 9 percent to 19^1/$_2$ percent of the urban population. S. I. Smetanin, "Razlozhenie soslovii i formirovanie klassovoi struktury gorodskogo naseleniia Rossii v 1800–1861 gg.," *IZ* 102 (1978): 153–82. On illegal residence in town and country, see Mironov, *Russkii gorod,* 87–88, 120–21.

97. I. F. Pavlovskii, "Statisticheskie svedeniia o Poltavskoi gubernii sto let nazad," *TPlUAK,* vypusk 2 (1906): 73.

98. Troitskii, *Russkii absoliutizm,* 39–40, 152–53; Zaionchkovskii, *Pravitel'stvennyi apparat,* 44–53.

99. Becker, *"Raznochintsy,"* 69–70.

100. *Sbornik postanovlenii po Sanktpeterburgskomu obshchestvennomu upravleniiu* (St. Petersburg, 1860).

101. On social categories as an administrative tool, see Freeze, "The *Soslovie* (Estate) Paradigm," 24–25; Hildermeier, *Bürgertum und Stadt,* 48, 124–37, 183–217, 307–22; McFarlin, "The Extension of the Imperial Russian Civil Service"; idem, "Recruitment Norms."

102. Kimerling [Wirtschafter], "Soldiers' Children."

103. For some suggestive comments in this direction, see Abbott Gleason, "The Terms of Russian Social History," in Clowes, Kassow, and West, eds., *Between Tsar and People,* 15–27; Alfred J. Rieber, "The Sedimentary Society," in ibid., 343–66.

104. Anatole Leroy-Beaulieu, *The Empire of the Tsars and the Russians,* ed. and trans. Zenaida A. Ragozin (New York, 1902), 1:309–10.

105. Harold Perkin, *The Origins of Modern English Society, 1780–1880* (London, 1969).

106. Mack Walker, *German Home Towns: Community, State, and General Estate, 1648–1871* (Ithaca, N.Y., 1971), 43–44.

107. John P. LeDonne argues that the insecurity of the elite led it to define social boundaries more precisely by forming an imperial ruling class with a common interest in the extension of serfdom. LeDonne, *Ruling Russia,* 21–22.

108. The authorities actually tolerated orderly individual petitions, but treated collective statements as rebellion. Michael Cherniavsky, *Tsar and People: Studies in Russian Myths* (New Haven, 1961); Daniel Field, *Rebels in the Name of the Tsar* (Boston, 1976); Wirtschafter, *Russian Soldier,* 120–23.

109. Rieber, "The Sedimentary Society" (see n. 103 above).

110. Colin M. MacLachlan and Jaime E. Rodríguez, *The Forging of the Cosmic Race: A Reinterpretation of Colonial Mexico* (Berkeley, 1980).

CHAPTER 3: ADMINISTRATIVE APPLICATIONS AND THE ORIGINS OF
RAZNOCHINTSY

1. On problems with the statistical sources, see Kahan, *Russian Economic History,* 199–214; A. D. Povalshin, *Sostoianie Riazanskoi gubernii v polovine 19 stoletiia (1848–1873 gg.)* (Riazan, 1895), 3–4.

2. Chartier, "Intellectual History or Sociocultural History?" 39–40 (see chap. 1, n. 56).

3. The best discussion of the statistical sources is in Mironov, *Russkii gorod,* and Kabuzan, *Narodonaselenie Rossii.* On the Muscovite data, see Ia. E. Vodarskii, *Naselenie Rossii v kontse XVII–nachale XVIII veka* (Moscow, 1977).

4. Kabuzan, *Narodonaselenie Rossii;* V. M. Kabuzan and N. M. Shepukova, "Tabel' pervoi revizii narodonaseleniia Rossii (1718–1727 gg.)," *Istoricheskii arkhiv,* no. 3 (May–June 1959): 126–65; RGADA, f. 248, kn. 1163, ch. 2, ll. 964–1017.

5. RGADA, f. 248, kn. 695; 711; 1117; 1163, ch. 1–2; 1920.

6. RGADA, f. 248, kn. 711; op. 10, kn. 908; f. 291, op. 1, ch. 1, dd. 53, 67, 517, 1720; f. 540, op. 1, d. 1101. In the case of Cossacks, the distinction continued until the collapse of the tsarist regime, whereas the single householders became part of the free rural population of the postemancipation era. McNeal, *Tsar and Cossack.*

7. RGADA, f. 291, op. 1, ch. 1, d. 5 (1720 g.).

8. A law of 1723 required a minimum capital of five hundred rubles (three hundred for St. Petersburg) for registration in the *posad.*

9. In 1744 the Pskov municipal council *(ratusha)* petitioned the Main Magistracy to permit registration of local *raznochintsy* who were married to merchant widows and daughters and who possessed homes, shops, and factories located on city (referred to as "merchant") lands. Local officials were eager to ascribe these people; because of the 980 male souls registered in Pskov during the first revision, only 364 remained to pay all the taxes and perform service obligations that required eighty-six persons at any given time. RGADA, f. 291, op. 1, ch. 1, d. 639. For similar cases, see RGADA, f. 291, op. 1, ch. 1, dd. 521, 888, 1252, 2397, 2399, 2839, 3783.

10. RGADA, f. 291, op. 1, ch. 1, d. 3654.

11. One retired soldier as much as admitted to illegal trading in 1770, when he petitioned to register as a Moscow merchant. Although he possessed a capital of five hundred rubles, he considered his unregistered involvement in trade dangerous. RGADA, f. 291, op. 1, ch. 4, d. 16133. For the case of a Briansk merchant who

lived and traded in Moscow before changing his legal residence, see RGADA, f. 713, op. 1, d. 827. For a full discussion of the economic issues associated with the *raznochintsy,* see chapter 4.

12. RGADA, f. 291, op. 1, ch. 1, dd. 765, 1709, 1085, 1252. On the registration of *raznochintsy* who had escaped the capitation in St. Petersburg and Astrakhan, see RGADA, f. 291, op. 1, ch. 1, d. 633.

13. The Main Magistracy vigorously refused to register illegitimate children and persons of uncertain birth unless their adoptive fathers clearly belonged to the community. RGADA, f. 291, op. 1, ch. 1, dd. 1215, 1432.

14. RGADA, f. 248, kn. 1163, ch. 2, ll. 858ob.–859ob.; f. 291, op. 1, ch. 1, dd. 1215, 1252, 1432, 1940, 2014, 2101, 2211, 2409, 2470, 2698, 2911; TsGIAgM, f. 32, op. 17, d. 1275. On continued local resistance to the registration of persons who posed a welfare problem, see TsGIAgM, f. 16, op. 13, d. 236.

15. Ironically, in the frontier town of Astrakhan, where social categories were even more fluid, *raznochintsy* clearly belonged to the *posad* and came under the authority of the magistracy. *SIRIO,* 134:136–37, 216–17.

16. For *raznochintsy* joining the urban taxpaying community, see RGADA, f. 291, op. 1, ch. 4, dd. 15329, 16831. For the children of ecclesiastical ranks, see RGADA, f. 291, op. 1, ch. 4, d. 18187; f. 713, op. 1, d. 440; TsGIAgM, f. 54, op. 1, dd. 524, 539, 1859. For the petition of a coiner *(monetchik)* released from state service because of illness, see RGADA, f. 291, op. 1, ch. 4, d. 18040.

17. In 1782 authorities in Nizhnii Novgorod province discovered forty Crown peasants who were not registered in the tax rolls. V. I. Snezhnevskii, "Opis' zhurnalam nizhegorodskogo namestnicheskogo pravleniia (za 1781–1783 gg.)," *DNGUAK: Sbornik statei soobshchenii, opisei, del i dokumentov,* t. 3 (Nizhnii Novgorod, 1898): 129. In 1794 one gypsy family sought to register as townspeople of Moscow, but because a Senate ukase of 1783 equated them with state peasants, authorities assigned them to the economic peasantry of Moscow province. TsGIAgM, f. 54, op. 1, d. 1098. In 1795 a former monastery servitor requested registration in a Moscow craft guild. The archival record does not indicate the outcome of this case, but the Moscow monastery where the petitioner had served had been closed earlier in the reign of Catherine the Great, and in the fourth revision he and his family had been registered to a village in Kazan *namestnichestvo*—a village they had never even visited. TsGIAgM, f. 54, op. 1, d. 1088.

18. In 1777 the Main Magistracy appealed to the Senate in a dispute with the Tula provincial administration *(namestnicheksoe pravlenie)* concerning the sons of a deceased former coachman who had registered as a Moscow merchant. To obtain a release from the services he performed for the *iam* (community of coachmen), the former coachman had agreed to pay seven rubles a year. In 1781 the community of coachmen demanded that his three sons make a similar payment of 750 rubles for the period 1767–1779. According to the Main Magistracy, the sons possessed a capital of over three thousand rubles and on the basis of Catherinean legislation were no longer subject to the capitation or under any obligation to the coachmen. The outcome of this appeal is not known, but in 1782 the Senate still had not responded. RGADA, f. 291, op. 1, ch. 4, d. 18211. For references to *raznochintsy* as illegal traders, see RGADA, f. 291, op. 1, ch. 4, d. 15330 (1769 g.), d. 19880 (1779 g.); TsGIAgM, f. 1036, op. 1, d. 10 (1792 g.). This usage also appears frequently in the urban instructions to the Legislative Commission.

19. LeDonne, *Ruling Russia,* 269–90.

20. RGADA, f. 248, kn. 3356, ll. 328–59ob.; f. 633, op. 2, dd. 25, 40; f. 494, op. 1, dd. 2836, 2904, 3073; f. 291, op. 1, ch. 4, d. 16934. During the second revision, there were significant numbers of *raznochintsy* in Astrakhan, at that time still a border town where runaways were permitted to settle freely. RGADA, f. 291, op. 1, ch. 1, d. 2060.

21. RGADA, f. 494, op. 1, d. 2843.

22. *SIRIO,* 134:432–33.

23. Ibid., 402–4.

24. RGADA, Gosarkhiv, razriad 24, op. 2, d. 35. Similar conditions existed in European Russia, but on a smaller scale. Mironov, *Russkii gorod.*

25. RGADA, f. 494, op. 1, d. 3108. A few years later in 1772, *raznochintsy* in Tuturskaia *sloboda* (Ilimsk administration) were identified along with peasants as farmers and tradesmen. Of twenty *raznochintsy,* twelve had a trade *(remeslo)* but only five did not possess arable land. RGADA, f. 494, op. 1, d. 3332.

26. At that time, the local authorities argued, the Cossacks had not been properly subjected to tax and service obligations; in addition, landless hired laborers and urban *raznochintsy* needed to be resettled and given land. RGADA, f. 494, op. 1, d. 3365.

27. *PSZ* (II), vol. 27, no. 26891.

28. RGIA, f. 571, op. 1, d. 1414. For the 1790s, see also TsGIAgM, f. 16, op. 1, d. 762.

29. A law of 1832 added children of personal nobles and unranked administrative office employees, retired lower military ranks, sacristans *(tserkovniki),* and when they reached age twenty-five, children purchased from "Kirghizes, Kalmyks, and other Asiatics." *PSZ* (II), vol. 7, no. 5842.

30. K. F. German, *Statisticheskie issledovaniia otnositel'no Rossiiskoi imperii,* ch. 1 (St. Petersburg, 1819), 149–50; Petr Keppen, *Deviataia reviziia: Issledovanie o chisle zhitelei v Rossii v 1851 godu* (St. Petersburg, 1857), 2, 8; A. Glagolev, "Zakony narodonaseleniia v Rossii," in Ministerstvo vnutrennikh del. Statisticheskoe otdelenie. *Materialy dlia statistiki Rossiiskoi imperii* (St. Petersburg, 1841): otdelenie 1, 218; Kabuzan, *Narodonaselenie Rossii;* Kabuzan and Shepukova, "Tabel' pervoi revizii"; Anisimov, *Podatnaia reforma,* 101–15.

31. In many cases the term *raznochintsy* did not even appear, though groups legally defined as such were included. For tables summarizing some of these data, see John P. LeDonne, "Police Reform in Russia: A Project of 1762," *CMRS* 32 (1991): 249–74; Hildermeier, *Bürgertum und Stadt,* 360–61, 364–65; P. G. Ryndziunskii, "Gorodskoe naselenie," in M. K. Rozhkova, ed., *Ocherki ekonomicheskoi istorii Rossii pervoi poloviny XIX veka* (Moscow, 1959), 284; idem, *Gorodskoe grazhdanstvo,* 225, 263–66, 300, 338, 371; Kopanev, *Naselenie Peterburga,* 25, 43–46; Kizevetter, *Posadskaia obshchina,* 155. See also "Vedomost' o narodonaselenii Rossii za 1851 god, po 9 narodnoi perepisi," *ZMVD* (November 1853): otdelenie 3, 61–76.

32. Hildermeier discusses the inconsistent application of legal terminology to the urban population. Hildermeier, *Bürgertum und Stadt,* 81–83.

33. Using police data from Moscow, V. Androssov included *raznochintsy* and unranked administrative personnel in a single category. Elsewhere, however, he indicated that *raznochintsy* belonged to the lower classes along with peasants, townspeople, and soldiers. V. Androssov, *Statisticheskaia zapiska o Moskve* (Moscow, 1832),

52–53, 63. Ivan Pushkarev defined *raznochintsy* as "retired lower Court employees, children of personal nobles and unranked administrative personnel, and in general persons who are not registered to a trading or taxpaying category *(zvanie)*." Ivan Pushkarev, *Opisanie Sanktpeterburga i uezdnykh gorodov Sanktpeterburgskoi gubernii*, ch. 1 (St. Petersburg, 1839), 43–50.

34. German, *Statisticheskie issledovaniia*, 164–65; Keppen, *Deviataia reviziia*, 8; Kopanev, *Naselenie Peterburga*, 43–45. For the failure to define the category *raznochintsy*, despite its repeated use in provincial data, see Ministerstvo vnutrennikh del, *Materialy dlia statistiki Rossiiskoi imperii*, vol. 1 (St. Petersburg, 1839); idem, *Panorama Sanktpeterburga*, ch. 2 (St. Petersburg, 1834), 84–86.

35. A. Bushen, "Nalichnoe naselenie imperii za 1858 god," in Ministerstvo vnutrennikh del, Tsentral'nyi statisticheskii komitet, *Statisticheskie tablitsy Rossiiskoi imperii*, vypusk 2 (St. Petersburg, 1863), 264.

36. Ibid., 265–66, 288–89, 292–93, 314.

37. According to Peter the Great's Table of Ranks, promotion to rank eight in civil service automatically conferred hereditary nobility; whereas ranks nine through fourteen entitled the bearer to personal nobility. Beginning in 1845 rank five conferred hereditary nobility; ranks nine through six, personal nobility; and ranks fourteen through ten, personal honored citizenship. A decree of 1856 then raised the attainment of hereditary nobility to rank four. The title of honored citizen *(pochetnyi grazhdanin)*, created in 1832, brought exemption from conscription, the capitation, and corporal punishment. Shepelev, *Otmenennye istorii*, 11–16, 47–101.

38. "Obshchie gorodskie vybory v S.-Peterburge, po novomu ustroistvu," *ZMVD*, ch. 16 (1846): 311–54; *Sbornik postanovlenii po Sanktpeterburgskomu obshchestvennomu upravleniiu* (St. Petersburg, 1860).

39. The urban histories discussed in chapter 1 follow this usage.

40. Although legal sources and population counts did not specifically identify ecclesiastical ranks released from the church domain as *raznochintsy*, they would have been incorporated in various secular categories depending on their current occupation, service, and type of education. *Sbornik rasporiazhenii po ministerstvu narodnogo prosveshcheniia*, 2 vols. (St. Petersburg, 1866), 1: 801–2. For the relevant legislation, see chapter 2.

41. Official data on students and revolutionaries are summarized in Brower, *Training the Nihilists*, 44; Zaionchkovskii, *Pravitel'stvennyi apparat*, 25–26; Pushkin, "*Raznochintsy* in the University," 34, 52–57, 62–63; Brym, "A Note on the *Raznochintsy*," 85; Leikina-Svirskaia, *Intelligentsiia v Rossii*, 52–53, 60–65, 104–5, 110, 137–38, 150–51, 156–57, 162–63, 177, 298–99, 307–17. See also *Tablitsy uchebnykh zavedenii vsekh vedomstv Rossiiskoi imperii s pokazaniem otnosheniia chisla uchashchikhsia k chislu zhitelei* (St. Petersburg, 1838).

42. *PSZ* (I), vol. 10, no. 7226; *Opisanie dokumentov i del, khraniashchikhsia v arkhive Sv. Sinoda*, 35 vols. (St. Petersburg, 1869–1916), vol. 20, prilozhenie 10; Mironov, *Russkii gorod*, 81–88, 148–49.

43. Population data of 1843 from Iaroslavl also included nobles, civil servants with rank, and *raznochintsy* under the same rubric. "Inventarnoe opisanie gubernskogo goroda Iaroslavlia v 1843 godu," *ZMVD*, ch. 3 (1843): 249. The *razsyl'shchiki* were not police troops in the modern sense of security forces. Their duties as described by John P. LeDonne were closer to those of the U.S. marshall; that is, they

executed administrative-judicial decisions involving the seizure of property and the collection of fines or monetary settlements. LeDonne, *Absolutism and Ruling Class.*

44. The usual meaning of *dvorovye liudi* as household serfs is clearly inadequate here. The term also may refer to petty servicemen, such as Polish and Ukrainian *szlachta,* whose claims to noble status were not recognized by the tsarist government. When these people failed to document their nobility within a specified period of time, they became peasants or lower-class townspeople.

45. TsGIAgM, f. 54, op. 1, d. 911; f. 203, op. 754, d. 1296.

46. TsGIAgM, f. 203, op. 744, d. 1518.

47. TsGIAgM, f. 16, op. 1, d. 337.

48. Some parishes had a significant proportion of *raznochintsy,* but this may have resulted from local differences in applying the terminology. The only way to account for the fluctuations would be to undertake microstudies of specific communities. Even so, because it is not always clear which groups were regarded as *raznochintsy,* the results would be questionable.

49. This is precisely what Mironov does when he "purifies" the *raznochinnyi* rubric by removing "non-*raznochintsy*" (e.g., nobles) in order to make the church statistics comparable to other types of population data. Mironov, *Russkii gorod,* 81–85.

50. Throughout the eighteenth century ecclesiastical sons repeatedly sought and obtained releases from the church domain in order to become coiners and employees of printing houses. TsGIAgM, f. 203, op. 753, dd. 162, 295, 1011, 1442; op. 754, d. 554.

51. Four christenings also were not included in the data because, even though at least one of the godparents was from a *raznochinnyi* subcategory, the parents were either merchants, townspeople, or members of craft guilds.

52. The printed form for confessional lists used by the churches of Zamoskvoretskii "forty" *(sorok)* in 1856 included the rubrics ecclesiastical domain; military; state; merchants, townspeople, members of craft guilds, and other urban inhabitants; household serfs; and peasants. TsGIAgM, f. 203, op. 747, d. 1712.

53. TsGIAgM, f. 203, op. 747, d. 392, ll. 15, 91; d. 422, ll. 13, 196, 265; d. 603, l. 14; d. 872, l. 10.

CHAPTER 4: STATE BUILDING, ECONOMIC DEVELOPMENT, AND THE CREATION OF *RAZNOCHINTSY*

1. In Petrine Russia the term of military service was for life; it was reduced to twenty-five years in 1793 and to twenty in 1834.

2. Retired soldiers were expected to have their passports stamped by the appropriate authorities in any locality where they took up residence. On the right of retired soldiers to change their place of residence, see *PVM,* 9 January 1843, no. 4. On the right not to choose a permanent residence, see TsGIAgM, f. 32, op. 12, d. 386.

3. *PVM,* 17 August 1842, no. 90. Some soldiers may have had *artel'* monies that became their personal property at the time of retirement. Wirtschafter, *Russian Soldier,* 79.

4. The condition of retired soldiers is treated more concretely in Wirtschafter, "Social Misfits."

5. Local archives contain numerous records of official discharges indicating the return of soldiers to their families. RGADA, f. 441, op. 1, dd. 379, 774; TsGI-AgM, f. 32, op. 12, d. 386; f. 54, op. 1, dd. 1194, 1501, 1795. On the acceptance of returnees by peasant communities and on their easy integration into the social order, see N. Cherniakovskii, "Statisticheskoe opisanie ishimskogo okruga Tobol'-skoi gubernii," *ZMVD*, ch. 2 (1843): 251–52.

6. Fedor Enskii, *Otstavnye soldaty* (St. Petersburg, 1873), xxxvii–xxxviii.

7. Androssov, *Statisticheskaia zapiska,* 181–82. On soldiers' wives as prostitutes and traffickers in foundlings, see David L. Ransel, *Mothers of Misery: Child Abandonment in Russia* (Princeton, 1988), 21–22, 154–58. The wives of retired soldiers, former wards of imperial foundling homes, and state administrative employees faced similar problems and also could receive passports permitting free residence when their husbands died, disappeared, or no longer were able to provide for them. TsGIAgM, f. 54, op. 1, dd. 809, 901, 1486, 1795, 2479. In 1799 authorities in Moscow refused to grant a passport to a woman who claimed to be the legal wife of a former ward of the foundling home. Although she presented a statement from a priest verifying her marriage, she could not document where she had lived with this alleged husband, who had been sent to a workhouse *(smiritel'nyi dom)*. Ibid., d. 1602.

8. In one case, a state official who had employed a soldier's wife and fathered her illegitimate children claimed that she was the wife of his household serf and sold her to another noble. The woman eventually was freed, after her original owners testified that she was indeed a soldier's wife. Her children, however, remained serfs, for they had been raised and fed by her first employer and registered to him in the sixth revision. V. I. Snezhnevskii, "Opis' delam arzamasskogo uezdnogo suda, 1804–1847," *DNGUAK*, vypusk 6 (Nizhnii Novgorod, 1889): 270–71. Similarly, "Opis' delam arzamasskogo uezdnogo suda," *DNGUAK*, vypusk 5 (Nizhnii Novgorod, 1889): 188; V. I. Snezhnevskii, "K istorii pobegov krepostnykh v poslednei chetverti XVIII i v XIX stoletiiakh," *Nizhegorodskii sbornik* 10 (Nizhnii Novgorod, 1890): 566–67.

9. M. D. Chulkov, "Prigozhaia povarikha ili pokhozhdenie razvratnoi zhenshchiny," in A. V. Kokorev, ed., *Khrestomatiia po russkoi literature XVIII veka* (Moscow, 1965).

10. Kimerling [Wirtschafter], "Soldiers' Children"; Wirtschafter, *Russian Soldier,* 35–38; Beatrice Farnsworth, "The Soldatka: Folklore and Court Record," *SR* 49 (1990): 58–73.

11. The correlation between illegitimate birth and indeterminate social status obviously was not limited to cases involving soldiers' children, but because the government was interested in these children as a source of manpower for the army—legally they belonged to the military domain—the documentation for this group is abundant. For comprehensive treatment of the category soldiers' children, see Kimerling [Wirtschafter], "Soldiers' Children." For the larger problem of unwanted children, see Ransel, *Mothers of Misery.*

12. For detailed discussion of the 1816 legislation, see Kimerling [Wirtschafter], "Soldiers' Children." For the petition of a household serf who discovered he was the illegitimate child of a soldier's wife and believed as a result that he was entitled to choose a station in life (i.e., register in a taxpaying category), see TsGI-AgM, f. 54, op. 1, d. 2021.

13. "Opis' delam arzamasskogo uezdnogo suda," vypusk 5 (1889): 178, 186,

195–96 (see n. 8 above); Snezhnevskii, "Opis' delam arzamasskogo uezdnogo suda, 1804–1847," 254 (see n. 8 above); idem, "Opis' delam arzamasskogo uezdnogo suda," *DNGUAK,* t. 1, vypusk 7 (Nizhnii Novgorod, 1890): 288, 299. For similar disputes from the 1840s, see TsGIAgM, f. 16, op. 13, dd. 188, 449.

14. Snezhnevskii, "Opis' delam arzamasskogo uezdnogo suda, 1804–1847," 259–60, 265.

15. "Opis' del Permskoi uchenoi arkhivnoi kommissii vyslannykh iz Senatskogo arkhiva," *TPUAK,* vypusk 3, otdel 2 (Perm, 1897): 56–57.

16. In one case from the 1840s, the illegitimate son of a soldiers' wife sought emancipation from his landlord at the age of forty, which precluded induction into the army. TsGIAgM, f. 16, op. 13, d. 238. Snezhnevskii, "Opis' delam arzamasskogo uezdnogo suda, 1804–1847," 266 (see n. 8 above). On efforts of soldiers' wives to conceal their illegitimate sons, see TsGIAgM, f. 54, op. 1, d. 1478; Kimerling [Wirtschafter], "Soldiers' Children."

17. RGADA, f. 441, op. 1, d. 946; TsGIAgM, f. 54, op. 1, dd. 1662, 2060. For efforts by retired soldiers and soldiers' wives to obtain the release of their sons from the military, see TsGIAgM, f. 16, op. 13, dd. 1489, 1499.

18. "Opis' delam arzamasskogo uezdnogo suda," vypusk 5 (1889): 181, 191–93 (see n. 8 above); V. I. Snezhnevskii, "Opis' delam nizhegorodskogo gorodovogo magistrata, 1745–1775," *DNGUAK* t. 1, vypusk 12–14 (Nizhnii Novogorod, 1894): 41; "Opis' del Permskoi uchenoi arkhivnoi kommissii vyslannykh iz Senatskogo arkhiva," 57–58 (see n. 15 above).

19. On levies of excess clergy, the social condition of ecclesiastical ranks, and the institutional needs of the church, see Freeze, *The Parish Clergy;* Gregory L. Freeze, *The Russian Levites: Parish Clergy in the Eighteenth Century* (Cambridge, Mass., 1977). For petitions requesting assignment to state service, submitted by sons of priests, unordained churchmen, and administrative employees of the church, see TsGIAgM, f. 203, op. 753, dd. 162, 295, 1011; op. 754, dd. 554, 1060, 1061; RGADA, f. 291, op. 1, ch. 4, dd. 20388, 21399. For the petition of a deacon's son whom the Moscow consistory refused to discharge in 1761, see TsGIAgM, f. 203, op. 753, d. 1442. For the case of a sexton sent to the army in 1785 for refusing to go to church, see TsGIAgM, f. 203, op. 754, d. 1007. On the expulsion of a monk, subsequently registered in the townspeople, see TsGIAgM, f. 16, op. 13, d. 295. On the priority accorded the military in assignments of excess sacristans, see TsGIAgM, f. 54, op. 1, d. 2718. On the release and subsequent acceptance of ecclesiastical progeny and employees into the townspeople and merchant categories, see TsGIAgM, f. 54, op. 1, dd. 911, 1831. On a sacristan who became a state peasant because he could not obtain an official church position, see "Opis' del Permskoi uchenoi arkhivnoi kommissii vyslannykh iz Senatskogo arkhiva," 16 (see n. 15 above). On the appointment of seminarians to teaching positions in state schools, see Snezhnevskii, "Opis' zhurnalam nizhegorodskogo namestnicheskogo pravleniia (za 1781–1783 gg.), 216, 133 (see chap. 3, n. 17 above).

20. On state administrative employees discharged from service for unacceptable behavior or incompetence, see TsGIAgM, f. 54, op. 1, d. 1907; V. I. Snezhnevskii, "Opis' delam makar'evskogo uezdnogo suda (1750–1806)," *DNGUAK* t. 1, vypusk 8 (Nizhnii Novgorod, 1890): 368; idem, "Opis' delam i dokumentam nizhegorodskogo gorodovogo magistrata, 1782–1786," *DNGUAK* t. 1, vypusk 12–14

(Nizhnii Novgorod, 1894): 113; idem, "Opis' zhurnalam nizhegorodskogo namest-nicheskogo pravleniia (za 1781–1783 gg.)," 102–3, 105, 108, 142, 180, 200 (see chap. 3, n. 17 above).

21. In the instructions to the Legislative Commission from the city of Nizhnii Novgorod, five copyists requested that the merchants who served as permanent members of the magistracy receive a salary and be excluded from the poll tax registers; so that they no longer would be formally registered as merchants. *SIRIO*, 134:15–16.

22. LeDonne, *Absolutism* and *Ruling Russia.*

23. For questions concerning the absolute authority of noble landowners over their serfs, see Isabel de Madariaga, "Catherine II and the Serfs: A Reconsideration of Some Problems," *SEER* 52, no. 126 (January 1974): 34–62. On the ambiguities of noble status, see *Noblesse, état et société en Russie XVI*ᵉ–début du XIXᵉ siècle, *CMRS* 34 (1993). Even John P. LeDonne, who depicts a ruling class "with privileges giving it a status sharply different from the rest of the population," also notes that the secretarial and clerical staff of the civilian apparatus and the noncommissioned officers of the military "formed a human reserve, blurring somewhat the sharp distinction between ruling class and dependent population, but through them the ruling class multiplied its points of contact with that population and magnified its power over them." LeDonne, *Absolutism*, vii, 60.

24. Some of these data are summarized in Troitskii, *Russkii absoliutizm*, and in Zaionchkovskii, *Pravitel'stvennyi apparat.*

25. RGVIA, f. 395, op. 325, d. 10, ll. 10–11.

26. *Otchet ministerstva iustitsii za 1845* (St. Petersburg, 1846), xix; *Otchet ministerstva iustitsii za 1846* (St. Petersburg, 1847), xli.

27. RGVIA, f. 801, op. 60, d. 29, ll. 6ob.–8. Polish *szlachta* who failed to document their ancestry became "single householders" with the right to regain noble status through military service on the same basis as their Russian counterparts. *Otchet ministerstva iustitsii za 1845*, li.

28. Wirtschafter, *Russian Soldier*, 33–34, 44–49.

29. Thus, in 1782 two factory owners in Nizhnii Novgorod requested exclusion from the poll tax registers and enrollment in the noble lists on a hereditary basis. Snezhnevskii, "Opis' zhurnalam nizhegorodskogo namestnicheskogo pravleniia (za 1781–1783 gg.)," 156 (see chap. 3, n. 17 above).

30. On loss of noble rights due to criminal convictions, see TsGIAgM, f. 54, op. 1, d. 1139 (1797 g.). See also the courts-martial discussed in Wirtschafter, *Russian Soldier.*

31. TsGIAgM, f. 54, op. 1, d. 256.

32. RGVIA, f. 801, op. 61/2, d. 250, ll. 947–55ob.

33. For comprehensive study of the social consequences of imperial expansion, including its impact on the delimitation of elites, see Andreas Kappeler, *Russland als Vielvölkerreich;* idem, *Russlands Erste Nationalitäten;* and *Noblesse, état et société en Russie.*

34. RGVIA, f. 801, op. 61, d. 202, ll. 390–93.

35. This comes out clearly in Sergei Aksakov's novel *A Russian Gentleman.*

36. John P. LeDonne believes that the category of personal nobles was only implied in the legislation establishing the Table of Ranks and was not actually introduced until the 1785 Charter to the Nobility. Even so, the Table of Ranks did state

that the children of civil servants of non-noble origin who had not reached rank eight were not nobles; whether or not these officials were called personal nobles, the consequences of their status for the larger problem of social categorization was the same. LeDonne, *Absolutism*, 318, n. 5.

37. Troitskii, *Russkii absoliutizm*, 208–9, 242–43.

38. RGVIA, f. 14414, op. 10/291, sv. 60, d. 326, ch. 21.

39. Another source of uncertainty was the recognition of individual claimants by provincial noble assemblies on the basis of fraudulent evidence; this practice continued into the nineteenth century and allowed members of the ruling class to extend and consolidate the patronage networks upon which their power rested. Bribery obviously also played a role here. LeDonne, *Absolutism*, 9–11. In the period before 1782, regimental commanders in the Smolensk area illegally admitted single householders to military service as nobles. *PSZ* (I), vol. 21, no. 15500.

40. LeDonne, *Absolutism*, 60.

41. Ibid., 13–15. As late as 1764 even serfs released by their masters received appointments to state service. RGADA, f. 248, op. 42, d. 3574, l. 245.

42. RGADA, f. 248, kn. 3301, ll. 528–31ob.; kn. 3353, ll. 484–89; LeDonne, *Absolutism*, 14, 56–58.

43. Robert E. Jones, *The Emancipation of the Russian Nobility, 1762–1785* (Princeton, 1973).

44. *SIRIO*, 90:485–86.

45. *SIRIO*, 90:572.

46. For the legislation governing enserfment and rights to serf ownership, see chapter 2.

47. "Opis' delam arzamasskogo uezdnogo suda," vypusk 5 (1889): 176–77 (see n. 8 above).

48. Ibid., 174–75.

49. Ibid.

50. Snezhnevskii, "Opis' zhurnalam nizhegorodskogo namestnicheskogo pravleniia (za 1781–1783 gg.)," 225 (see chap. 3, n.17 above). For a smiliar report dated 1787, see idem, "Opis' delam nizhegorodskogo gorodovogo magistrata, 1780–1798," *DNGUAK*, t. 1, vypusk 11 (Nizhnii Novgorod, 1891): 578–79.

51. The child's mother had worked for her mistress only five years. "Opis' delam arzamasskogo uezdnogo suda," vypusk 5 (1889): 191 (see n. 8 above). For a similar case, see Snezhnevskii, "K istorii pobegov," 559–60.

52. V. I. Snezhnevskii, "Opis' del i dokumentov nizhegorodskogo gorodovogo magistrata za 1787–1861 gg.," *DNGUAK. Sbornik statei, soobshchenii, opisei, del i dokumentov*, t. 2, vypusk 15 (Nizhnii Novgorod, 1895): 65–66; idem, "Opis' delam arzamasskogo uezdnogo suda," vypusk 5 (1889): 192–93 (see n. 8 above).

53. Snezhnevskii, "Opis' delam arzamasskogo uezdnogo suda, 1804–1847," 260–61 (see n. 8 above). Lengthy judicial proceedings repeatedly kept individuals in illegal bondage. In one instance a townsman in Nizhnii Novgorod illegally possessed a female serf for twenty years, the judicial proceedings lasting ten of these. Ibid., 269–70. Similarly, in April 1782 the Nizhnii Novgorod city magistracy began to investigate the status of several household serfs whose father, a townsman, claimed that he and his children had been freed in 1753 by their merchant master but the merchant's heir had repossessed the children. Snezhnevskii, "Opis' zhurnalam nizhegorodskogo namestnicheskogo pravleniia (za 1781–1783 gg.)," 129 (see chap. 3, n. 17 above).

54. RGIA, f. 1149, op. 2, d. 20, l. 25–25ob.

55. *Raznochintsy* also used forged letters of credit to document rights of ownership. Snezhnevskii, "Opis' delam arzamasskogo uezdnogo suda, 1804–1847," 269–70 (see n. 8 above). In 1804 authorities in Nizhnii Novgorod province assigned a former shoemaker's apprentice to the state peasantry after discovering that an officer had held him in illegal bondage for eleven years. V. I. Snezhnevskii, "Opis' delam vasil'skogo uezdnogo suda," *DNGUAK*, vypusk 5 (Nizhnii Novgorod, 1889): 173–74.

56. If discovered, the guilty parties faced fines. See the 1831 case involving a priest and noble landowner in V. I. Snezhnevskii, "Opis' delam nizhegorodskogo uezdnogo politseiskogo upravleniia," *DNGUAK*, t. 1, vypusk 7 (Nizhnii Novgorod, 1890): 318–19. On the continued illegal exploitation of serf labor based on letters of credit, see Snezhnevskii, "K istorii pobegov," 551–52.

57. For a complicated case (1808) that involved two merchants and three nobles, replete with legal documentation bearing the names of the nobles, see Snezhnevskii, "Opis' delam arzamasskogo uezdnogo suda, 1804–1847," 260–61; "Opis' delam arzamasskogo uezdnogo suda," vypusk 5 (1889): 176–77 (see n. 8 above).

58. In 1791 one such operation involved a merchant, a noble, and a runaway soldier. "Opis' delam arzamasskogo uezdnogo suda," vypusk 5 (1889): 179 (see n. 8 above). On the capture and sale of townspeople and persons excluded from the ecclesiastical domain as conscripts in the late eighteenth and mid-nineteenth centuries, see ibid., 183–84; V. I. Snezhnevskii, "Opis' delam nizhegorodskogo uezdnogo suda, 1846–1868," *DNGUAK*, t. 1, vypusk 11 (Nizhnii Novgorod, 1891): 555–56.

59. TsGIAgM, f. 54, op. 1, d. 1775.

60. RGIA, f. 1149, op. 2, d. 44, l. 39ob.

61. RGIA, f. 1149, op. 2, d. 20, ll. 14–17ob.; d. 44, ll. 27ob.–28.

62. RGIA, f. 1149, op. 2, d. 44, l. 27–27ob.

63. RGIA, f. 1149, op. 1, d. 12, ll. 2–3ob.

64. Such abuses were sufficiently widespread to prompt the government, beginning in 1816, to attempt regulation of the nature and duration of these labor contracts. Serfs were to be entrusted only to registered artisans for a maximum of five years; however, renewals of these contracts were permitted. RGIA, f. 1149, op. 2, d. 44. See also *SIRIO*, 4:365.

65. Wirtschafter, *Russian Soldier*, 19–20; Victoria E. Bonnell, *Roots of Rebellion: Workers' Politics and Organizations in St. Petersburg and Moscow, 1900–1914* (Berkeley, 1983), 20–71; Victoria E. Bonnell, ed., *The Russian Worker: Life and Labor under the Tsarist Regime* (Berkeley, 1983).

66. "Opis' del Permskoi uchenoi arkhivnoi kommissii vyslannykh iz Senatskogo arkhiva," 59–60 (see n. 15 above).

67. V. I. Snezhnevskii, "Opis' delam makar'evskogo uezdnogo suda, 1811–1863," *DNGUAK*, t. 1, vypusk 9 (Nizhnii Novgorod, 1890): 418.

68. Ibid., 418–19.

69. V. I. Snezhnevskii, "Opis' delam semenovskogo uezdnogo suda (1831–1867)," *DNGUAK*, t. 1, vypusk 7 (Nizhnii Novgorod, 1890): 329.

70. On the importance of runaways as a source of hired labor, see N. V.

Kozlova, "Naemnyi trud v gorodakh Podmoskov'ia vo vtoroi chetverti XVIII v.," *Russkii gorod*, vypusk 6 (Moscow, 1983), 102–26.

71. Shipov, *Istoriia moei zhizni* (see chap. 1, n. 49 above). On forged passports, see RGADA, f. 633, op. 2, d. 26 (1751 g.); Snezhnevskii, "Opis' delam nizhegorodskogo uezdnogo suda, 1846–1868," 555–56 (see n. 58 above); idem, "K istorii pobegov," 527–28. On late eighteenth-century efforts by the Senate to regulate local registration of deserters from the army, see TsGIAgM, f. 16, op. 1, d. 195.

72. Snezhnevskii, "Opis' zhurnalam nizhegorodskogo namestnicheskogo upravleniia (za 1781–1783 gg.)," 89–93 (see chap 3, n. 17 above). One peasant runaway who requested registration in 1780 fell into the hands of a local official who enserfed him to his relative, a village priest. The runaway complained to the local governor, who in 1783 ruled in his favor. Ibid., 189. Similarly, Snezhnevskii, "K istorii pobegov," 517–95.

73. Snezhnevskii, "K istorii pobegov," 526–27, 574–75.

74. The court decision did not mention the woman's other children, except for one daughter whose freedom she had purchased for twenty rubles. Presumably, the others, whose fathers were private serfs, remained the property of the landlords. Snezhnevskii, "Opis' delam vasil'skogo uezdnogo suda," 161–62 (see n. 55 above).

75. Snezhnevskii, "Opis' del i dokumentov nizhegorodskogo gorodovogo magistrata za 1787–1861 gg.," 73–74 (see n. 52 above).

76. There is a serious need for systematic study of marriage across social boundaries, which memoir and judicial sources suggest was a significant phenomenon.

77. Snezhnevskii, "Opis' del i dokumentov nizhegorodskogo gorodovogo magistrata za 1787–1861 gg.," 32–34 (see n. 52 above).

78. RGIA, f. 1149, op. 1, d. 12; op. 2, dd. 20, 44, 90; op. 3, d. 125.

79. Once a former serf was registered in a free category, he could not be returned to legal servitude. RGIA, f. 1149, op. 2, d. 44.

80. RGIA, f. 1149, op. 2, dd. 20, 90.

81. These basic points are covered in William Blackwell, ed., *Russian Economic Development from Peter the Great to Stalin* (New York, 1974); Ian Blanchard, *Russia's "Age of Silver": Precious-Metal Production and Economic Growth in the Eighteenth Century* (New York, 1989); Olga Crisp, *Studies in the Russian Economy before 1914* (London, 1976); Alexander Gerschenkron, "Problems and Patterns of Russian Economic Development," in Cyril Black, ed., *The Transformation of Russian Society: Aspects of Social Change since 1861* (Cambridge, Mass., 1960), 42–72; Arcadius Kahan, *The Plow, the Hammer, and the Knout: An Economic History of Eighteenth-Century Russia* (Chicago, 1985); Thomas C. Owen, *The Corporation under Russian Law, 1800–1917: A Study in Tsarist Economic Policy* (Cambridge, 1991); Walter McKenzie Pintner, *Russian Economic Policy under Nicholas I* (Ithaca, N.Y., 1967); Peter Lyashchenko, *History of the National Economy of Russia* (New York, 1949); Rozman, *Urban Networks;* Mikhail I. Tugan-Baranovsky, *The Russian Factory in the Nineteenth Century* (Homewood, Ill., 1970).

82. According to John P. LeDonne, patronage networks served primarily to consolidate the power of the ruling class. LeDonne, *Absolutism.*

83. RGADA, f. 291, op. 1, ch. 1, d. 2923.

84. The *raznochintsy* in question came under the authority of the district administrative office or the Dmitrov ecclesiastical authorities. The Main Magistracy

sent an official to investigate the matter, but the outcome is not known. TsGIAgM, f. 32, op. 17, d. 1275.

85. Peasants and *raznochintsy* sometimes retained property located on taxed lands without registering in the formal urban community, provided they reached an agreement with local authorities to pay the appropriate taxes *(obrochnye den'gi)*. They, in effect, leased property from the city and paid a form of rent comparable to that owed by state peasants. RGADA, f. 291, op. 1, ch. 1, d. 67. For similar reports from other localities, see RGADA, f. 291, op. 1, ch. 1, dd. 397, 1795, 2374, 2580, 2698, 3783.

86. RGADA, f. 291, op. 1, ch. 1, d. 639. *Raznochintsy* in the city of Tara (Tobol'sk government) worked primarily as artisans. Ibid., d. 3783.

87. RGADA, f. 713, op. 1, d. 827.

88. Three such serfs from the estate of Prince M. M. Golitsyn were expelled from the St. Petersburg merchant community only after their master identified them and petitioned for their return. RGADA, f. 291, op. 1, ch. 1, d. 397.

89. Ibid., d. 888.

90. The following discussion is based on *SIRIO*, vols. 8, 93, 107, and 134.

91. *SIRIO*, 93:299–300.

92. Kahan, *The Plow*, 343–45.

93. On *raznochintsy* as a source of workers for mining and manufacturing enterprises, see RGADA, f. 248, kn. 3356, ll. 328–59ob.

94. In 1769 a merchant from Cheboksary petitioned the Main Magistracy to grant him the authority to enforce restrictions on trade by *raznochintsy*, because local officials were doing nothing to prevent the illegal transactions. RGADA, f. 291, op. 1, ch. 4, d. 15330. For complaints by the Main Magistracy regarding the failure of provincial administrative offices *(voevodskie kantseliarii)* to consult city officials in the assignment of quartering obligations, see ibid., d. 15486.

95. Administrative boundaries and jurisdictions also shifted repeatedly, at least until the ministerial reforms of Alexander I established a more stable structure. For the specifics, see LeDonne, *Absolutism*.

96. RGADA, f. 291, op. 1, ch. 4, d. 19880 (1779 g.); TsGIAgM, f. 1036, op. 1, d. 10 (1792 g.).

97. For evidence of similar conditions in the 1790s and 1800s, see Snezhnevskii, "Opis' del i dokumentov nizhegorodskogo gorodovogo magistrata za 1787–1861 gg.," 8–9, 20, 30–32, 85 (see n. 52 above).

98. *Sbornik svedenii i materialov po vedomstvu ministerstva finansov*, t. 3, no. 11 (St. Petersburg, 1865): 281–317; RGIA, f. 1167, op. 16, d. 102.

99. The same can be said of peasants, retired soldiers, and soldiers' wives. Androssov, *Statisticheskaia zapiska*, 31, 180–82.

100. *Ministerstvo finansov, 1802–1902*, ch. 1 (St. Petersburg, 1902), 74–88; RGIA, f. 1167, op. 16, d. 102. For a proposal to allow free domestic trade for a fee of fifty rubles, see ibid., d. 224.

101. Shipov, *Istoriia moei zhizni* (see chap. 1, n. 49 above).

102. On geographical mobility, see Mironov, *Russkii gorod*, and Hildermeier, *Bürgertum und Stadt*.

103. Two economically successful groups in Russian society, Jews and Old Believers, were effective precisely because of the strength of their autonomous (albeit not always legal) community structures.

104. Repression obviously played a role in perpetuating weak organization.

CHAPTER 5: SOCIETAL REPRESENTATIONS: THE *RAZNOCHINTSY* AS OUTSIDERS

1. Quoted in Rose L. Glickman, "The Literary Raznochintsy in Mid-Nineteenth Century Russia" (Ph.D. diss., University of Chicago, 1968), 104.

2. In contrast to the legislative sources and the published versions of instructions to the Legislative Commission, which I am relatively certain to have read in full, I make no such claim with respect to the literary, journalistic, and memoir accounts upon which much of this chapter is based.

3. *SIRIO,* 147:26–27.

4. *SIRIO,* 134:470–73. For comparable usages, see *SIRIO,* 144:79–84.

5. *SIRIO,* 8:189–90.

6. The urban instructions are published in *SIRIO,* vols. 4, 8, 14, 32, 36, 123, 134, 144, and 147.

7. *SIRIO,* 8:98–101, 182–83; 68:509; 144:29–33, 104–5, 345–51, 377–83, 417–23, 438; 147:119.

8. *SIRIO,* 14:331, 469, 474; 32:527–31; 43:604–5; 68:361, 557–59.

9. *SIRIO,* 4:342–43; 68:627, 636–38, 645–50.

10. The association of *raznochintsy* with lower service classes is more explicit in the instruction from the city of Belev (Belgorod province). *SIRIO,* 144:417–18.

11. Esper, "The Odnodvortsy"; Wirtschafter, *Russian Soldier,* 33–34, 45–56; M. T. Beliavskii, *Odnodvortsy chernozem'ia* (Moscow, 1984).

12. Noble instructions did not employ the term *odnodvortsy,* but the *uezdnye raznochintsy* they mentioned clearly consisted of groups comprising the *odnodvortsy.* By contrast, not all *odnodvortsy* described themselves as *raznochintsy.* Moreover, in the first half of the nineteenth century, the legislation clearly distinguished the two categories. See chapter 2. See also Ia. Abramov, "Soslovnye nuzhdy, zhelaniia i stremleniia v epokhu Ekaterininskoi kommissii," *Severnyi vestnik,* no. 8 (August 1886): 159–87, esp. 159–79.

13. The widow of a general had taken control of these lands, and her serfs were now farming them. *SIRIO,* 115:102–104. For similar claims from single householders and other traditional categories of military servicemen in Moscow and Kazan governments, see *SIRIO,* 115:3–12, 180–82, 191–92.

14. *SIRIO,* 115:213–14. Similarly, *SIRIO,* 32:453. Two deputies from the ploughing soldiers well understood the necessity of education if these groups were to avoid falling into the status of state peasants. *SIRIO,* 32:410–12, 429–32, 452–54. On the Ukrainian frontier force, see Keep, *Soldiers of the Tsar,* 136–38, 147–48, 276–81.

15. *SIRIO,* 93:575; 107:107–14, 155, 476–82, 511–14; 134:12–16, 106–8, 293–98; 144:217–36, 259, 400–3, 440–41. For the legislation prohibiting non-nobles from owning serfs or populated estates, see chapter 2.

16. *SIRIO,* 107:14.

17. *SIRIO,* 107:51–56.

18. *SIRIO,* 93:573–76; 107:22–25; 144:194–211, 382–83, 409–10.

19. *SIRIO,* 134:293–96.

20. *SIRIO,* 144:211, 235–36, 409–10. Some argued that by granting symbols of *otlichnost',* the government would attract more nobles to state service. *SIRIO,* 144:401. Merchants also were concerned about *podlost'* and so sought to occupy a

position just below the nobility that would distinguish them from the less privileged *raznochintsy*, military servicemen, and lower (military) ranks. *SIRIO*, 144:423.

21. For the legal usages, see chapter 2.

22. *SIRIO*, 8:448, 457–58, 495; 68:622–23. For the definition of *raznochintsy* as persons who were forbidden to own populated estates and serfs: *SIRIO*, 4:276–77.

23. *SIRIO*, 4:460.

24. N. V. Gogol', *Zapiski sumasshedshego* in idem, *Sochineniia N. V. Gogolia*, 5 vols. (St. Petersburg 1894), 1:382. See also Becker, "*Raznochintsy*," 69–70; Albert Kaspin, "Ostrovsky and the Raznochinets in His Plays" (Ph.D. diss., University of California, Berkeley, 1957), 50–51.

25. F. F. Vigel', whose service career was less than brilliant, also felt that he had not received his just deserts as a hereditary nobleman. F. F. Vigel', *Zapiski*, 2 vols. (Moscow, 1928; reprint, Cambridge, 1974).

26. I. S. Turgenev, *Nakanune* in *Izbrannye proizvedeniia v dvukh tomakh* (Leningrad, 1958). See also Becker, "*Raznochintsy*," 69–70.

27. I. S. Turgenev, "Punin i Baburin," in *Sobranie sochinenii*, 10 vols. (Moscow, 1961–1962), 8:142–88. See also Becker, "*Raznochintsy*," 70.

28. Ibid.

29. A. I. Gertsen, *Byloe i dumy*, 2 vols. (Moscow, 1962), 1:532.

30. Boborykin generally is credited with having introduced the category intelligentsia into Russian social and cultural discourse. P. D. Boborykin, *Vospominaniia v dvukh tomakh*, ed. E. Vilenskaia and L. Roitberg, 2 vols. (Moscow, 1965), 1:135, 174, 302; E. A. Shtakenshneider, *Dnevniki i zapiski (1854–1886)*, (Moscow, 1934; reprint, Newtonville, Mass., 1980), 446–47.

31. Stackenschneider was speaking of M. M. Stasiulevich, editor of *Vestnik evropy*, and F. Berg, editor of *Niva*.

32. Shtackenshneider, *Dnevniki i zapiski*, 269–70.

33. Here Belinskii's use of the term *raznochinets* suggests a distinct social grouping. V. G. Belinskii, "Mysli i zametki o russkoi literature," in *Polnoe sobranie sochinenii* (Moscow, 1955) 9: 430–57. See also Becker, "*Raznochintsy*," 70.

34. Shtrange, *Demokraticheskaia intelligentsiia;* Kurmacheva, *Krepostnaia intelligentsiia;* Brower, *Training the Nihilists;* James C. McClelland, *Autocrats and Academics: Education, Culture, and Society in Tsarist Russia* (Chicago, 1979); Anthony Netting, "Russian Liberalism: The Years of Promise, 1842–1855" (Ph.D. diss., Columbia University, 1967); Jeffrey Brooks, *When Russia Learned to Read: Literacy and Popular Literature, 1861–1917* (Princeton, 1985); McReynolds, *The News under Russia's Old Regime*.

35. Boborykin, *Vospominaniia*, 1:45–47, 54, 91, 135, 174, 302.

36. The serfs either paid *obrok* to their masters or were "indentured" to merchants as redemption. Karpov, *Vospominaniia*, 164–67 (see chap.1, n. 49 above).

37. Arkadii's father was a district treasurer *(kaznachei)*, an office that granted rank nine. Polevoi—writer, translator, and publicist—was the son of a merchant; and although he lacked formal education, he succeeded in pursuing a literary career. Nikolai Polevoi, "Zhivopisets," in *Mechty i zhizn'* (Moscow, 1988), 41; idem, "Avtobiografiia N. A. Polevogo," in ibid., 286–300.

38. Ostrovskii's grandfather was a seminary graduate and archpriest. His father, Nikolai, graduated from the Moscow Ecclesiastical Academy and pursued a successful career in the civil service. By 1839 Nikolai reached rank eight, and he

and his children were inscribed in the register of the Moscow nobility. He died a middle noble, the owner of four estates and 279 serfs. Aleksandr himself graduated from a Moscow gymnasium and attended Moscow University for three years; after dropping out, he spent the next eight years as a civil servant in judicial posts before becoming a full-time writer. Kaspin, "Ostrovsky and the *Raznochinets*," 26–37; "Ostrovskii," *KLE*, 5:490–500.

39. A. N. Ostrovskii, *Puchina* in *Polnoe sobranie sochinenii*, 16 vols. (Moscow, 1949–1953), 4:200–251.

40. By the end of the play Polugaev becomes a successful lawyer in private practice, as had Ostrovskii's father.

41. A. N. Ostrovskii, *Ne ot mira sego*, in *Polnoe sobranie sochinenii*, 9:220–64.

42. For a summary description of Ostrovskii's *raznochinnye* characters, see Kaspin, "Ostrovsky and the *Raznochinets*."

43. On the life and work of Pomialovskii, see Glickman, "The Literary Raznochintsy," chapter 2.

44. Becker, "*Raznochintsy*," 70. When officials of the Third Section identified *raznochintsy*, they referred to one of several unprivileged, lower-class groups or semieducated, low-level servicemen and specialists who sometimes achieved hereditary nobility through service and who sometimes participated in revolutionary activities and peasant disturbances. Thus they viewed the *raznochintsy* as a social category in the traditional legal-administrative sense and in no way equated them with the revolutionary democratic intelligentsia. GARF, f. 109, op. 3, d. 69 (1851); op. 223, d. 27 (1862), d. 31 (1866); op. 1, d. 2226 (1880). A. P. Mal'shinskii, *Obzor sotsial'no-revoliutsionnogo dvizheniia v Rossii* (St. Petersburg, 1880). At least two other writers, associates of Chernyshevskii and the sons of non-noble civil servants, also did not use the category *raznochintsy* when describing the milieu of their childhood. M. A. Voronov and S. A. Makashin, *Rasskazy o starom Saratove* (Saratov, 1937).

45. Glickman, "The Literary Raznochintsy," 119–20.

46. N. G. Pomialovskii, *Brat i sestra* in *Sochineniia v dvukh tomakh*, 2 vols. (Moscow-Leningrad, 1965), 2:191–258.

47. Ibid.

48. Pomialovskii's *raznochintsy* included impoverished nobles, lower-class townspeople, retired noncommissioned officers, petty officials, and sacristans who were not on permanent staff. Boborykin also applied this definition, among others.

49. A. I. Gertsen, "1831–1863" and "VIII let," in *Sochineniia v deviati tomakh*, vol. 8 (Moscow, 1958), 31–51 and 211–18.

50. "Pis'mo k 'odnomu iz mnogikh,' " *Kolokol*, 15 September 1864, no. 189, pp. 1550–53; 15 October 1864, no. 190, pp. 1561–62; 1 April 1865, no. 196, pp. 1605–7.

51. Ibid., 15 October 1864, no. 190, p. 1562.

52. N. K. Mikhailovskii, "Iz literaturnykh i zhurnal'nykh zametok 1874 goda," in *Sochineniia N. K. Mikhailovskogo* (St. Petersburg, 1896), 2: 600–76.

53. Ibid.

54. In an article from 1911 Plekhanov described Herzen as a *raznochinets* in his *soslovie* outlook. G. V. Plekhanov, *Sochineniia*, 24 vols. (Moscow, 1923–1927), 20:128–30; idem, "A. I. Gertsen i krepostnoe pravo," in ibid., 23:332.

55. V. I. Lenin, "Iz proshlogo rabochei pechati v Rossii" and "Rol' soslovii i

klassov v osvoboditel'nom dvizhenii," in *Polnoe sobranie sochinenii,* 55 vols. (Moscow, 1958–1965), 25:93–95 and 23:397–99.

56. On "the outsider as insider," see Peter Gay, *Weimar Culture: The Outsider as Insider* (New York, 1968).

57. The *raznochintsy* who were invading the village included tavern owners, innkeepers, renters of grain mills, and others from whose ranks came "kulaks and bloodsuckers [*miroedy*]." Francis William Wcislo, *Reforming Rural Russia: State, Local Society, and National Politics, 1855–1914* (Princeton, 1990), 89–90. An earlier legal reference to rural *raznochintsy* as outsiders appeared in a law of 1854 that required "nobles, *raznochintsy,* ecclesiastical ranks, and other outsiders [*storonnye liudi*]" who lived on state peasant lands to conclude agreements with local communities concerning the conditions of use. *PSZ* (II), vol. 29, no. 28132.

58. *Spiski naselennykh mest Saratovskoi gubernii* (Saratov, 1912).

59. Obviously, the notion of the *raznochintsy* as non-nobles would have continued to make legal sense until 1917.

60. The *inochintsy* identified by Pososhkov included nobles, military servicemen, civil servants, peasants, and lesser church deacons *(tserkovnye prichetniki).* I. T. Pososhkov, *Kniga o skudosti i bogatstve, i drugie sochineniia,* reprint, ed. B. B. Kafengauz (Moscow, 1951), 114–15. For a good translation, see Ivan Pososhkov, *The Book of Poverty and Wealth,* ed. and trans. A. P. Vlasto and L. R. Lewitter (London, 1987).

61. In his study of the service records of ten thousand officials in the reign of Nicholas I, Walter Pintner found very few examples of individuals who called themselves *raznochintsy* by social origin; rather, they identified themselves by the occupation or service function of their fathers: the son of a deacon, soldier, official, and so on.

62. The district court regarded the former serf as a vagrant and ordered that he be assigned to the army or to settlement in Siberia. The provincial authorities, however, gave him the benefit of the doubt and allowed him to register as a state peasant without any punishment. V. I. Snezhnevskii, "Opis' delam arzamasskogo uezdnogo suda," *DNGUAK,* t. 1, vypusk 7 (Nizhnii Novgorod, 1890): 288.

63. Keep, *Soldiers of the Tsar;* Wirtschafter, *Russian Soldier;* McNeal, *Tsar and Cossack;* J. E. O. Screen, *The Helsinki Yunker School, 1846–1879: A Case Study of Officer Training in the Russian Army,* Studia Historica 22 (Helsinki, 1986); Emmanuel Flisfish, *Kantonisty* (Tel Aviv, 1983); Michael Stanislawski, *Tsar Nicholas I and the Jews: The Transformation of Jewish Society in Russia, 1825–1855* (Philadelphia, 1983).

64. RGVIA, f. 11, op. 6, d. 146, ll. 245–245ob. (1802 g.); op. 73, d. 1 (1856 g.); op. 85/29, d. 5 (1856 g.); op. 87, d. 4 (1856 g.); d. 5 (1857 g.).

65. *SIRIO,* 115:305–15; 144:79–84.

66. On the *raznochintsy* as parishioners, see chapter 3.

67. RGADA, f. 633, op. 2, dd. 42, 43, 61.

68. RGADA, f. 713, op. 1, d. 592.

69. For complaints that local police forced Moscow University's printers and their wives to work excessively on roads and bridges, see TsGIAgM, f. 54, op. 1, d. 254.

70. TsGIAgM, f. 105, op. 1, d. 779 (1800 g.); *Atlas Moskovskoi gubernii* (Moscow, 1787), Nauchno-tekhnicheskii arkhiv "Mosoblstroirestavratsiia," N 176–B (1, 2, 3). In St. Petersburg the property of *raznochintsy* was located in areas removed from the city center. K. Veselovskii, "Statisticheskie issledovaniia o nedvizhimykh

imushchestvakh v Sanktpeterburge," *Otechestvennye zapiski* 57, no. 3 (1848): otdelenie 2, 5–9.

CHAPTER 6: SELF-DEFINITION AND IDENTITY

1. For the legislation governing emancipation of illegally enserfed persons, see chapter 2.

2. V. N. Trapeznikov, "O liudiakh, iskavshikh vol'nosti iz vladeniia gospod svoikh," *TPUAK,* vypusk 4 (Perm, 1901): 142–52. Similar cases are summarized in "Opis' del Permskoi uchenoi arkhivnoi kommissii vyslannykh iz Senatskogo arkhiva," 54, 60–61 (see chap. 4, n. 15 above). For additional petitions from peasants seeking emancipation, including at least one that was forwarded to the Senate, see TsGIAgM, f. 16, op. 1, dd. 427, 477; op. 13, dd. 176, 215, 967, 992. Unfortunately, local archival records do not always indicate the outcome of a case.

3. Snezhnevskii, "K istorii pobegov," 528–30 (see chap. 4, n. 8 above).

4. GA RF, f. 109, op. 3, d. 1885.

5. Trapeznikov, "O liudiakh, iskavshikh vol'nosti" (see n. 2 above).

6. This contrasts sharply with the prereform army, where officers faced court-martial and punishment for similar abuses. Wirtschafter, *Russian Soldier.*

7. "Opis' del Permskoi uchenoi arkhivnoi kommissii vyslannykh iz Senatskogo arkhiva," 14 (see chap. 4, n. 15 above).

8. Snezhnevskii, "Opis' zhurnalam nizhegorodskogo namestnicheskogo pravleniia (za 1781–83 gg.)," 185–86 (see chap. 3, n. 17 above).

9. Ibid., 124–25. On the category *razsyl'shchiki,* see LeDonne, *Absolutism,* 135.

10. Snezhnevskii, "Opis' del i dokumentov nizhegorodskogo gorodovogo magistrata za 1787–1861 gg.," 46–59 (see chap. 4, n. 52 above).

11. A. V. Selivanov, "Opis' del arkhiva Vladimirskogo gubernskogo pravleniia," *TVUAK,* kn. 5 (Vladimir, 1903): 1–3. For the case of a printer's wife who fled her husband, presented herself as a soldier's wife and remarried, see TsGIAgM, f. 203, op. 733, d. 687 (1752 g.).

12. TsGIAgM, f. 32, op. 1, d. 232, t. 1–4. Quote is from ibid., t. 4, l. 64.

13. For discussion of these issues, see LeDonne, *Absolutism.*

14. On the concept of "self-fashioning," see Greenblatt, *Renaissance Self-Fashioning.*

15. Otto Müller's study, which represents the only comprehensive linguistic analysis, covers the period 1860–1890, when the term *intelligentsia* became established. Otto Müller, *Intelligencija: Untersuchungen zur Geschichte eines politischen Schlagwortes* (Frankfurt, 1971), 11–49. For a brief treatment, see Pollard, "The Russian Intelligentsia."

16. M. M. Shtrange examines the non-noble educated elite and Marc Raeff the provincial nobility. Shtrange, *Demokraticheskaia intelligentsiia;* Raeff, *Origins.* See also Laran, "La Première Génération de l'"intelligentsia.'"

17. On the intellectual origins of the intelligentsia in the circles of the 1830s and 1840s, see Malia, "What Is the Intelligentsia?" (see chap. 1, n. 35 above); Isaiah Berlin, "A Remarkable Decade: I. The Birth of the Russian Intelligentsia," reprinted in idem, *Russian Thinkers* (New York, 1978), 114–35. Nicholas Riasanovsky attributes the emergence of the intelligentsia to a split between the educated public

and the government in the 1840s and 1850s that is best understood as a consequence of Westernization and modernization. He defines the intelligentsia as critical, usually oppositionist intellectuals based in higher education, the periodical press, book publishing, and so on. Nicholas V. Riasanovsky, *A Parting of Ways: Government and the Educated Public in Russia, 1801–1855* (Oxford, 1976). See also Richard Pipes, "The Historical Evolution of the Russian Intelligentsia," in Pipes, ed., *The Russian Intelligentsia,* 47–62; George Fischer, "The Intelligentsia and Russia," in Black, ed., *The Transformation of Russian Society,* 253–74. Michael Confino argues that only with the "generation of the sons" in the late 1850s and the nihilist movement of the 1860s can one speak of "the first generation of the Russian intelligentsia." Michael Confino, "On Intellectuals." For a psychological interpretation that identifies the birth of the intelligentsia with the persons of Belinskii, Chernyshevskii, and Dobroliubov, see Vladimir C. Nahirny, *The Russian Intelligentsia: From Torment to Silence* (New Brunswick, N.J., 1983); idem, "The Russian Intelligentsia: From Men of Ideas to Men of Convictions," *Comparative Studies in Society and History* 4 (1962): 403–35.

18. Confino defines the characteristic features of the intelligentsia as "(1) a deep concern for problems and issues of public interest—social, economic, cultural, and political; (2) a sense of guilt and personal responsibility for the state and the solution of these problems and issues; (3) a propensity to view political and social questions as moral ones; (4) a sense of obligation to seek ultimate logical conclusions—in thought as well as in life—at whatever cost; (5) the conviction that things are not as they should be, and that something should be done." Confino, "On Intellectuals," 117–18.

19. Daniel R. Brower, "The Problem of the Russian Intelligentsia," *SR* 26 (1967): 638–39, 646.

20. Khasanova, "K voprosu ob izuchenii intelligentsii."

21. Quoted from Brower, "The Problem of the Russian Intelligentsia," 640.

22. Müller, *Intelligencija.*

23. Ibid., 195–207, 220–29, 246–51.

24. The classic and unsurpassed example of such analysis remains Martin Malia, *Alexander Herzen and the Birth of Russian Socialism* (Cambridge, Mass., 1961).

25. Confino, "On Intellectuals," esp. 128–37, 142–43.

26. Ibid., 60.

27. Some Soviet historians avoid this problem by treating the *raznochintsy* and the intelligentsia as virtually synonymous. Thus by the mid-nineteenth century, the *raznochintsy* as a legal and social category became submerged in the intelligentsia. To treat these very different concepts as one is to misunderstand the meaning of the category *raznochintsy.* Such analysis rests on a very narrow definition of the *raznochintsy* as educated commoners and leads to a second erroneous conclusion that the intelligentsia and the professions or educated elites were synonymous. Shtrange, *Demokraticheskaia intelligentsiia;* V. R. Leikina-Svirskaia, *Intelligentsiia v Rossii vo vtoroi polovine XIX veka* (Moscow, 1971); Vul'fson, "Poniatie 'raznochinets'," 107–24; Sidorova, "Polozhenie raznochintsev."

28. Daniel T. Orlovsky, "State Building in the Civil War Era: The Role of the Lower Middle Strata," in Koenker, Rosenberg, and Suny, eds., *Party, State, and Society,* 180–209.

29. Gregory L. Freeze, "The Orthodox Church and Serfdom in Prereform

Russia," *SR* 48 (1989): 361–87; Daniel Field, "Peasants and Propagandists in the Russian Movement to the People of 1874," *JMH* 59 (1987): 415–38.

30. Shtrange, *Demokraticheskaia intelligentsiia.* Shtrange's definition of the *raznochinskaia* intelligentsia is based on social origin, but he also includes in the group poor nobles who held the correct "oppositionist" views.

31. "Otryvki iz dnevnika," *Iz literaturnogo naslediia F. M. Reshetnikova* in *Literaturnyi arkhiv,* vypusk 1 (Leningrad, 1932), 244–45.

32. On primary education in the postemancipation period, see Eklof, *Russian Peasant Schools.*

33. Daniel Field attributes the failure of the movement primarily to repression. Field, "Peasants and Propagandists."

34. On the strong similarities in Slavophile and populist thinking, see Abbott Gleason, *Young Russia: The Genesis of Russian Radicalism in the 1860s* (New York, 1980).

35. Müller, *Intelligencija.*

36. Alan Kimball sees the roots of the revolutionary movement in the politics of the reform era, specifically in the frustrated efforts of educated society to form stable cultural organizations and professional associations. Kimball, "Russian Civil Society."

37. I am grateful to Marc Raeff for formulating the subtitle for this section.

38. Vatro Murvar, "Max Weber's Urban Typology and Russia," *Sociological Quarterly* 8 (1967): 481–94. On patrimonialism, see Pipes, *Russia under the Old Regime.* On the seventeenth century, see Samuel H. Baron, "The Weber Thesis and the Failure of Capitalist Development in 'Early Modern' Russia," *JGO* 18 (1970): 321–36.

39. The lack of effective power is developed in Raeff, *The Well-Ordered Police State.*

40. Rieber, *Merchants and Entrepreneurs;* idem, "The Sedimentary Society" (see chap. 2, n. 103 above); Thomas C. Owen, "Impediments to Bourgeois Consciousness in Russia, 1880–1905: The Estate Structure, Ethnic Diversity, and Economic Regionalism," in Clowes, Kassow, and West, eds., *Between Tsar and People,* 75–89.

41. Hildermeier, *Bürgertum und Stadt,* esp. 81–83, 124–32, 183–217, 366–69.

42. S. M. Troitskii, "Dvorianskie proekty sozdaniia 'tret'ego china' " in *Obshchestvo i gosudarstvo feodal'noi Rossii* (Moscow, 1975), 226–36; David M. Griffiths, "Eighteenth-Century Perceptions of Backwardness: Projects for the Creation of a Third Estate in Catherinean Russia," *CASS* 13 (1979): 452–72. For a summary of the relevant literature, see Freeze, "The *Soslovie* (Estate) Paradigm," 15–16, esp. n. 16.

43. Griffiths, "Eighteenth-Century Perceptions," 470–71.

44. For a translation of the 1785 Charter to the Towns, see David M. Griffiths and George E. Munro, eds. and trans., *Catherine II's Charters of 1785 to the Nobility and the Towns* (Bakersfield, Calif., 1990).

45. For a translation of Catherine the Great's instruction, see Paul Dukes, ed. and trans., *Russia under Catherine the Great,* vol. 2: *Catherine the Great's Instruction (Nakaz) to the Legislative Commission, 1767* (Newtonville, Mass., 1977).

46. RGADA, f. 291, op. 1, ch. 4, d. 14960. Printed in *SIRIO,* 36:179–232.

47. *PSZ* (I), vol. 22, no. 16188.

48. The term *meshchane* was used in two ways: to describe all formal urban residents and to describe a subcategory within the larger group.

49. Walker, *German Home Towns.*

50. Those seeking to register in an urban category needed permission from their communities of origin, the communities they sought to enter, and local state officials.

51. *M. M. Speranskii: Proekty i zapiski* (Moscow-Leningrad, 1961), 178–89.

52. Ibid., 178–79.

53. Ibid., 186–89.

54. *SIRIO*, 90:363–85.

55. *SIRIO*, 90:366–67. For a proposal that sought to enhance the stability of the "middle estate" (merchants, factory owners, and skilled craftsmen/artists) by making them hereditary citizens, to be distinguished from ordinary townspeople *(meshchane)*, see RGIA, f. 1167, op. 16, d. 101.

56. *SIRIO*, 90:441, 482, 486, 605–7.

57. *SZ* (1832), t. 9, kn. 1, razdel 3, gl. 1, otdelenie 1, st. 240–45. In annual reports submitted to Nicholas I by A. K. Benkendorf, chief of the Third Section, official confusion about the "middle classes" *(srednie klassy)* continued. Described in the 1827 report as the loyal patriotic "soul of the empire," the "middle class" (here the singular was used) included landlords who lived in towns, nonserving nobles, merchants of the first guild, the educated, and literati. Reports of 1829 and 1830 identified the "middle classes" as the petty nobility, bureaucracy, and merchants. A. Sergeev, ed., "Gr. A. K. Benkendorf o Rossii v 1827–1830 gg.," *Krasnyi arkhiv* (1929), vol. 6 (37): 146, 168; (1930), vol. 1 (38): 109, 133, 138.

58. On developments in education, see Vladimirskii-Budanov, *Gosudarstvo i narodnoe obrazovanie;* Rozhdestvenskii, *Istoricheskii obzor;* Leikina-Svirskaia, *Intelligentsiia v Rossii;* Frieden, *Russian Physicians,* 21–52; Samuel C. Ramer, "The Transformation of the Russian Feldsher, 1864–1914," in Ezra Mendelsohn and Marshall S. Shatz, eds., *Imperial Russia, 1700–1917: State, Society, Opposition* (DeKalb, Ill., 1988), 136–60; Rieber, "The Rise of Engineers," 539–41.

59. L. A. Bulgakova, "Soslovnaia politika v oblasti obrazovaniia vo vtoroi chetverti XIX v.," in *Voprosy politicheskoi istorii SSSR* (Moscow, 1974), 105–24. This view is challenged in James T. Flynn, "Tuition and Social Class in the Russian Universities: S. S. Uvarov and 'Reaction' in the Russia of Nicholas I," *SR* 35 (1976): 232–48.

60. *Sbornik rasporiazhenii po ministerstvu narodnogo prosveshcheniia,* 2 vols. (St. Petersburg, 1866), vol. 1, 6 and 14 September 1813, p. 223; *Sbornik postanovlenii po ministerstvu narodnogo prosveshcheniia,* 2 vols. (St. Petersburg, 1875–1876), vol. 2, 19 August 1827, no. 1308, pp. 71–73; 9 May 1837, no. 10,217; 29 December 1846.

61. Ibid., vol. 2, 9 May 1837, no. 10,217. The government did not in fact deny lower-class pupils access to the classical gymnasium course, which could lead to a university education. Rather, pupils from categories subject to the capitation were required to obtain releases from the communities to which they were registered, and serfs had to be freed by their landlords. Even in 1845, however, these criteria were not always being met. Ibid., vol. 2, 19 August 1827, no. 1308, pp. 71–73; *Sbornik rasporiazhenii po ministerstvu narodnogo prosveshcheniia,* vol. 2, 10 October 1844, pp. 768–70; 30 June 1845, pp. 825–26; 31 December 1845, p. 882.

62. Rozhdestvenskii, *Istoricheskii obzor,* 196–98.

63. On exclusion from the capitation, see *Zhurnal departamenta narodnogo pro-sveshcheniia*, ch. 3 (1821): 234–35; *Sbornik postanovlenii po ministerstvu narodnogo pro-sveshcheniia*, 2:765, 870–71.

64. Before undergoing a formal change of status in the form of a specialized calling, graduates of state schools who came from social categories liable for the capitation had to obtain a release from their communities of origin. During the reign of Alexander I, at least two townsmen from Nizhnii Novgorod successfully sought releases to become teachers. The community granted the first in 1808 only after the governor intervened and the second in 1821 after receiving a guarantee that the former townsman would continue to pay taxes until the next census. Snezh-nevskii, "Opis' del i dokumentov nizhegorodskogo gorodovogo magistrata za 1787–1861 gg.," 86, 97 (see chap. 4, n. 52 above).

65. Amitai Etzioni, ed., *The Semi-Professions and Their Organization: Teachers, Nurses, and Social Workers* (New York, 1969); William J. Goode, "The Theoretical Limits of Professionalization," in ibid., 266–313.

66. Dietrich Geyer, "Zwischen Bildungsbürgertum und Intelligencija: Staats-dienst und akademische Professionalisierung im vorrevolutionären Russland," in Werner Conze and Jürgen Kocka, eds., *Bildungsbürgertum im 19. Jahrhundert*, Teil 1: *Bildungssystem und Professionalisierung in Internationalen Vergleichen* (Stuttgart, 1985), 207–30; McClelland, *Autocrats and Academics;* Frieden, *Russian Physicians.*

67. Goode, "The Theoretical Limits of Professionalization," 291–94 (see n. 65 above); Amitai Etzioni, "Preface," in Etzioni, ed., *The Semi-Professions*, xiii.

68. Many historians make this point. Most notably, Pipes, *Russia under the Old Regime*, and Müller, *Intelligencija.*

69. Clowes, Kassow, and West, eds., *Between Tsar and People.*

70. Geyer, "Zwischen Bildungsbürgertum und Intelligencija."

71. Nancy Frieden's study of public-sector physicians (about three-fourths of all physicians) illustrates the pattern. Frieden, *Russian Physicians.*

72. Marc Raeff makes the point that the absence of autonomous intermedi-ary bodies exacerbated the explosive tensions of the late imperial period. Marc Raeff, *Understanding Imperial Russia: State and Society in the Old Regime* (New York, 1984), 217–25.

73. A parallel idea of classlessness existed in the official notion that the au-tocracy stood above class interests. On the notion of a classless intelligentsia, see Pollard, "The Russian Intelligentsia," 13–17; Müller, *Intelligencija*, 307–15.

74. Belinskii, "Mysli i zametki o russkoi literature," 431 (see chap. 5, n. 33 above).

75. Clowes, Kassow, and West, eds., *Between Tsar and People.*

76. On this process in urban society in the second half of the nineteenth century, see Brower, "Estate, Class, and Community." On the instability of student circles in the 1860s, see idem, *Training the Nihilists.*

77. On intelligentsia, state, and peasant utopianism, see Stites, *Revolutionary Dreams.*

78. Haimson, "Civil War and the Problem of Social Identities," 24–30 (see chap. 1, n. 6 above).

CONCLUSION

1. G. V. Plekhanov, "M. P. Pogodin i bor'ba klassov," in *Sochineniia,* 23:97.

2. Until 1841 church sources used the term to describe all nonmilitary service categories, including some nobles. See above, chapter 3.

3. The reported peasant practice of referring to any educated person as *barin* likewise attested to the need for deliberate delimitation.

4. Hayden White, *Tropics of Discourse: Essays in Cultural Criticism* (Baltimore, 1978), 91.

5. Quoted in Raymond Williams, *Culture and Society: 1780–1950* (New York, 1958, 1983), 50.

6. In stressing the lack of clear delimitation between civil administration and social institutions, Dietrich Geyer effectively questions the appropriateness of the notion "state *and* society." Dietrich Geyer, " 'Gesellschaft' als staatliche Veranstaltung: Sozialgeschichtliche Aspekte des russischen Behördenstaats im 18. Jahrhundert," in Dietrich Geyer, ed., *Wirtschaft und Gesellschaft im vorrevolutionären Russland* (Cologne, 1975), 20–52.

7. Christoph Schmidt offers a partial example. In a discussion of social mobility based upon the 1897 census, Schmidt identifies horizontal and vertical estates *(Stände)* distinguished by education, economic position, and access to state service. Christoph Schmidt, "Dokumentation: Stände," in Henning Bauer, Andreas Kappeler, and Brigitte Roth, eds., *Die Nationalitäten des Russischen Reiches in der Volkzählung von 1897* (Stuttgart, 1991), 380–81.

S e l e c t   B i b l i o g r a p h y

This select bibliography does not include individual files from archival collections, encyclopedia entries, or articles from prerevolutionary Russian journals identified in the list of abbreviations. Isolated articles from prerevolutionary serials that are cited only sporadically do appear, as do articles from current scholarly journals. Also not included are the many inventories *(opisi)* describing the contents of archival collections *(fondy)* that were examined but that did not yield relevant documents.

ARCHIVES

Rossiiskii gosudarstvennyi arkhiv drevnikh aktov, Moscow (RGADA):
      f. 248   Senat i ego uchrezhdeniia
      f. 291   Glavnyi magistrat
      f. 441   Sviiazhskaia provintsial'naia kantseliariia
      f. 450   Uglichskaia provintsial'naia kantseliariia
      f. 494   Ilimskaia voevodskaia kantseliariia
      f. 540   Novoladozhskaia voevodskaia kantseliariia
      f. 566   Riazhskaia voevodskaia kantseliariia
      f. 633   Tomskaia voevodskaia kantseliariia
      f. 713   Brianskaia ratusha i gorodovoi magistrat
      f. 717   Vologodskii gorodovoi magistrat
     Gosarkhiv, Razriad XXIV, Sibirskii prikaz i upravlenie Sibir'iu
  Tsentral'nyi gosudarstvennyi istoricheskii arkhiv goroda Moskvy, Moscow TsGIAgM):
      f. 16   Kantseliariia Moskovskogo general-gubernatora
      f. 32   Moskovskii gorodovoi magistrat
      f. 54   Moskovskoe gubernskoe pravlenie
      f. 105   Moskovskaia uprava blagochiniia
      f. 203   Moskovskaia dukhovnaia konsistoriia

f. 1036   Serpukhovskaia gorodskaia shestiglasnaia duma
f. 1633   Dmitrovskaia shestiglasnaia duma
f. 2121   Tserkvi Zamoskvoretskogo soroka g. Moskvy
Rossiiskii gosudartsvennyi voenno-istoricheskii arkhiv, Moscow (RGVIA):
f. 395   Inspektorskii departament voennogo ministerstva
f. 801   Auditoriatskii departament voennogo ministerstva
f. 14414 Glavnyi shtab vtoroi armii
f. Voenno-uchenyi arkhiv
Gosudarstvennyi arkhiv Rossiiskoi federatsii, Moscow (GARF, formerly TsGAOR):
f. 109   Tret'e otdelenie sobstvennoi ego imperatorskogo velichestva kantseliarii
f. 1155   Ia. I. Rostovtsev (personal fond)
Rossiiskii gosudarstvennyi istoricheskii arkhiv, St. Petersburg (RGIA):
f. 571   Departament raznykh sborov i podatei ministerstva finansov
f. 1149   Departament zakonov Gosudarstvennogo soveta
f. 1167   Komitet 6 dekabria 1826 goda
f. 1284   Departament obshchikh del ministerstva vnutrennikh del
f. 1287   Khoziaistvennyi departament ministerstva vnutrennikh del
Nauchno-tekhnicheskii arkhiv "Mosoblstroirestavratsiia," Moscow:
Atlas Moskovskoi gubernii. Moscow, 1787. [N 176–B (1, 2, 3)]

PRINTED SOURCES

Abramov, Ia. "Soslovnye nuzhdy, zhelaniia i stremleniia v epokhu Ekaterininskoi
komissii." *Severnyi vestnik* (1886), no. 4: 145–80; no. 6: 47–84; no. 7: 69–99;
no. 8: 159–87; no. 10: 131–66; no. 12: 17–32.
*Absoliutizm v Rossii (XVII–XVIII vv.): Sbornik statei k semidesiatiletiiu so dnia rozhdeniia
B. B. Kafengauza.* Moscow, 1964.
Akademiia nauk SSSR. *Slovar' Akademii rossiiskoi.* 6 vols. St. Petersburg, 1806–1822.
———. *Slovar' tserkovno-slavianskogo i russkogo iazyka.* 4 vols. St. Petersburg, 1847.
Aksakov, S. T. *A Russian Gentleman.* Translated by J. D. Duff. Oxford: Oxford Univer-
sity Press, 1982.
Alekseev, A. A. "O sotsial'noi differentsiatsii russkogo iazyka v 18 veke." *Wiener
slavistisches Jahrbuch* 31 (1985): 9–28.
Alexander, John T. *Bubonic Plague in Early Modern Russia: Public Health and Urban
Disaster.* Baltimore: Johns Hopkins University Press, 1980.
Anderson, C. Arnold, and Bowman, Mary Jean, eds. *Education and Development.* Chi-
cago: Aldine, 1965.
Androssov, V. *Statisticheskaia zapiska o Moskve.* Moscow, 1832.
Anisimov, E. V. *Podatnaia reforma Petra I.* Leningrad, 1982.
Antonov, V. S. "K voprosu o sotsial'nom sostave i chislennosti revoliutsionerov
70-kh godov." In *Obshchestvennoe dvizhenie v poreformennoi Rossii: Sbornik.*
Edited by L. M. Ivanov. Moscow, 1965.
Arkhiv Gosudarstvennogo Soveta. 5 vols. St. Petersburg, 1869–1904.
Arsen'ev, K. I. "Istoriko-statisticheskii ocherk narodnoi obrazovannosti v Rossii do
kontsa XVIII veka." *Uchenye zapiski vtorogo otdeleniia imperatorskoi Akademii
nauk* 1, otdelenie 2 (St. Petersburg, 1854): 1–32.

Avakumovic, Ivan. "A Statistical Approach to the Revolutionary Movement in Russia, 1878–1887." *Slavic Review* 18 (1959): 182–86.

Baron, Samuel H. "The Weber Thesis and the Failure of Capitalist Development in 'Early Modern' Russia." *Jahrbücher für Geschichte Osteuropas* 18 (1970): 320–36.

Bauer, Henning, Kappeler, Andreas, and Roth, Brigitte, eds. *Die Nationalitäten des Russischen Reiches in der Volkzählung von 1897.* Stuttgart: F. Steiner, 1991.

Becker, Christopher. "*Raznochintsy:* The Development of the Word and of the Concept." *Slavic Review* 18 (1959): 63–74.

Beliavskii, M. T. *Odnodvortsy chernozem'ia.* Moscow, 1984.

Belinskii, V. G. *Polnoe sobranie sochinenii.* 13 vols. Moscow, 1953–1959.

Bennett, Helju Aulik. "The *Chin* System and the *Raznochintsy* in the Government of Alexander III, 1881–1894." Ph.D. diss., University of California, Berkeley, 1971.

———. "Evolution of the Meanings of *Chin:* An Introduction to the Russian Institution of Rank Ordering and Niche Assignment from the Time of Peter the Great's Table of Ranks to the Russian Revolution." *California Slavic Studies* 10 (1977): 1–43.

Berkov, P. N., ed. *Russkaia komediia i komicheskaia opera XVIII veka.* Moscow, 1950.

Berlin, Isaiah. *Russian Thinkers.* New York: Viking, 1978.

Besançon, Alain. *Éducation et société en Russie dans le second tiers du XIXe siècle.* Paris and La Haye: Mouton, 1974.

Black, Cyril, ed. *The Transformation of Russian Society: Aspects of Social Change since 1861.* Cambridge: Harvard University Press, 1960.

Blackwell, William L., ed. *Russian Economic Development from Peter the Great to Stalin.* New York: Franklin Watts, 1974.

Blanchard, Ian. *Russia's "Age of Silver": Precious-Metal Production and Economic Growth in the Eighteenth Century.* New York: Routledge, 1989.

Blum, Jerome. *Lord and Peasant in Russia from the Ninth to the Nineteenth Century.* Princeton: Princeton University Press, 1961.

Boborykin, P. D. *Vospominaniia v dvukh tomakh.* Edited by E. Vilenskaia and L. Roitberg. 2 vols. Moscow, 1965.

Bonnell, Victoria E. *Roots of Rebellion: Workers' Politics and Organizations in St. Petersburg and Moscow, 1900–1914.* Berkeley: University of California Press, 1983.

———, ed. *The Russian Worker: Life and Labor under the Tsarist Regime.* Berkeley: University of California Press, 1983.

Brooks, Jeffrey. *When Russia Learned to Read: Literacy and Popular Literature, 1861–1917.* Princeton: Princeton University Press, 1985.

Brower, Daniel R. "The Problem of the Russian Intelligentsia." *Slavic Review* 26 (1967): 638–47.

———. "Fathers, Sons, and Grandfathers: Social Origins of Radical Intellectuals in Nineteenth-Century Russia." *Journal of Social History* 2 (1968–1969): 333–55.

———. "Student Political Attitudes and Social Origins: The Technological Institute of Saint Petersburg." *Journal of Social History* 6 (1972–1973): 202–13.

———. *Training the Nihilists: Education and Radicalism in Tsarist Russia.* Ithaca, N.Y.: Cornell University Press, 1975.

———. "Estate, Class, and Community: Urbanization and Revolution in Late Tsarist Russia." *The Carl Beck Papers in Russian and East European Studies.* Paper no. 302. Pittsburgh: University of Pittsburgh Press, 1983.

———. "Urbanization and Autocracy: Russian Urban Development in the First Half of the Nineteenth Century." *Russian Review* 42 (1983): 377–402.

———. *The Russian City between Tradition and Modernity, 1850–1900.* Berkeley: University of California Press, 1990.

Brunner, Otto, Conze, Werner, and Koselleck, Reinhart, eds. *Geschichtliche Grundbegriffe: Historisches Lexikon zur politisch-sozialen Sprache in Deutschland.* 7 vols. Stuttgart: Ernst Klett, 1972–1992.

Brym, Robert J. "A Note on the *Raznochintsy.*" *Journal of Social History* 10 (1976–1977): 354–59.

Bulgakova, L. A. "Soslovnaia politika v oblasti obrazovaniia vo vtoroi chetverti XIX v." In *Voprosy politicheskoi istorii SSSR.* Moscow, 1974, 104–24.

———. "Intelligentsiia v Rossii vo vtoroi chetverti XIX veka: sostav, pravovoe i material'noe polozhenie." Kand. diss., Leningrad, 1983.

Burshen, A. *Statisticheskie tablitsy Rossiiskoi imperii za 1858 god.* St. Petersburg, 1863.

Catherine II's Charters of 1785 to the Nobility and the Towns. Edited and translated by David M. Griffiths and George E. Munro. Bakersfield, Calif.: C. Schlacks, Jr., 1990.

Chechulin, N. D. *Russkoe provintsial'noe obshchestvo vo vtoroi polovine XVIII v.* St. Petersburg, 1889.

Cherniavsky, Michael. *Tsar and People: Studies in Russian Myths.* New Haven: Yale University Press, 1961.

Chulkov, Mikhail D. *Slovar' iuridicheskii ili svod rossiiskikh uzakonenii, vremiannykh uchrezhdenii, suda i rasprava.* 5 vols. Moscow, 1792–1796.

———. "Prigozhaia povarikha ili pokhozhdenie razvratnoi zhenshchiny." In *Khrestomatiia po russkoi literature XVIII veka.* Edited by A. V. Kokorev. Moscow, 1965.

Clowes, Edith W., Kassow, Samuel D., and West, James L., eds. *Between Tsar and People: Educated Society and the Quest for Public Identity in Late Imperial Russia.* Princeton: Princeton University Press, 1991.

Confino, Michael. *Domaines et seigneurs en Russie vers la fin du XVIIIe siècle.* Paris: Institut d'études slaves de l'Université de Paris, 1963.

———. *Systèmes agraires et progrès agricole.* Paris and La Haye: Mouton, 1969.

———. "On Intellectuals and Intellectual Traditions in Eighteenth- and Nineteenth-Century Russia." *Daedalus* 101 (1972): 117–49.

———. "Révolte juvénile et contre-culture." *Cahiers du Monde russe et soviétique* 31 (1990): 489–538.

———. "Servage russe, esclavage américain (note critique)." *Annales Économies, Sociétés, Civilisation* 45 (1990): 1119–41.

———. *Société et mentalités collectives en Russie sous l'ancien régime.* Paris: Institut d'études slaves de l'Université de Paris, 1991.

Conze, Werner, and Kocka, Jürgen, eds. *Bildungsbürgertum im 19. Jahrhundert.* Teil 1: *Bildungssystem und Professionalisierung in Internationalen Vergleichen.* Stuttgart: Klett-Cotta, 1985.

Coquin, François-Xavier. *La Grande Commission Législative, 1767–1768: Les cahiers de doléances urbains (Province de Moscou).* Paris: Beatrice-Nauwelaerts, 1972.

Crisp, Olga. *Studies in the Russian Economy before 1914.* London: Macmillan, 1976.

Crisp, Olga, and Edmondson, Linda, eds. *Civil Rights in Imperial Russia.* New York: Oxford University Press, 1989.

Dal', V. I. *Tolkovyi slovar' Velikorusskogo iazyka.* 4 vols. St. Petersburg, 1912.

Daniel, Wallace. "The Merchantry and the Problem of Social Order in the Russian State: Catherine II's Commission on Commerce." *Slavonic and East European Review* 55 (1977): 185–203.

——. "The Merchants' View of the Social Order in Russia as Revealed in the Town *Nakazy* from Moskovskaia Guberniia to Catherine's Legislative Commission." *Canadian-American Slavic Studies* 11 (1977): 503–22.

——. "Grigorii Teplov and the Conception of Order: The Commission on Commerce and the Role of the Merchants in Russia." *Canadian-American Slavic Studies* 16 (1982): 410–31.

Deiateli revoliutsionnogo dvizheniia v Rossii. 5 vols. Moscow, 1927–1934.

Delo petrashevtsev. 3 vols. Moscow, 1937–1951.

Del'vig, A. I. *Polveka russkoi zhizni.* 2 vols. Moscow, 1930.

Desiatiletie ministerstva narodnogo prosveshcheniia 1833–1843. St. Petersburg, 1864.

Dobroliubov, N. A. *Polnoe sobranie sochinenii v shesti tomakh.* 6 vols. Moscow, 1934–1941.

Doklady Moskovskoi gorodskoi upravy. Moscow, 1866.

Dostoevskii, F. M. *Dnevnik pisatelia za 1873 i 1876 gody.* Moscow, 1929.

Dukes, Paul, ed. and trans. *Russia under Catherine the Great.* 2 vols. Newtonville, Mass.: Oriental Research Partners, 1977–1978.

Eighteenth-Century Russian Publications. Watertown, Mass.: General Microfilm, n.d.

Egorov, B. F. *Petrashevtsy.* Leningrad, 1988.

Eklof, Ben. *Russian Peasant Schools: Officialdom, Village Culture, and Popular Pedagogy, 1861–1914.* Berkeley and Los Angeles: University of California Press, 1986.

Elishev, A. I. "Vnutrennee obozrenie." *Russkoe obozrenie* (September 1896): 445–58; (March 1897): 525–35; (May 1897): 477–86; (February 1898): 986–88.

Enskii, Fedor. *Otstavnye soldaty.* St. Petersburg, 1873.

Erman, L. K. *Intelligentsiia v pervoi russkoi revoliutsii.* Moscow, 1966.

Eroshkin, N. P. *Krepostnicheskoe samoderzhavie i ego politicheskie instituty.* Moscow, 1981.

Esper, Thomas. "The Odnodvortsy and the Russian Nobility." *Slavonic and East European Review* 45 (1967): 124–34.

Etzioni, Amitai, ed. *The Semi-Professions and Their Organization: Teachers, Nurses, and Social Workers.* New York: Free Press, 1969.

Farnsworth, Beatrice. "The Soldatka: Folklore and Court Record." *Slavic Review* 49 (1990): 58–73.

Farrell, Dianne Ecklund. "Popular Prints in the Cultural History of Eighteenth-Century Russia." Ph.D. diss., University of Wisconsin, Madison, 1980.

Field, Daniel. *Rebels in the Name of the Tsar.* Boston: Houghton Mifflin, 1976.

——. "Peasants and Propagandists in the Russian Movement to the People of 1874." *Journal of Modern History* 59 (1987): 415–38.

Fitzpatrick, Anne Lincoln. *The Great Russian Fair: Nizhnii Novgorod, 1840–1890.* New York: St. Martin's Press, 1990.

Flisfish, Emmanuel. *Kantonisty.* Tel Aviv: Effect, 1983.

Flynn, James T. "The Universities, the Gentry, and the Imperial Russian Services, 1815–1825." *Canadian Slavic Studies* 2 (1968): 486–503.

——. "Tuition and Social Class in the Russian Universities: S. S. Uvarov and 'Reaction' in the Russia of Nicholas I." *Slavic Review* 35 (1976): 232–48.

Foucault, Michel. *The Archaeology of Knowledge and the Discourse on Language.* Translated by A. M. Sheridan Smith. New York: Pantheon Books, 1972.

————. *Madness and Civilization: A History of Insanity in the Age of Reason.* Translated by Richard Howard. New York: Vintage Books, 1988.

Freeze, Gregory L. *The Russian Levites: Parish Clergy in the Eighteenth Century.* Cambridge: Harvard University Press, 1977.

————. *The Parish Clergy in Nineteenth-Century Russia: Crisis, Reform, Counter-Reform.* Princeton: Princeton University Press, 1983.

————. "The *Soslovie* (Estate) Paradigm in Russian Social History." *American Historical Review* 91 (1986): 11–36.

————. "The Orthodox Church and Serfdom in Prereform Russia." *Slavic Review* 48 (1989): 361–87.

————. "Bringing Order to the Russian Family: Marriage and Divorce in Imperial Russia, 1760–1860." *Journal of Modern History* 62 (1990): 709–46.

Frieden, Nancy Mandelker. *Russian Physicians in an Era of Reform and Revolution, 1856–1905.* Princeton: Princeton University Press, 1981.

Frierson, Cathy A. *Peasant Icons: Representations of Rural People in Late Nineteenth-Century Russia.* New York: Oxford University Press, 1993.

Fuller, William C., Jr. *Strategy and Power in Russia, 1600–1914.* New York: Free Press, 1992.

Garrard, J. G. *Mixail Čulkov: An Introduction to His Prose and Verse.* The Hague: Mouton, 1970.

Gay, Peter. *Weimar Culture: The Outsider as Insider.* New York: Harper and Row, 1968.

Geertz, Clifford. *The Interpretation of Cultures.* New York: Basic Books, 1973.

————. "Art as a Cultural System." *Modern Language Notes* 91 (1976): 1473–99.

————. *Local Knowledge: Further Essays in Interpretive Anthropology.* New York: Basic Books, 1983.

Gelfond, Toby. "From Guild to Profession: The Surgeons of France in the Eighteenth Century." *Texas Reports on Biology and Medicine* 32 (1974): 121–34.

German, Ivan. "O chisle zhitelei v Rossii." *Statisticheskii zhurnal,* t. 1, ch. 1–2 (St. Petersburg 1806), 2:11–32.

German, K. F. *Statisticheskie issledovaniia otnositel'no Rossiiskoi imperii.* Ch. 1: *O narodonaselenii.* St. Petersburg, 1819.

Gertsen, A. I. *Sochineniia v deviati tomakh.* Vol. 8. Moscow, 1958.

————. *Byloe i dumy.* 2 vols. Moscow, 1962.

Geyer, Dietrich. "Zwischen Bildungsbürgertum und Intelligencija: Staatsdienst und akademische Professionalisierung im vorrevolutionären Russland." In *Bildungsbürgertum im 19. Jahrhundert.* Edited by Werner Conze and Jürgen Kocka. Stuttgart: Klett–Cotta, 1985, 207–30.

————, ed. *Wirtschaft und Gesellschaft im vorrevolutionären Russland.* Cologne: Kiepenheuer und Witsch, 1975.

Ginzburg, Carlo. *The Cheese and the Worms: The Cosmos of a Sixteenth-Century Miller.* Translated by John and Anne C. Tedeschi. Baltimore: Johns Hopkins University Press, 1980.

————. *Clues, Myths, and the Historical Method.* Translated by John and Anne C. Tedeschi. Baltimore: Johns Hopkins University Press, 1989.

Gleason, Abbott. *Young Russia: The Genesis of Russian Radicalism in the 1860s.* New York: Viking Press, 1980.

Glickman, Rose B. "The Literary Raznochintsy in Mid-Nineteenth Century Russia." Ph.D. diss., University of Chicago, 1968.

Gogol', N. V. *Sochineniia N. V. Gogolia.* 5 vols. St. Petersburg, 1894.

Golikova, N. B. *Ocherki po istorii gorodov Rossii kontsa XVII–nachala XVIII v.* Moscow, 1982.

Golitsyn, N. N. *Istoriia sotsial'no-revoliutsionnogo dvizheniia v Rossii, 1861-1881.* St. Petersburg, 1887.

Goroda feodal'noi Rossii: Sbornik statei pamiati N. V. Ustiugova. Moscow, 1966.

Greenblatt, Stephen Jay. *Renaissance Self-Fashioning: From More to Shakespeare.* Chicago: University of Chicago Press, 1980.

Griffiths, David M. "Eighteenth-Century Perceptions of Backwardness: Projects for the Creation of a Third Estate in Catherinean Russia." *Canadian-American Slavic Studies* 13 (1979): 452–72.

Griffiths, David M., and Munro, George E., eds. See *Catherine II's Charters of 1785 to the Nobility and the Towns,* above.

Guroff, Gregory, and Starr, S. Frederick. "A Note on Urban Literacy in Russia, 1890–1914." *Jahrbücher für Geschichte Osteuropas* 19 (1971): 520–31.

Haimson, Leopold H. "Social Identities in Early Twentieth Century Russia." *Slavic Review* 47 (1988): 1–21.

Hellie, Richard. *Enserfment and Military Change in Muscovy.* Chicago: University of Chicago Press, 1971.

———. "The Stratification of Muscovite Society: The Townsmen." *Russian History* 5 (1978): 119–75.

———. *Slavery in Russia, 1450–1725.* Chicago: University of Chicago Press, 1982.

Hildermeier, Manfred. "Was war das meščanstvo? Zur rechtlichen und sozialen Verfassung des unterenstädtischen Standes in Russland." *Forschungen zur osteuropäischen Geschichte* 36 (1985): 15–53.

———. *Bürgertum und Stadt in Russland, 1760–1860: Rechtliche Lage und soziale Struktur.* Cologne: Böhlau, 1986.

———. "Gesellschaftsbild und politische Artikulation der Kaufmannschaft im vor- und frühindustriellen Russland." *Forschungen zur osteuropäischen Geschichte* 38 (1986): 392–418.

Hittle, J. M. *The Service City: State and Townsmen in Russia, 1600–1800.* Cambridge: Harvard University Press, 1979.

Hudson, Hugh D., Jr. "Urban Estate Engineering in Eighteenth-Century Russia: Catherine the Great and the Elusive 'Meshchanstvo.'" *Canadian-American Slavic Studies* 18 (1984): 393–410.

Istochniki po istorii russkogo obshchestvennogo soznaniia perioda feodalizma. Novosibirsk, 1986.

Istoricheskaia geografiia Rossii XII–nachala XX v. Moscow, 1978.

Iukhneva, N. V. *Staryi Peterburg: istoriko-etnograficheskie issledovaniia.* Leningrad, 1982.

Jarausch, Konrad Hugo, ed. *The Transformation of Higher Learning, 1860–1930: Expansion, Diversification, Social Opening, and Professionalization in England, Germany, Russia, and the United States.* Chicago: University of Chicago Press, 1983.

Jones, Robert E. *The Emancipation of the Russian Nobility, 1762–1785.* Princeton: Princeton University Press, 1973.

Kabuzan, V. M. *Narodonaselenie Rossii v XVIII–pervoi polovine XIX v. (Po materialam revizii).* Moscow, 1963.

———. *Izmeneniia razmeshchenii naseleniia Rossii v XVIII–pervoi polovine XIX v. (Po materialam revizii).* Moscow, 1971.

Kabuzan, V. M., and Shepukova, N. M. "Tabel' pervoi revizii narodonaseleniia Rossii (1718–1727 gg.)." *Istoricheskii arkhiv*, no. 3 (May–June 1959): 126–65.

Kahan, Arcadius. *The Plow, the Hammer, and the Knout: An Economic History of Eighteenth-Century Russia*. Chicago: University of Chicago Press, 1985.

———. *Russian Economic History: The Nineteenth Century*. Edited by Roger Weiss. Chicago: University of Chicago Press, 1989.

Kaipsh, E. I. "Dvizhenie narodonaseleniia v Rossii s 1848 po 1852 gg.." *Sbornik statisticheskikh svedenii o Rossii, izdavaemyi statisticheskim otdeleniem russkogo geograficheskogo obshchestva*, no. 3 (1858): 429–64.

Kamenskii, A. *"Pod seniiu Ekateriny . . .": Vtoraia polovina XVIII veka*. St. Petersburg, 1992.

Kamesko, L. V. "Izmeneniia soslovnogo sostava uchashchikhsia srednei i vysshei shkoly Rossii (30–80-e gody XIX v.)." *Voprosy istorii*, no. 10 (1970): 203–7.

Kappeler, Andreas. *Russlands Erste Nationalitäten: Das Zarenreich und die Völker der Mittleren Wolga vom 16. bis 19. Jahrhundert*. Cologne-Vienna: Böhlau, 1982.

———. *Russland als Vielvölkerreich: Entstehung, Geschichte, Zerfall*. Munich: Beck, 1992.

Kaspin, Albert. "Ostrovsky and the Raznochinets in His Plays." Ph.D. diss., University of California, Berkeley, 1957.

Keep, John L. H. *Soldiers of the Tsar: Army and Society in Russia, 1462–1874*. New York: Oxford University Press, 1985.

Keppen, P. I. *Deviataia reviziia: Issledovanie o chisle zhitelei v Rossii v 1851 godu*. St. Petersburg, 1857.

Khasanova, S. I. "K voprosu ob izuchenii intelligentsii dorevoliutsionnoi Rossii." In *Revoliutsionno-osvoboditel'noe dvizhenie v XIX–XX vv. v Povolzh'e i Priural'e*. Edited by G. N. Vul'fson. Kazan, 1974, 37–54.

Khodarkovsky, Michael. *Where Two Worlds Met: The Russian State and the Kalmyk Nomads, 1600–1771*. Ithaca, N.Y.: Cornell University Press, 1992.

Kimball, Alan. "Russian Civil Society and Political Crisis in the Era of the Great Reforms, 1859–1863." Unpublished manuscript. Eugene, Oregon, 1989.

Kimerling [Wirtschafter], Elise. "Soldiers' Children, 1719–1856: A Study of Social Engineering in Imperial Russia." *Forschungen zur osteuropäischen Geschichte* 30 (1982): 61–136.

Kizevetter, A. A. *Posadskaia obshchina Rossii XVIII st.* Moscow, 1903.

———. *Istoricheskie ocherki*. Moscow, 1912.

Kliuchevskii, V. O. *Istoriia soslovii v Rossii*. Reprinted in *Sochineniia v deviati tomakh*. Vol. 6. Moscow, 1989.

Klyuzhev, Ivan. "Elementary Public Instruction in Russia (Part I)." *The Russian Review* 3 (1914): 60–72.

Knabe, Bernd. "Die Struktur des russischen Posadgemeindes und das Katalog der Beschwerden und Forderungen der Kaufmannschaft, 1762–1767." *Forschungen zur osteuropäischen Geschichte* 22 (Berlin 1975).

Kocka, Jürgen. *Weder Stand noch Klasse: Unterschichten um 1800*. Bonn: J. H. W. Dietz, 1990.

Koenker, Diane P., Rosenberg, William G., and Suny, Ronald Grigor, eds. *Party, State, and Society in the Russian Civil War: Explorations in Social History*. Bloomington: Indiana University Press, 1989.

Kopanev, A. I. *Naselenie Peterburga v pervoi polovine XIX veka.* Moscow and Leningrad, 1957.

Korkorev, A. V., ed. *Khrestomatiia po russkoi literature XVIII veka.* Moscow, 1965

Kurmacheva, M. D. *Krepostnaia intelligentsiia Rossii: Vtoraia polovina XVIII–nachalo XIX veka.* Moscow, 1983.

Kuz'mina, V. D. "Neizvestnoe proizvedenie russkoi demokraticheskoi satiry XVIII v." *Izvestiia AN SSSR. Otdelenie literatury i iazyka* 14, vypusk 4 (July–August 1955): 374–83.

LaCapra, Dominick, and Kaplan, Steven L., eds. *Modern European Intellectual History: Reappraisals and New Perspectives.* Ithaca, N.Y.: Cornell University Press, 1982.

Laran, Michel. "La Première Génération de l'"intelligentsia' roturière en Russie (1750–1780)." *Revue d'histoire moderne et contemporaine* 13 (1966): 137–56.

LeDonne, John P. *Ruling Russia: Politics and Administration in the Age of Absolutism, 1762–1796.* Princeton: Princeton University Press, 1984.

———. *Absolutism and Ruling Class: The Formation of the Russian Political Order, 1700–1825.* New York: Oxford University Press, 1991.

———. "Police Reform in Russia: A Project of 1762." *Cahiers du Monde russe et soviétique* 32 (1991): 249–74.

Leikina-Svirskaia, V. R. "Formirovanie raznochinskoi intelligentsii v Rossii v 40-kh godakh XIX v." *Istoriia SSSR,* no. 1 (1958): 83–104.

———. *Intelligentsiia v Rossii vo vtoroi polovine XIX veka.* Moscow, 1971.

Lenin, V. I. *Polnoe sobranie sochinenii.* 55 vols. Moscow, 1958–1965.

Leroy-Beaulieu, Anatole. *The Empire of the Tsars and the Russians.* Translated and edited by Zenaida A. Ragozin. 3d ed. 3 vols. New York, 1902.

Luppov, S. L. *Kniga v Rossii v poslepetrovskoe vremia.* Leningrad, 1976.

Lyashchenko, Peter. *History of the National Economy of Russia.* Translated by L. M. Herman. New York: Macmillan, 1949.

Lyotard, Jean-François. *The Postmodern Condition: A Report on Knowledge.* Translated by Geoff Bennington and Brian Massumi. Minneapolis: University of Minnesota Press, 1984.

M. M. Speranskii: Proekty i zapiski. Moscow and Leningrad, 1961.

McClelland, James C. *Autocrats and Academics: Education, Culture, and Society in Tsarist Russia.* Chicago: Univeristy of Chicago Press, 1979.

McFarlin, Harold A. "Recruitment Norms for the Russian Civil Service in 1833: The Chancery Clerkship." *Societas—A Review of Social History* 3 (1973): 61–73.

———. "The Extension of the Imperial Russian Civil Service to the Lowest Office Workers: The Creation of the Chancery Clerkship, 1827–1833." *Russian History* 1 (1974): 1–17.

MacLachlan, Colin M., and Rodríguez, Jaime E. *The Forging of the Cosmic Race: A Reinterpretation of Colonial Mexico.* Berkeley: University of California Press, 1980.

McNeal, Robert H. *Tsar and Cossack, 1855–1914.* London: Macmillan, 1987.

McReynolds, Louise. *The News under Russia's Old Regime: The Development of a Mass-Circulation Press.* Princeton: Princeton University Press, 1991.

Madariaga, Isabel de. "Catherine II and the Serfs: A Reconsideration of Some Problems." *Slavonic and East European Review* 52 (1974): 34–62.

———. *Russia in the Age of Catherine the Great.* New Haven: Yale University Press, 1981.

Malia, Martin. *Alexander Herzen and the Birth of Russian Socialism.* Cambridge: Harvard University Press, 1961.

Mal'shinskii, A. P. *Obzor sotsial'no-revoliutsionnogo dvizheniia v Rossii.* St. Petersburg, 1880.

Mart'ianov, P. "Obezpechenie nizhnikh chinov po otstavke." *Voennyi sbornik* 47, no. 1 (1866): 123–31.

Materialy dlia geografii i statistiki Rossii: Smolenskaia guberniia. St. Petersburg, 1862.

Mel'nik, I. S., ed. *Sibir', ee sovremennoe sostoianie i ee nuzhdy. Sbornik statei.* St. Petersburg, 1908.

Mendelsohn, Ezra, and Shatz, Marshall S., eds. *Imperial Russia, 1700–1917: State, Society, Opposition.* DeKalb: Northern Illinois University Press, 1988.

Merton, Robert K. *Social Theory and Social Structure.* New York: Free Press, 1968.

Mikhailovskii, N. K. *Sochineniia N. K. Mikhailovskogo.* Vol. 2. St. Petersburg, 1896.

Ministerstvo finansov. *Ministerstvo finansov, 1802–1902.* St. Petersburg, 1902.

Ministerstvo narodnogo prosveshcheniia. *Sbornik materialov dlia istorii prosveshcheniia v Rossii.* 3 vols. St. Petersburg, 1893–1898.

Ministerstvo vnutrennikh del. *Panorama Sanktpeterburga.* Kn. 1–2. St. Petersburg, 1834.

———. *Statisticheskie svedeniia o Sanktpeterburge.* St. Petersburg, 1836.

———. *Materialy dlia statistiki Rossiiskoi imperii.* St. Petersburg, 1839 and 1841.

———. Tsentral'nyi statisticheskii komitet. *Statisticheskie tablitsy Rossiiskoi imperii.* Vypusk 2. St. Petersburg, 1863.

———. Tsentral'nyi statisticheskii komitet. *Sanktpeterburg po perepisi 10 dekabria 1869 goda.* Vypusk 1–3. St. Petersburg, 1872–1875.

Mironov, B. N. "Russkii gorod vo vtoroi polovine XVIII–pervoi polovine XIX veka: tipologicheskii analiz." *Istoriia SSSR,* no. 5 (September–October 1988): 150–68.

———. *Russkii gorod v 1740–1860-e gody.* Leningrad, 1990.

Moon, David. *Russian Peasants and Tsarist Legislation on the Eve of Reform: Interaction between Peasants and Officialdom, 1825–1855.* London: Macmillan, 1992.

Morrison, Daniel. "'Trading Peasants' and Urbanization in Eighteenth Century Russia: The Central Industrial Region." Ph.D. diss., Columbia University, 1981.

Müller, Otto. *Intelligencija. Untersuchungen zur Geschichte eines politischen Schlagwortes.* Frankfurt: Athenaum, 1971.

Murvar, Vatro. "Max Weber's Urban Typology and Russia." *Sociological Quarterly* 8 (1967): 481–94.

Nahirny, Vladimir C. "The Russian Intelligentsia: From Men of Ideas to Men of Convictions." *Comparative Studies in Society and History* 4 (July 1962): 403–35.

———. *The Russian Intelligentsia: From Torment to Silence.* New Brunswick, N.J.: Transaction Books, 1983.

Nakhimovsky, Alexander D., and Nakhimovsky, Alice Stone, eds. *The Semiotics of Russian Cultural History.* Ithaca, N.Y.: Cornell University Press, 1985.

Netting, Anthony. "Russian Liberalism: The Years of Promise, 1842–1855. Ph.D. diss., Columbia University, 1967.

Nikitin, V. N. "Vek prozhit'—ne pole pereiti (iz rasskazov otstavnogo soldata)." *Evreiskaia biblioteka* 4 (1873): 164–213.

Noblesse, état et société en Russie XVIe-début du XIXe siècle. Cahiers du Monde russe et soviétique 34 (1993).

Obshchestvo i gosudarstvo feodal'noi Rossii. Moscow, 1975.

Obzor deiatel'nosti ministerstva narodnogo prosveshcheniia i podvedomstvennykh emu uchrezhdenii v 1862, 63 i 64 godakh. St. Petersburg, 1865.

Opisanie del arkhiva ministerstva narodnogo prosveshcheniia. Vol. 1. Petrograd, 1917.

Opisanie dokumentov i del, khraniashchikhsia v arkhive Sv. Sinoda. 35 vols. St. Petersburg, 1869–1916.

Ostrovskii, A. N. *Polnoe sobranie sochinenii.* 16 vols. Moscow, 1949–1953.

Otchety ministerstva iustitsii za 1842–1859. St. Petersburg, 1843–1861.

Ovsianiko-Kulikovskii, D. N. *Istoriia russkoi intelligentsii.* St. Petersburg, 1909.

Owen, Thomas C. *Capitalism and Politics in Russia: A Social History of the Moscow Merchants, 1855–1905.* New York: Cambridge University Press, 1981.

———. *The Corporation under Russian Law, 1800–1917: A Study in Tsarist Economic Policy.* Cambridge: Cambridge University Press, 1991.

Paperno, Irina. *Chernyshevsky and the Age of Realism: A Study in the Semiotics of Behavior.* Stanford, Calif.: Stanford University Press, 1988.

Perkin, Harold. *The Origins of Modern English Society, 1780–1880.* London: Routledge, 1969.

Perkins, Etta Louise. "Careers in Art: An Exploration in the Social History of Post-Petrine Russia." Ph.D. diss., Indiana University, 1980.

———. "Mobility in the Art Profession in Tsarist Russia." *Jahrbücher für Geschichte Osteuropas* 39 (1991): 225–33.

Peterburg i guberniia: Istoriko-etnograficheskie issledovaniia. Leningrad, 1989.

Pintner, Walter M. *Russian Economic Policy under Nicholas I.* Ithaca, N.Y.: Cornell University Press, 1967.

———. "The Social Characteristics of the Early Nineteenth-Century Russian Bureaucracy." *Slavic Review* 29 (1970): 429–43.

———. "The Russian Higher Civil Service on the Eve of the 'Great Reforms.'" *Journal of Social History* (Spring 1975): 55–68.

Pintner, Walter M., and Rowney, Don Karl, eds. *Russian Officialdom: The Bureaucratization of Russian Society from the Seventeenth to the Twentieth Century.* Chapel Hill: University of North Carolina Press, 1980.

Pipes, Richard. "Narodnichestvo: A Semantic Inquiry." *Slavic Review* 23 (1964): 441–58.

———. "Russia's Exigent Intellectuals." *Encounter* 22 (1964): 79–84.

———. *Russia under the Old Regime.* New York: Scribner's, 1974.

———, ed. *The Russian Intelligentsia.* New York: Columbia University Press, 1961.

Pirumova, N. M. *Zemskaia intelligentsiia i ee rol' v obshchestvennoi bor'be.* Moscow, 1986.

Pisarev, D. I. *Literaturnaia kritika v trekh tomakh.* 3 vols. Leningrad, 1981.

Plekhanov, G. V. *Sochineniia.* 24 vols. Moscow, 1923–1927.

Ploshinskii, L. O. *Gorodskoe ili srednee sostoianie russkogo naroda, v ego istoricheskom razvitii, ot nachala Rusi do noveishikh vremen.* St. Petersburg, 1852.

Polevoi, Nikolai. *Izbrannye proizvedeniia i pis'ma.* Leningrad, 1986.

———. *Mechty i zhizn'.* Moscow, 1988.

Pollard, Alan. "The Russian Intelligentsia: The Mind of Russia." *California Slavic Studies* 3 (1964): 1–32.

Polnoe sobranie zakonov Rossiiskoi imperii. 1st ser.: 1649–1825. 46 vols. St. Petersburg,

1830; 2d ser.: 1825–1881. 55 vols. St. Petersburg, 1830–1884; 3d ser.: 1881–1913. 33 vols. St. Petersburg, 1885–1916.

Pomeranz, William E. "Justice from Underground: The History of the Underground *Advokatura.*" *Russian Review* 52 (July 1993): 321–40.

Pomialovskii, N. G. *Sochineniia v dvukh tomakh.* 2 vols. Moscow and Leningrad, 1965.

Pososhkov, I. T. *Kniga o skudosti i bogatstve, i drugie sochineniia.* Edited by B. B. Kafengauz. Moscow, 1951.

———. *The Book of Poverty and Wealth.* Edited and translated by A. P. Vlasto and L. R. Lewitter. London: Athlone, 1987.

Povalshin, A. D. *Sostoianie Riazanskoi gubernii v polovine 19 stoletiia (1848–1873 gg.).* Riazan, 1895.

Prikazy voennogo ministra. St. Petersburg, 1809–1868.

Pullat, R. N., ed. *Problemy istoricheskoi demografii SSSR: Sbornik statei.* Tallin, 1977.

Pushkarev, I. *Opisanie Sanktpeterburga i uezdnykh gorodov Sanktpeterburgskoi gubernii.* Ch. 1–3. St. Petersburg, 1839–1841.

Pushkin, Michael. "The Professions and the Intelligentsia in Nineteenth-Century Russia." *University of Birmingham Historical Journal* 12 (1969–1970): 72–99.

———. "*Raznochintsy* in the University: Government Policy and Social Change in Nineteenth-Century Russia." *International Review of Social History* 26 (1981): 25–65.

Rabinovich, M. G. *Ocherki etnografii russkogo feodal'nogo goroda: Gorozhane, ikh obshchestvennyi i domashnii byt.* Moscow, 1978.

Raeff, Marc. *Siberia and the Reforms of 1822.* Seattle: University of Washington Press, 1956.

———. *Michael Speransky: Statesman of Imperial Russia, 1772–1839.* The Hague: Martinus Nijhoff, 1957.

———. *Origins of the Russian Intelligentsia: The Eighteenth-Century Nobility.* New York: Harcourt, Brace and World, 1966.

———. *The Well-Ordered Police State: Social and Institutional Change through Law in the Germanies and Russia, 1600–1800.* New Haven: Yale University Press, 1983.

———. *Understanding Imperial Russia: State and Society in the Old Regime.* Translated by Arthur Goldhammer. New York: Columbia University Press, 1984.

Rakhmatullin, M. A. *Krest'ianskoe dvizhenie v velikorusskikh guberniiakh v 1826–1857 gg.* Moscow, 1990.

Ransel, David L. *Mothers of Misery: Child Abandonment in Russia.* Princeton: Princeton University Press, 1988.

Repin, I. *Dalekoe blizkoe.* Moscow, 1986.

Reshetnikov, F. M. "Iz literaturnogo naslediia F. M. Reshetnikova." *Literaturnyi arkhiv.* Vypusk 1. Leningrad, 1932.

Riasanovsky, Nicholas. *A Parting of Ways: Government and the Educated Public in Russia, 1801–1855.* Oxford: Oxford University Press, 1976.

Rieber, Alfred J. *Merchants and Entrepreneurs in Imperial Russia.* Chapel Hill: University of North Carolina Press, 1982.

———. "The Rise of Engineers in Russia." *Cahiers du Monde russe et soviétique* 31 (1990): 539–68.

Rockwell, Joan. *Fact in Fiction: The Use of Literature in the Systematic Study of Society.* London: Routledge, 1974.

Roshchevskaia, L. P. *Revoliutsionery-raznochintsy v zapadnosibirskom izgnanii.* Leningrad, 1983.

Rossov, Captain. "Istoricheskii ocherk prizreniia otstavnykh voennykh chinov v proshlom veke i v nachale nyneshniago stoletiia." *Voennyi sbornik* 30, no. 4 (April 1863): 375–98.

Rozhanov, F. S. *Zapiski po istorii revoliutsionnogo dvizheniia v Rossii.* St. Petersburg, 1913.

Rozhdestvenskii, S. V. *Istoricheskii obzor deiatel'nosti ministerstva narodnogo prosveshcheniia, 1802–1902.* St. Petersburg, 1902.

―――. "Materialy dlia istorii uchebnykh reform v Rossii v XVIII–XIX vekakh." *Zapiski istoriko-filologicheskogo fakul'teta imperatorskogo S.-Peterburgskogo universiteta.* Ch. 96. Vypusk 1. St. Petersburg, 1910.

―――. *S.-Peterburgskii universitet v pervoe stoletie ego deiatel'nosti. Materialy po istorii S.-Petersburgskogo universiteta.* Vol. 1, 1819–1835. St. Petersburg, 1919.

Rozhkova, M. K., ed. *Ocherki ekonomicheskoi istorii Rossii pervoi poloviny XIX veka.* Moscow, 1959.

Rozman, Gilbert. *Urban Networks in Russia, 1750–1800, and Premodern Periodization.* Princeton: Princeton University Press, 1976.

Rubenshtein, N. L. "Ulozhennaia komissiia 1754–1766 gg. i ee proekt novogo ulozheniia 'O sostoianii poddannykh voobshche' (K istorii sotsial'noi politiki 50-kh–nachala 60-kh godov XVIII v.)." *Istoricheskie zapiski* 38 (1951): 208–51.

Ruckman, Jo Ann. *The Moscow Business Elite: A Social and Cultural Portrait of Two Generations, 1840–1905.* DeKalb: Northern Illinois University Press, 1984.

Russkii gorod (issledovaniia i materialy). Vypusk 1–9. Moscow, 1976–1990.

Russkoe naselenie Pomor'ia i Sibiri (period feodalizma). Moscow, 1973.

Ryndziunskii, P. G. *Gorodskoe grazhdanstvo doreformennoi Rossii.* Moscow, 1958.

Sanninskii, B. "Kto takie raznochintsy?" *Voprosy literatury*, no. 4 (1977): 232–40.

Sarup, Madan. *An Introductory Guide to Post-structuralism and Postmodernism.* 2d ed. Athens: University of Georgia Press, 1993.

Sbornik Akademiku B. D. Grekovu ko dniu semidesiatiletiia. Moscow, 1952.

Sbornik imperatorskogo Rossiiskogo istoricheskogo obshchestva. 148 vols. St. Petersburg, 1867–1916.

Sbornik postanovlenii po ministerstvu narodnogo prosveshcheniia. 2 vols. St. Petersburg, 1875–1876.

Sbornik postanovlenii po Sanktpeterburgskomu obshchestvennomu upravleniiu. Ch. 1–2. St. Petersburg, 1860.

Sbornik rasporiazhenii po ministerstvu narodnogo prosveshcheniia. 2 vols. St. Petersburg, 1866.

Sbornik svedenii i materialov po vedomstvu ministerstva finansov. St. Petersburg, 1865.

Schliefman, Nurit. "A Russian Daily Newspaper and Its Readership: Severnaia pchela 1825–1840." *Cahiers du Monde russe et soviétique* 28 (1987): 127–44.

Schmidt, Christoph. "Über die Bezeichnung der Stände *(sostojanie-soslovie)* in Russland seit dem 18. Jahrhundert." *Jahrbücher für Geschichte Osteuropas* 38 (1990): 199–211.

Screen, J. E. O. *The Helsinki Yunker School, 1846–1879: A Case Study of Officer Training in the Russian Army.* Studia Historica 22. Helsinki, 1986.

Sergeev, A., ed. "Graf A. Kh. Benkendorf o Rossii v 1827–1830 gg." *Krasnyi arkhiv* 6(37) (1929): 138–74; 1(38) (1930): 109–47.

Shaganova, O. M. "Terminy rodstva v revizskikh skazkakh." *Russkaia rech'*, no. 2 (March–April 1979): 89–94.

Shchetinina, G. I. "Retsenziia na kn. V. R. Leikina-Svirskaia, Intelligentsiia v Rossii vo vtoroi polovine XIX veka." *Istoriia SSSR*, no. 1 (January–February 1972): 180–82.

Shebeka, N. I., ed. *Khronika sotsialisticheskogo dvizheniia v Rossii, 1878–1887. Ofitsial'nyi otchet.* Moscow, 1906.

Shepelev, L. E. *Otmenennye istorii—chiny, zvaniia i tituly v Rossiiskoi imperii.* Leningrad, 1977.

Shtakenshneider, E. A. *Dnevniki i zapiski (1854–1886).* Moscow, 1934. Reprint, Newtonville, Mass.: Oriental Research Partners, 1980.

Shtrange, M. M. *Demokraticheskaia intelligentsiia Rossii v XVIII veke.* Moscow, 1965.

Sidorova, I. B. "Kto takie raznochintsy? (Polemika v literature)." In *Voprosy otechestvennoi, zarubezhnoi istorii, literaturovedeniia i iazykoznaniia.* Ch. 1 (Kazan, 1981), 24–33.

———. "Otrazhenie nuzhd raznochintsev v gorodskikh nakazakh 1767 goda." In *Voprosy otechestvennoi, zarubezhnoi istorii, literaturovedeniia i iazykoznaniia.* Ch. 1 (Kazan, 1981), 33–40.

———. "Polozhenie raznochintsev v russkom obshchestve (XVIII–pervaia polovina XIX v.)." Kand. diss., Kazan, 1982.

Sinel, Allen. *The Classroom and the Chancellery: State Educational Reform in Russia under Count Dmitrii Tolstoi.* Cambridge: Harvard University Press, 1973.

Sivkov, K. V. "Krepostnye khudozhniki v sele Arkhangel'skom: Stranitsa iz istorii krepostnoi intelligentsii nachala XIX v." *Istoricheskie zapiski* 6 (1940): 195–214.

———. "O sud'be krepostnykh khudozhnikov sela Arkhangel'skogo." *Istoricheskie zapiski* 38 (1951): 270–72.

Sladkevich, I. G. "O soslovnykh proektakh Komiteta 6 dekabria 1826." In *Issledovaniia po otechestvennomu istochnikovedeniiu.* Moscow and Leningrad, 1964.

Smetanin, S. I. "Razlozhenie soslovii i formirovanie klassovoi struktury gorodskogo naseleniia Rossii v 1800–1861 gg." *Istoricheskie zapiski* 102 (1978): 153–82.

Snezhnevskii, V. I. "K istorii pobegov krepostnykh v poslednei chetverti XVIII i v XIX stoletiiakh." *Nizhegorodskii sbornik* 10 (Nizhnii Novgorod, 1890): 566–67.

Solovkov, I. A. *Antologiia pedagogicheskoi mysli Rossii XVIII v.* Moscow, 1985.

Speranskii, M. M. See *M. M. Speranskii: Proekty i zapiski,* above.

Spiski naselennykh mest Saratovskoi gubernii. Saratov, 1912.

Stackenschneider, E. A. See Shtakenshneider, E. A., above.

Stanislawski, Michael. *Tsar Nicholas I and the Jews: The Transformation of Jewish Society in Russia, 1825–1855.* Philadelphia: Jewish Publication Society, 1983.

Stites, Richard. *Revolutionary Dreams: Utopian Vision and Experimental Life in the Russian Revolution.* New York: Oxford University Press, 1989.

Sviachenko. "Khronika zhizni soldatskogo syna Dmitriia Zhurby." *Sovremennik* 110, no. 9 (September 1865): 33–113; no. 10 (October 1865): 283–361.

Svod voennykh postanovlenii. 12 vols. St. Petersburg, 1838.

Svod zakonov Rossiiskoi imperii. 15 vols. 1st, 2d, and 3d redactions. St. Petersburg, 1832, 1842, and 1857.

Szeftel, Marc. "La Condition juridique des déclassés dans la Russie ancienne." *Archives d'histoire du droit oriental* 2 (Brussels, 1938): 431–42.

Tablitsy uchebnykh zavedenii vsekh vedomstv Rossiiskoi imperii s pokazaniem otnosheniia chisla uchashikhsia k chislu zhitelei. St. Petersburg, 1838.

Tolstoi, D. A. *Gorodskie uchilishcha v tsarstvovanie Imperatritsy Ekateriny Velikoi.* St. Petersburg, 1886.

Torke, Hans-Joachim, "Das russische Beamtentum in der ersten Hälfte des 19. Jahrhunderts." *Forschungen zur osteuropäischen Geschichte* 13 (1967): 7–345.

———. *Die Staatsbedingte Gesellschaft im Moskauer Reich: Zar und Zemlja in der altrussischen Herrschaftsverfassung, 1613–1789.* Leiden: E. J. Brill, 1974.

Troitskii, I. "Mekhanik-samouchka Kulibin." *Narodnoe chtenie,* kn. 6 (St. Petersburg, 1860): 56–106.

Troitskii, S. M. *Russkii absoliutizm i dvorianstvo v XVIII v.: Formirovanie biurokratii.* Moscow, 1974.

Trubnikov, V. V. "Resultaty narodnykh perepisei v Ardatovskom uezde Simbirskoi gubernii." *Sbornik statisticheskikh svedenii o Rossii, izdavaemyi statisticheskim otdeleniem imperatorskogo russkogo geograficheskogo obshchestva,* kn. 3 (St. Petersburg, 1858): 343–427.

Tugan-Baranovsky, Mikhail I. *The Russian Factory in the Nineteenth Century.* Homewood, Ill.: American Economic Association, by R. D. Irwin, 1970.

Turgenev, I. S. *Izbrannye proizvedeniia v dvukh tomakh.* 2 vols. Leningrad, 1958.

———. *Sobranie sochinenii.* 10 vols. Moscow, 1961–1962.

"Ukaz Senata 29 noiabria 1819." *Zhurnal departamenta narodnogo prosveshcheniia,* ch. 3 (St. Petersburg, 1821): 234–35.

V. N. Karpov, Vospominaniia—N. N. Shipov, Istoriia moei zhizni. Reprint, Moscow and Leningrad, 1933.

Veselovskii, K. S. "Statisticheskie issledovaniia o nedvizhimykh imushchestvakh v Sanktpeterburge." *Otechestvennye zapiski* 57, no. 3, otdelenie 2 (1848): 1–27.

Vigel', F. F. *Zapiski.* 2 vols. Moscow, 1928. Reprint, Cambridge: Oriental Research Partners, 1974.

Vinogradov, V. V. "Vozniknovenie i razvitie slova soslovie." *Etimologiia 1966* (Moscow, 1968): 133–37.

Vladimirskii-Budanov, M. *Gosudarstvo i narodnoe obrazovanie v Rossii XVIII v.* Vol. 1. Iaroslavl, 1874. Reprint, Cambridge: Oriental Research Partners, 1972.

Vodarskii, Ia. E. *Naselenie Rossii v kontse XVII-nachale XVIII veka: chislennost', soslovno-klassovyi sostav, razmeshchenie.* Moscow, 1977.

Voprosy voennoi istorii. Moscow, 1965.

Voronov, M. A., and Makashin, S. A. *Rasskazy o starom Saratove.* Saratov, 1937.

Vul'fson, G. N. "Poniatie 'raznochinets' v XVIII–pervoi polovine XIX veka." In *Ocherki istorii narodov Povolzh'ia i Priural'ia.* Vypusk 1. Kazan, 1967, 107–24.

Vvedenskii, P. M. "Metodika analiza pasportnoi statistiki Rossii pervoi poloviny XIX v." *Istochnikovedenie otechestvennoi istorii 1981* (Moscow, 1982): 167–77.

Walker, Mack. *German Home Towns: Community, State, and General Estate, 1648–1871.* Ithaca, N.Y.: Cornell University Press, 1971.

Wcislo, Francis William. *Reforming Rural Russia: State, Local Society, and National Politics, 1855–1914.* Princeton: Princeton University Press, 1990.

Weber, Max. *From Max Weber: Essays in Sociology.* Edited and translated by H. H. Gerth and C. Wright Mills. New York: Oxford University Press, 1946.

White, Hayden. *Metahistory: The Historical Imagination in Nineteenth-Century Europe.* Baltimore: Johns Hopkins University Press, 1973.

————. *Tropics of Discourse: Essays in Cultural Criticism.* Baltimore: Johns Hopkins University Press, 1978.

Williams, Raymond. *Culture and Society: 1780–1950.* New York: Columbia University Press, 1958 and 1983.

Wirtschafter, Elise Kimerling. *From Serf to Russian Soldier.* Princeton: Princeton University Press, 1990.

————. "Problematics of Status Definition in Imperial Russia: The *Raznočincy.*" *Jahrbücher für Geschichte Osteuropas* 40 (1992): 319–39.

————. "Social Misfits: Veterans and Soldiers' Families in Servile Russia." *The Journal of Military History* (forthcoming, July 1995).

Wortman, Richard S. *The Development of a Russian Legal Consciousness.* Chicago: University of Chicago Press, 1976.

Yaney, George L. *The Systematization of Russian Government: Social Evolution in the Domestic Administration of Imperial Russia, 1711–1905.* Urbana: University of Illinois Press, 1973.

Zaionchkovskii, P. A. *Pravitel'stvennyi apparat samoderzhavnoi Rossii v XIX v.* Moscow, 1978.

Index

tributary natives *(iasachnye),* 20, 24, 45,
    95. *See also* minorities
Troitskii, S. M., 74
tsarist myth, 37
Tsaritsyn, 43
Tula, 171n
Turgenev, I. S., 99–100
Turks, 100
Tver, 49

Ukrainian frontier force, 40–41, 96, 122
Ukrainians, 95–96, 110
Ulitin, serf, 83–84
unranked administrative employees. *See*
    bureaucracy
Ural'sk, 90
urban "citizens," xi, 21, 33, 50, 87, 135–
    37, 164n. *See also* craft guilds; mer-
    chants; townspeople; urban com-
    munity
urban community *(posad),* 12–13, 19–
    24, 27, 31, 40–41, 48, 54, 86–87,
    109, 163n, 181n; registration in,
    43–45
Uspenie Bogoroditsy, 58
Uspenskii cathedral, 60
Uspenskii, N. V., 129

Varangians, 36
Vasil', 122
Vasil'evskii island, 32
Vedernikov, administrative clerk, 121
Viatka, 168n
Vitebsk, 80
Vladimir, 120
Volga, xiv, 90
Volokolamsk, 116
Voronezh, 83, 97
Voskresenie Khristova, 57
Voznesenie Gospodnia, 57
"volunteers," 23
Vse Skorbiashie, 57
Vul'fson, G. N., 6–7

War Ministry, Inspectors' Department,
    71
Weber, Max, 133
westernization, 74
White, Hayden, 148
woman question, 141

zakladchiki, 166n
Zamoskvoretskii *sorok,* 55–56, 58, 61–62
zemstvo, 109, 139
zvanie (calling), xii, 50, 134–37, 141,
    149, 162n